I FORGOT
TO GET OLD

I FORGOT TO GET OLD

Helen Lewison

Helen Lewison

Library of Congress Number: 2002092440
ISBN :   Hardcover   1-4010-6139-7
                Softcover   1-4010-6138-9

To order additional copies of this book, contact:
Xlibris Corporation
1-888-795-4274
www.Xlibris.com
Orders@Xlibris.com
15530

INTRODUCTION

"*This is a book of recollections of childhood; reminiscences of events important and unimportant in the scheme of things, poetry (humorous) or otherwise, essays on life in general and mine in particular. A random walk through my life story, stopping now and then to laugh, to cry, to remember and most of all to look back and say "Hey, look at me I'm still dancing".*"

CONTENTS

HELEN LEWISON

AUTHOR OF

"SEDUCTION OF SILENCE"

AND

"THE WACO KIDS"

I FORGOT TO GET OLD

I have always prided myself on having a good memory but suddenly I looked in the mirror and saw a woman with white hair. Who was she? She looked familiar, but was she someone I knew? Internally, I am still this nubile creature anxiously awaiting another day, another adventure and every person a puzzle. Did I have all the adventures? Did I solve all the puzzles? Did I have a memory lapse? Did I move to another dimension? When did I get older? When did I grow up? Am I really wiser and mellower? I don't think so.

All the people I have known and met have seen my face and that is where I've been. The reflection of how others perceived me is the image I have of myself. There have been a variety of faces over the years but I seem to remember only the smiling, happy ones. I must have an "erase mode" that wipes out all the negative images I received.

I feel the same as I did, ten, twenty, thirty years ago—or I think I do. There is always, not necessarily a fire in my belly, but certainly there are an abundant number of embers that with a little fanning begins to glow. There is still the mischievous five year old, the sober twelve year old, and the earnest twenty-one and on it goes, but who is that woman I now see in the mirror. I guess I will just have to get in touch with my "inner child" and tell it "You don't have to act your age but try to be considerate of that woman in the mirror. It could turn out to be you".

THE ARSONIST

Seated in the tall grass in our yard, Peter Rabbit was a very bad influence on me when I was about five. We would sit together in the yard and plan our strategy. We both loved fires, dancing flames—they were so exciting. I would take out matches and gather small piles of dried leaves. I never seemed to get a fire started. The ground was too moist or perhaps the leaves weren't dry enough. Every now and then my mother would call out from the house, "Helen, what are you doing?" My response was always the same, "Playing with Peter Rabbit".

Frustrated by my feeble attempts, I decided to leave Peter and venture out on my own. Passing a neighbor's open garage with the car still inside, a brilliant idea enter my mind. No one will see me in the darkness under the car. I will have complete privacy. After crawling under the car, I proceeded to make a small pile of any objects that looked flammable. As I was finishing my project, my brother passed the garage and spotted me. He called "What are you doing, I'm going to get Mother". Guilt overtook me and I started to run around the block, down the alley, over the fence, up the steps into our house; quickly, into the bathroom where I bolted the door. I climbed upon the rim of the bathtub and saw my brother, my mother fast approaching. I pulled the window down and latched it securely. At last I was safe for the time being. Totally exhausted, I placed a bath towel on the floor and fell into a deep sleep.

The smell of dinner began drifting under the door and the sound of dishes. Quietly opening the door, I moved ever so nonchalantly into the dining room. No words were spoken, no reprimands, just silence. I finished my meal and said, "You know, Peter Rabbit made me do it". I went out and talked to Peter, "We can't start fires anymore," and I never did.

The Waco Kids

GONE WITH THE WIND

Growing up in Texas gives people a different perspective of American history. Our lessons were filled with stories about the Alamo and the Lone Star State. General Sam Houston's cry "Remember the Alamo" still rings in my ear from time to time.

I never seemed comfortable with this chauvinistic pride in being a Texan or a Southerner. I was the daughter of European immigrants and my roots were not deep enough to feel at home. The use of the phrase "Damn Yankees" was bandied about, but I had no idea what a Yankee was. Who was I? I was a girl, an American, a Texan, a Jew—but in what order.

In junior high school we were all given a holiday from our classes to attend the movie "Gone With The Wind" showing the spectacle of the glory of the south. I remember going to the Orpheum Theater and being pushed as the crowds rushed in. I ended up in the balcony, over to the far side where the screen was distorted. I saw the movie at a very oblique angle. This must have been a forerunner of my view of life. I did become a devotee of chili and matzo balls. I could not endure the "rah, rah, team" of football, but I did love to ride a bicycle. I did sometimes sit in the back row of a tabernacle and sing "Rock of Ages" and go to Hebrew School. The only thing I remember about the movie "Gone With the Wind" is Scarlet O'Hara saying "I'll think about it tomorrow". These have been words I live by.

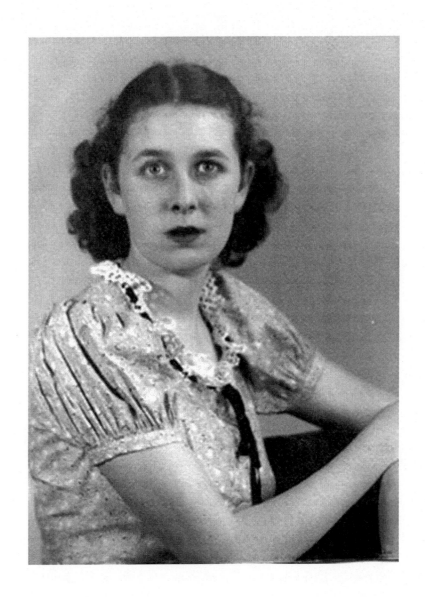

THE BRIDE WORE BLACK

"Why in the world would you want to be married in black?" My mother asked me looking puzzled. I did not reply. My aunt was brought into the discussion. She said, "It doesn't have to be white, a lovely pastel would be nice." My mother again inquired, "You are only twenty, much too young to be wearing a black dress." I refused to change my mind. Dramatically, I intoned, "I am going to my doom."

Wedding plans proceeded. An army chaplain at Fort Mason was to perform the service. My younger cousin was to be the best man. I was marrying a soldier I had met at a dance when I was seventeen and had not seen again until ten days before. The war in Europe had just ended and he had been liberated from two years in a prisoner of war camp. His letter had been filled with words about our impending marriage and here he was waiting for me to make the ultimate commitment. It seemed that I had no choice. He had survived the war and had come home to claim his prize. It was flattering and disconcerting. Yet, here I was getting married.

I can still see my cousin, Joe winking at me through his thick glasses during the ceremony. It reminded me of a fish staring out of a tank and I began to giggle. The chaplain stopped the ceremony and gave me a stern look. "Marriage is a serious step." He finished and the deed was done. I was married to a man I didn't know, leaving for a city I'd never seen and yet it seemed like the right thing to do. I was entering into the unknown and my wish to wear black was part of the mystery.

The stranger I had married remained an enigma the ten years we lived together. No one commented on my dress. Fate catapulted me into marriage a second time. Destiny again took me by the hand and I followed. I took no chances and wore a pastel dress.

One marriage in black had an unhappy ending. I had learned my lesson. The poet William Congreve said: "Marry in haste, we may repent at leisure." But, Robert Browning wrote, "I am grown peaceful as old age tonight, I regret little, I would change still less."

THE OTHER HALF

The minute your mate, spouse, husband, wife or whatever category fits your particular circumstance dies, you die with them. You become one of the walking dead. A life shared for many years is impossible to replace. You were attached in the most obvious fashion . . . living together. You are now detached and the lifeline between the two of you is broken never to be repaired.

Who can remember the small details that were unimportant except to the two of you? Who is always somewhere around? Where is the one you sat across from day after day? Ultimately, you come up against a blank wall that jars you into the reality of your life. You continue to eat, to sleep and all the ordinary daily doings but it all feels so pointless, so futile. Is the remainder of my life to be spent in vagrant careless breathing? I can touch myself and I am still warm; I can look out and see the sky but I am so empty. I will soon put on my face, the one I use for company. I will again go out and laugh. I will again give the appearance of a stable independent person. I am, I think, the only one that knows that my future ended a few years ago. I live on a day-to-day basis; no long term plans, no long-term dreams. How did this happen?

I know about death or thought I did. Hah! I knew nothing. The quiet surrounds me. I am absorbed in the quiet. The phone will ring and a voice brings me back during the conversation. As soon as I hang up, I cease to exist. Am I different from others who are left to grieve? Do I have to busy myself incessantly to forget?

I have no answers and my questions seem inadequate. How could I have spent so many years on this earth and not become aware of how death on a personal level changes what you were forever! The walking dead sounds very dramatic but it's far from being that simple. We walk the earth and no one recognizes us. We have joined a very exclusive club "The Other Half".

CANNABALISM (MULTIVITAMINS)

This morning I chewed up an elephant and a lion
You would think with such a diet
I wouldn't feel so fine
It seems, I should take vitamins
Each day, to keep my body going
Ergo, these small creatures
Will keep my step from slowing
I have a dickens of a time getting pills down my throat
So, I've resorted to children's chewable
I'll even eat a goat.
Why they make pills for children
In the shape of living creatures
I suppose they still feel primitive
And will be attracted to their features
I, too, enjoy green elephants
And pink lions and tigers, too.
Since my doctor said they are good for me
I'll chew and chew and chew.

SOMEWHERE

Somewhere between St. Marten and St. Thomas in the Caribbean in Stateroom 090 at 11:45 PM in the fall of 1993, I decided my journey had meaning besides eating and eating and shopping and shopping. I began to meet my shipmates. First Blossom and Marty from Newport Beach. Marty is almost 91 and they have been married for fifty years. She's about seventy something and looks like a well-fed silky cat. He looks pretty old but is eagerly hoping for another year or more. Rose and Melvin; she's Spanish, warm, loving and has a terrible back. Melvin is compassionate and kind. They live somewhere in Southern California. There is Mary Ellen who is still pretty and lives in a trailer park in Florida. She used to sell antiques, has four children, grandchildren and was divorced many years ago. Sally and Dean are from Oregon and they make furniture; they are comparatively young compared to the rest of the people on the ship.

Bob and Frances live on St. Croix; they are leaving the ship tomorrow. They have been married sixty years and have a daughter who lives in Austria (married to an Austrian painter). They both look so mellow that I feel I am looking at a lovely masterpiece hung in some museum.

There's the surgeon and his wife who are very sincere, down to earth but I don't remember their name. All I do remember is that she dotes on her son.

The blond woman whose last name is Wright that I talked to on the Upper Promenade Deck who lives in Malibu, Florida. I never heard of any Malibu except the one in California. She has a lovely Virginia accent and is celebrating her new marriage to husband #3. The Dutchman and his wife; he owns a forty foot long boat and sails alone out of Holland into the sea. His wife never goes with him but I don't think she tries to stop him.

Tonight I watched a hypnotist and talked to a distinguished bearded man from French Canada who said anyone could be hypnotized. He says we can hypnotize ourselves. I know a bit about the autosuggestion theory because it helped me with pain over the years even though I am not sure how I really did it. I will now to try and see if it works for insomnia. He says, think about something pleasant, push disturbing thoughts away. Don't think about going to sleep. Think about relaxing, letting go visualize your body relaxing, going into a downshift, drifting into an easy state of being. I will try but not too hard. If the effort is not effortless, then it is a no win situation as far as I am concerned. I have been holding on tight for many years but in this season of my life, it would be good to loosen my hold and at the end of the day just float away and rejuvenate the inner me. I am out to sea now both literally and figuratively.

Oh yes, I have met more people. Jo-Ann from Dallas was on the Navigation Deck and has a son in the Texas Legislature. She knows "only slightly" the governor of Texas, Ann Richards and says she is as smart as a whip. She mentioned she had stayed at a place call the Heritage either in North or South Carolina with Kay Spreckle's (who was married to Clark Gable) sister or somebody that talks to her dogs when she's on the phone and never mentions her children. Jo-Ann has been married for 47 years and is still a very attractive blond. I am sure people must have said all her life "she's pretty as a picture". We spent two hours in the Crow's Nest (a bar) on the ship drinking nothing but glasses of ice water. I always drink what everybody else is drinking for the most part but I did think it very strange to order water from the waiter. (Repeat after me "water from the waiter.")

I also met a couple (Frances and Bill) from Alabama who

uttered the phrase "The Lord takes care, watches over" and a lot of other things the Lord does. I think he really took care of Frances and Bill. They have three daughters; one is married to a General. They have a condo and a boat in Sarasota, Florida and live in a restored plantation circa 1840 in Alabama. Bill believes people should not call the President by his first name. He is retired but is keeping his hand in by raising a herd of beef cattle (about 1,000 head). When I am talking to southerners, I find my old southern accent rears its head and I hear myself talking like I barely left Texas.

And then, there was Father William, a priest about sixty and I told him he was the best looking man on the ship. We spent time over champagne at the first formal evening with a couple of "fallen Catholics" (their words). On the day before debarking I met Father William over coffee, which is served in the Explorer Lounge. He was quite upset about his luggage and how it was to be handled when we left the ship. He asked me if I could clear up his confusion and concern. I said, "Father, it's really very simple, you just need faith, everything will go smoothly." He smiled and said, "That's very good, you've turned the tables on me. I guess I'm the one that needs faith this time."

I tried self-hypnosis as the man from French Canada had suggested. I thought pleasant thoughts (standing on the deck watching the beautiful blue ocean) . . . . (walking through a garden of beautiful flowers) . . . . (dancing under a full moon). Nothing worked, including the sleeping pills the ship's doctor provided. I had asked to be dropped off at one of the islands, so I could fly home early. She told me nobody dies from lack of sleep. I did survive quite nicely and welcomed my own bed in my own house. I don't know whether I'll venture out soon again but never say never.

POETRY CONTEST ON THE SHIP AT 3:00 AM—IN THE MIDDLE OF NOWHERE

A sailing, a sailing, I did go

The ship she was a sailing and
She did go too slow
I saw the briny deep
I saw the azure skies
I also saw the islands
So much beauty for my eyes
The warm winds they did charm me
The ship she was my friend
I would like to stay forever
But all good things must end.
A sailing, a sailing,
A sailing I did go
I will remember, I will remember
This ship that went so slow.

PART II The Trip Continues
A sailing, a sailing, a sailing I did go
And now the ship, she's swaying
She do go back and fro
When I stand, I do move about a bit
I be careful and take a little sit.
Out on the deck, the waves they
Throw themselves about
The sea, she is so beautiful
Of this I have no doubt.
A sailing, a sailing, and a sailing I did go
I'll soon be back at my homeport
And I, will go too slow.

WOE IS ME

I'm a painter without paint
A writer without a pen
A queen without a court
A rooster without a hen
A cook without a stove
An actress without a role
A mechanic without a tool
A destination without a goal
Woe is me!
An orphan without a storm
A cat without a mouse
A car without a driver
A family without a house
A book without a reader
A rug without a floor
This could go on forever
I think I'll walk out the door.

ZIPLOCK BAGS

I've read books about our ancestors
Who lived in long ago years?
The women were gatherers, collecting the berries
While the men folk went after the bears.
I've noticed the women of today
Take zip lock bags out of their purses

When attending large meals
They so quietly do steal
Bits of this, bits of that
I say "Curses".
I am a long way from my primitive sisters
I'm embarrassed by this behavior so crass
I know people are hungry all over the world
But, please ladies "Show a little class".

HOW VERY ODD

Where did they all go; the hours, the minutes, the days, where did they all go? Eventually you come face to face with the future, your future. All those years, those hours, the endless view you see over your shoulder, all that time spent that should have been carefully documented, and the meaning is lost in a haze of muddled memories. All the things you have acquired, all to be eventually relegated to someone else who could not possibly appreciate the effort and pleasure you found in your assortment of possessions.

It seems there really is no meaning of life, except for the now. Early on we didn't look for meaning. The future was something very distant that we never really thought about. We lived for the now, even then. We lived for the present and in retrospect we haven't changed. It is just that the future is within our "gun sights". We can take aim at the future and we feel sad. We're still smiling, we're still happy but the light of reality causes us to turn away from the glare. There is no escaping the future. We all have a common destiny but each of us feels like such an uncommon person. We are unique. There is no question about it. We are each separate entities but like anything, be it a box of cornflakes or a bottle of aspirin, we have an expiration date.

How odd that we are still acquiring; still wasting precious time. How odd we are programmed to be useful or useless depending on internal and external circumstances. How odd we are, how very odd!

ODE TO YVONNE

My changing life led me to accept an invitation from an aunt in Walnut Creek and her two daughters. I initiated this meeting; I've initiated many new sorties. This particular day upon going downtown and then waiting for the Bart train, I impulsively entered the Emporium, a department store, in my eternal search for something or other. My clothing expeditions are another story, which has no ending.

Behind the counter was a slim, calm intelligent face with very expressive eyes. We talked about almost everything except clothes, especially not about clothes. Here was a person who thought and spoke articulately about whatever it was we talked about. We exchanged phone numbers and as is common, neither was sure this conversation was to be continued.

I don't know who called first but it doesn't matter; first, we talked some—mostly about the world and the lonely crowd and the shallowness of our fellowman. Oh, we talked and we talked. People who think are parched like the desert and badly need the liquid of conversation to replenish their souls. We became friends, good friends.

My search for a garment I didn't need resulted in my finding a friend I did need. What a lucky happenstance to go shopping and find something money can't buy. We continue to talk and discover nuances in each other. As I told Yvonne yesterday, I've lived long she has lived deep.

P.S. Incidentally, I did go to Walnut Creek. I did meet my aunt's daughters. I did have an excellent Italian meal. I've never heard from them again. As Yvonne would say, does this tell you something?

To Eternal Friendship

From the Desert (Rat, Mouse) My Chinese Year

ON CRYING

I don't know if anyone bothers to remember crying. Since some people cry "at the drop of a hat" and some people cry at movies; others when the mood is either great happiness or great sadness. I've never really thought about crying as anything more than tears.

I was reading an article about unhappy moments and suddenly I remember *crying* as a point of reference in my never written autobiographical past. I don't remember crying as a child. I am sure I must have cried when I fell and hurt myself; maybe I cried I'm not sure. It seemed I used a lot of handkerchiefs in my young life but that was because there was no Kleenex and I had a perpetual cold.

I remember the first time I really cried. Tears poured from my eyes. I was about to get a divorce and had to leave my cat; that cat represented the life I wanted, a life with a constant companion complete with unwavering loyalty; all the qualities my marriage was missing. Many years have moved me beyond that time and now new tears appeared to replace them when my mother died.

I read her obituary in the newspaper the morning of her funeral. The tears flowed again. It was not an agitated crying, only a gentle flow of tears cascading down my cheeks for a gentle mother.

I once cried in the Gold Country in a small town called Dry Creek. This was a sobbing, an overwhelming sadness that my life was coming to a dead end and a desperate cry for help.

Now comes the end of crying. A husband dies, my husband of many years and where are the tears, the sobs, and the cries? Where is the mourning? Will I never cry again or is my inner self absorbing the tears? Am I becoming a sponge? I shed no tears, none absolutely none.

Someday, will something or someone touch me literally or figuratively and will tears emerge like a fountain or a spring or a geyser? It doesn't matter. I think the crying gene was never part of my persona. I always had the need to get on with life, sometimes slowly and perhaps I stumbled here and there but the road forward was always my destination. I think the greatest gift I received was "life" and the sharing of it was the best part. Now I am still here, still alive and that is nothing to cry about.

DEATH UNINVITED

Who asks death in? It permeates my life and it follows me in and out of my thoughts. I knew about death and dying but it was always someone else and somewhere else. How little I really knew about death. Now that I have come face to face, I am confused and spend a lot of time shaking my head saying, "No, no this isn't true".

I have not and doubt if I'll ever be reconciled with the knowledge that I will never see the one, death took away from me. Intellectually I know death is a cold fact of life. Emotionally, I still feel the presence of the one now dead. In fact, the presence is so strong that in the quiet of my home, there exists warmth that surrounds me and consoles me. Maybe when death came in it brought a companion. There seems to be something or someone standing in the shadows. I look around and see nothing, but when I look out the windows, I seem to be seeing with two pair of eyes and when I listen, it is with two pair of ears. Even my sense of smell seems to be increased. The sense of touch is mine alone. I reach out but its only empty air. No one asks death in. He is our uninvited guest.

Unfortunately, he is a frequent visitor and has been going from one place to another for thousands of years. How can I question the obvious and of course, why not? I have the right to be angry and frustrated with the grim reaper. In fact, it makes me feel better. Even if I can't stop death, at least I can show my ire and not take death lying down. Even if this is an existential approach to death, I get a certain amount of satisfaction in having a debate that I can't possibly win. I've confronted the inevitable and it has not found me wanting.

BIDING MY TIME

"I'm biding my time, hum . . . hum . . . hum . . . no regrets, no upsetting, and I'm biding my time".

The above from a song whose words I don't remember, but lyrics that apply to me. Each morning I slowly get up and sometimes knowing what I am going to do that day; sometimes there are no pressing appointments or pleasures awaiting me. Yesterday in conversation I talked about a play whose name escaped me. When I got home I searched my memory and researched my bookshelves. I found the name and the author. It was the play "Skin of My Teeth". It had touched me deeply years ago and in reading the summary of the play, a quote by the author struck a chord "the point of view of the wise observer who is not involved in what he sees but who does not, for that reason, despise what he is observing in the failures and triumphs of mankind".

I could for the most part been a character in this play. I do see and observe but I am basically uninvolved ergo I fault no one for their shortcomings and take casual enjoyment in their success. Whether I am a "wise observer" would have to be someone else's observation. This is what I am, what I was and what I will be. As the song goes, I'm basically "biding my time", seeing the world and watching the inhabitants moving about in their struggle to maintain some semblance of happiness and achievement. On the other hand, there are those of us the observers who are just "biding our time".

TIPS FOR TENDERNESS

Dedicated to all those who have lost their one and only, wife or husband and who need loving care.

1. Flannel sheets—It feels like sleeping on velvet, warm and cozy. You melt like chocolate over an ice cream sundae.
2. Good food—Any food your little heart desires. Unless you have a specific health problem indulge your taste buds. Spicy to enhance your taste, fried chicken, hamburgers, potato chips and even hot dogs to remind you of the good old days when people didn't worry about calories or cholesterol
3. Sound—Music that still makes you feel like dancing. Melodies that you can hum. Symphonies where your soul is enriched and your ears feel content.
4. Outside—Anywhere outside. If you feel like traveling, go for it. If you are not that ambitious, walk through the park or walk through the mall. You don't need a destination.
5. Books—If you find it hard to concentrate, don't fret. If you were once a reader, you'll probably wander back to immerse yourself in a book. Just relax and let your imagination take you into the world within the pages.
6. Quiet Time—To many being alone seems sad and depressing. Not necessarily. There is something very peaceful about quiet time. It restores some of the energy that is dissipated throughout the day. Reminisce a little but don't dwell on sadness. Think how lucky you are and were. You had a companion for many years and you were there to give them a

final tribute. As someone said to me last night. "You have to think about your future".

I thought about it and I have come to the conclusion that I am living my future. I've traveled a long road and intend to keep going. Long ago, I never dreamed about the future but I find each day has some pleasure to offer me, some smaller, some larger. I am grateful my future is still bright.

UNQUIET GRAVE

Waves of sadness flow, submerge me
Without warning. Winds snap at my
Face holding hands with anger
Gentle breezes take aim and
Tease me into bottomless pits.
Pulled up by bootstraps of courage
Determined to continue through
The next minute, the seconds are
Counted and stirred together to
Make an hour.
Deep, deep pain goes undiagnosed
No medicine man to cure an illness
With no name, again and again
To restart the wounded spirit
Remembered cries at approaching death
Always waiting around dark corners
Is the unquiet grave calling?

WHAT DID I WANT TO DO

I just finished listening to a program talking about the last line uttered by a character named Babbitt in the book by Sinclair Lewis "I've never done anything I ever wanted to do".

A lot of people could speak the same line and be speaking the truth. I think how sad that one goes through life never following their dreams, their joy or their desires.

I have indeed been lucky. I haven't consciously followed anything but some plan, some invisible wind blew me into the direction that pleased me and enveloped me with warm, loving hands; always seeming to steer me down roads, through mazes and up mountains of life. I feel I have given my senses a joy ride. I can remember many, many things I wanted to do and I did them. I've had setbacks but upon reflection they were positive because they broadened my knowledge and balanced my perspective.

For instance: If you've never been sick, how do you know what being well is all about. If you haven't felt pain, how can you appreciate the lack of it? To be perfectly honest, I have not done everything I ever wanted to do. At this moment, I am content and want to remain in this stagnant stage for a while but *this is what I want to do*. It is a good thing I am writing this at 12:30AM because by morning, I might think what I wrote was a lot of midnight oil being used to try to define the old question "Who am I"?

ADDENDUM 9:50 AM
MARCH 10, 1994

1. I never thought much about money or investing. I earned some, I spent some, I saved some but I never thought about it.
2. I never had a goal in my life, no grand ambition. I lived day by day and for some unknown reason, I attained contentment and happiness most of the time.
3. Now I wonder what I am going to do with the rest of my life. There must be a lot of things I never did that I can do. There is a magical essence to being alive and always the expectation of a surprise ending to the day, the week or maybe the year. I had no idea I would end up as "ye old philosopher" but what the heck, why not?

MEMORIES

Where do memories go? I have a large volume of stories about where I lived, how I lived, with whom I lived, whom I've met and what I did and didn't do. If memories could be incorporated into an art form what a wonderful colorful tapestry it would be. I think all of us have a large collectible assortment of memories.

Sometimes the word "memory" sounds trivial; its use so casually mouthed. When I start remembering, I am amazed at the experiences and the people involved in my life. They all have been incorporated into my life's resume. I can't remember the day I was born but since my mother's memory became part of mine, they have been added together with a grandmother I never knew and her life in another country.

What I would like to know is when I die, where will my memories go? Does it matter? It matters to me now and maybe that is all that's important. I have my own private library. There is no subject undocumented. Children's section, young adults, young married and the titles read—adventures, mystery, death, divorce, love, intrigue, pets and on it continues. How wonderful to open your mind and find any subject at any given moment. No leather bound library growing dusty on the shelves. Each of us has our own personal libraries for our own use and to share with others.

At least for our lifetime, we have accumulated a world (our world) of knowledge and by the time we leave, the pages will be frayed and well read with loving care.

INTESTINALLY CHALLENGED

I have muscular malformation
Congenital deformation
My inner sanctum does the twist
A new dance, I've added to the list
This is a brand new diagnosis
Certainly better than halitosis
The cure is no more problems
No more stress
Who's kidding, we're all a mess
I say, take it easy, have a giggle
Perhaps my belly will stop its jiggle
Another pill, perhaps a few
And in no time, as good as new.

THOUGHTS OF A
SENIOR CITIZEN

It is all so very amusing

It is all so very confusing

It seems I've attained a certain age

I read the book and turned the page

Life has not turned out as I thought it would

Mostly I've done better than I thought I could

I'm more content, sometimes I feel benign

Like a purring cat, I still feel fine.

WITHDRAWAL

I've felt this strange emotion for the last month and couldn't put a name to it. I don't think I ever felt this urgency to not want to talk, laugh or even think. This is so unlike me not to have the slightest desire to participate in the world around me.

Since I've been co-dependent with death for over a year this unsettling feeling must be a form of withdrawal. However, the usual addiction to alcohol or drugs might possibly have some similarity only in that each addiction has a negative effect on one's life and must be devastating in ways I will never know. I never thought I was addicted to death or sadness but since I've been living side by side with it, something within me is trying desperately to move away.

This brooding sense of nothingness I've been living with is a bridge I must cross and let the past go. How odd that I can sit here so calmly writing about something that has changed my life completely. When and if my withdrawal from the recent past becomes a reality, I very much hope I will become co-dependent with life.

MIDNIGHT THOUGHTS

Who will help me die? My husband stayed with my mother and helped her leave since I could no longer bear to hear or see her last painful moments. When my husband's turn came, I held fast and watched as he left as gently and tenderly as I could make possible. And now, I am wondering who will help me when I've reached the end of my life. Will I be aware and if so whose voice will I hear and whose touch will I feel?

By writing this morbid question, I do believe many of us from time to time would like to think someone would be there for our last moments of this glorious life that was bequeathed us. I find it so hard to think of leaving. I don't think I will have ever gotten my fill of life. Realistically, I know there is an end and I would hope someone is there to say goodbye. I will be going on the longest journey of my life and I would like a good send off; perhaps the words "Sweet dreams" would suffice.

I am in the twilight of my life and I suppose in the late evening when all is quiet, we come face to face with our own mortality. It is sad but a sadness of acceptance and quietness of the heart. I am trying to put my emotional books in order. Slowly over the past years I have neatly filed thoughts and deeds into convenient niches. I want to put my world in order. I don't want to have any regrets. I hope I can fill in all the blanks that haven't been examined yet. I would like to leave some legacy to the world but that is yet to be defined or even visualized. Even when I depart without the ceremonial trappings of a potentate, it would be comforting to think by my being, I had made a difference, a positive difference in some way. I think I have. I think I have done some good and perhaps that's enough. In retrospect and upon midnight ruminations, I think having done some good is quite acceptable as my legacy. No kindness or goodness should be taken lightly. Now as I wend my way to bed and to sleep, I can truly say, I haven't been half bad.

STRANGERS IN PARADISE

On our first trip to Europe, to Rome, the city of Eternal Light, I remember crossing the Atlantic from an altitude of 30,000 feet and was amazed that we seemed to be perpetually in bright sunshine. There was a period of night, possibly when the movie was being shown and the shades were drawn. I kept peaking around the shades and after a few hours of darkness, back we were again in the hilariously sunny skies welcoming me to a place I always wanted to go "sunny Italy".

It was sunny! We were efficiently collected like confused school children and driven to our hotel on the Via Veneto. The guide made amusing remarks about the driving habits of the Italians. We were in Italy, how fantastic, how magical. We were ushered to our room. It had a door painted a bilious green but we were in Rome. The bathtub was huge, so huge that I continued to feel very special as I splashed and luxuriated in the bubble bath that was generously supplied with the room. After inspecting our living quarters, I found the mini bar. This was my first introduction and I looked inside and saw all the bottles and cheeses. I thought perhaps this was an additional gift showered upon us by the Romans. I was hesitant to partake and gingerly removed a coke, drank it not wanting to be a greedy guest.

Eventually, over the next few days I learned the mini bar was there for our convenience, but it had a price. Every day the maid who cleaned the room inspected the contents, replaced what was used and noted it down to be placed upon our bill at the end of our stay.

The day we were leaving and our tour group was checking out, I heard howls of displeasure coming from the front desk. "What is this bill for?" "I don't understand these charges." It seems several of our fellow travelers had used much if not all of the contents of the mini bar in their rooms. We were not the only ones who were naïve but fortunately we had observed the ritual of replacement.

Looking back, we were strangers in Paradise, Rome was Paradise, Italy was Paradise—but as we all find out sooner or later even Paradise has a price.

THE LEANING TOWER

In Italy, there stands a famous leaning tower. It has been leaning for centuries. The soil was unstable or possibly the builder didn't make allowances for certain structural flaws. I really don't know why the leaning tower of Pisa is leaning.

I know that I am leaning a bit and so are many of my peer group—the alone group—the women who no longer have the balance of someone to hold them upright emotionally. Thus, we lean and since there are many of us we retain our stability by using each other as an invisible crutch to maintain our dignity. We don't think about our frail posture too often, as it is painful to realize we are dependent on others for our strength. It is true though without the support of others, we would be wavering and clutching at walls that don't exist.

I personally am very thankful that I am part of this tower that has enabled me to endure through the emptiness and sadness that is like a moat surrounding me. "Leaning Tower" or whatever metaphor I choose to describe my friends, we do hold each other together. If one falters another stands a little taller to compensate as we continue our journey through life.

DÉJÀ VU

The first time I took an airplane trip was a very traumatic event. My father was very ill, lived 2,000 miles across the country and I was compelled to travel by the most expeditious means. I was like many fearful, apprehensive and downright scared of sitting in a large object that soared above the earth.

I spent a sleepless night before the day of the flight and then the "day" was upon me. At the airport, I am sure I did the usual things, checked luggage, tickets, etc. I proceeded to go up the ramp or possibly up the steps to board the plane. The moment I walked aboard the plane, utter calm overtook me. I had been here before. I remembered how the aisles looked and the seats and the small windows. This was no threat to my safety; I had been here. I settled comfortably in my seat and in due time, the plane rolled down the runway and lifted gently and regally into the sky.

Even though my destination was one of sadness, my trip was one of pleasant elation and the ability to be sitting thousands of feet above the checkerboard earth; I felt the presence of those living in those infinitesimal houses below. I know why I felt so at ease in this strange vehicle in the air. I realized I had seen many movies of planes, people entering and departing planes. My imagination had transferred me from the movie screen to the real thing and for whatever reason; the transference was smooth and effortless.

I would wish all fear could be disposed of so easily. Flying through the white clouds, I remembering how mellow I felt. It was dreamlike. Now to become philosophical. Are dreams a reality or is reality a dream?

EXPIRATION DATE

I decided to bake something, which I haven't done in a very long time. Today, I felt ambitious. I would, for me, do something important. Cook! And then I decided to "bake". It was only muffins but I have avoided the kitchen for months except for brief moments so it became a major undertaking. It is time to befriend my kitchen, my stove, and my oven and make a commitment; have a relationship with all of the above.

I opened various cookbooks to determine which recipe was the most advantageous in arriving at the end result "good tasting muffins". I started assembling the ingredients and when I glanced at the top of the box of grain that was to be the main ingredient— lo and behold, the expiration date was a year and a half old. I opened the box and tasted and, yes, the taste was stale and tired.

All of a sudden I felt stale and tired, too! All of this new found energy was slowly draining away. The project was doomed, no muffins today. Expiration dates be damned! We all have one and I think, actually I know, that coming face to face with a date long past on a package of unopened cereal has stirred some subliminal emotion.

When did I put this box on my shelf? What happened all those past months? I suppose it boils down to a very simple fact. Don't worry about expiration dates, but do be aware that everyone and everything has one.

CALM BEFORE THE STORM

Today, I am calm. Benign and slowly moving in and out; doing small things and thinking large thoughts. How very, very nice to feel smooth, soft and serene. I am not foolish enough to think this mood will last but I will immerse myself in this warm soothing emotional bath until the *water* starts to turn cold. Even the silence around me is sweet—the only sound is the murmur of the refrigerator and a distant hum of traffic, alerting me to the outside world where noise is the flavor of the day.

I will carefully place this "calm" into a storage place in my memory and possibly on one of my whirling, dervish days be able to restore this day and relive it again. I still don't understand life or death. I still don't know why we are here and then we are gone. I still need to make some sense out of our existence. It can't be only for procreation and building a "better mouse trap". All the years I have lived I have seen the stumbling, bumbling of my fellow creatures. I feel we surely must be created for a better purpose. I have no answer and that is the answer. We are because we are but I would hope there is a better explanation.

I'M A CAUTION, TOO

"Finian, you're a caution". I said that to my senior citizen cat. It is an old fashioned phrase. I think it was used during the turn of the century. I use it now and then when speaking to my cat. He is a kind of a turn of the century cat himself; a very proud, private kind of cat. He has these little quirks, which seem to me old fashioned and very endearing. I think pet owners view themselves in their pet's behavior. Even though far fetched, it gives us pleasure to imagine that we know what they are thinking. Whenever I say, "Finian, you're a caution", I find myself momentarily back to summertime and cars with running boards and people spending Sunday in the park having picnics. All the long wide porches have big wooden swings and dogs run down the street without leashes and kids play hide-an-seek and wood tag.

I don't remember yesterday but I do remember yesterdays. I am sure they are not exactly as I remember them and I doubt if I was as I remember me.

A MOMENT OF SILENCE

For some reason, I have never noticed how little respect people pay to death. From the expression "You'll be the death of me" to the present day when dying is a commonplace occurrence in movies and television. Even the commercials on television talk about death and heaven as an amusing incident, not to be taken seriously. I take death very seriously.

Maybe, I didn't view death as a reality and was as indifferent as I now find the world around me. I suppose it's a protective coat we wear most of our lives to make our life bearable. I no longer wear the protective coat and death is the largest reality in my life. When the person closest to you dies, you come face to face with your own mortality. I find myself musing about my own death.

I find it very annoying to realize that so little homage is given death. Of course, if a moment of silence were awarded everyone who dies, there would never be another sound in the world.

I DIDN'T WIN AN OSCAR

I had a very strange dream. Once long ago when I was in school, I acted in several plays. My roles were very diverse. In one I was a student enrolled in an exclusive private school, a role of a spoiled, insolent girl. The other role was of an older person, perhaps a grandmother, who spent the entire play in her rocking chair dispensing wise words of advice, a mature counselor.

Last night in my dream, I was hurriedly going through old school notebooks looking for the plays and I was totally frustrated by not finding them. I then began acting out roles. It seems each scene I would find myself on stage acting out different roles. I would briefly be a character in a mystery, an emotional drama, a comedy and then as I recall an avant-garde play where chaos was the norm; the running back and forth, the speeches to everyone and no one, an abstract painting to capture many colors and moods.

Now that I am awake, bits and pieces of the dream keep making inroads into my brain. Dreams don't make sense, or mostly don't as far I am concerned. The conclusion I've finally come to is that all the roles in my life transferred into my dream world. Why now? Why not now? I am close to the rocking chair part that I had many years ago, and the play is coming to an end. I want to review my roles, I suppose, and applaud the good performances and be tolerant about the rest.

Role playing—was assigned when we were born. Genetically, environmentally, emotionally and then random chance polished the edges. In my dream, there was no conclusions drawn about the characters but in the light of day, the conclusions are more apparent. We gently and sometimes not gently wend our way from the cradle to the grave. As we grow older and move slower, we internalize our fear and hope we have a few more roles to play. Anyone can play dead.

NOTHING CERTAIN

I have always liked getting lost. Ever since I can remember it was not necessary for me to know exactly what I was going to do; whether it meant a certain show, a certain restaurant, a certain store—"nothing certain" should have been my motto. It is totally unnecessary to live your life in an orderly fashion to be happy; perhaps to be successful a certain amount of order is probably a good thing. Since ambition was never part of my vocabulary, I have lived my life on a daily basis, just doing what comes naturally.

I have lived for the most part an ordinary life; similar to most of the people I've known. The most obvious difference between the others and me is I don't mind getting lost and finding a road I've never been on before or a place that I've never heard of. Unfortunately, as you get older, getting lost isn't as interesting. I don't wander far from home anymore and my curiosity isn't as keen. I have enjoyed the unknown that I've discovered in the world. Around every corner, you can discover something new, something different; not an earth shattering phenomenon but just the wide-eyed wonderment that children seem to have. There is a child in all of us and I suppose I allowed her to play long after she grew up. Actually she's still there just waiting for another adventure.

BABIES ON MY KNEE

The babies on my knees are getting older. If you ever look at your knees, they have baby faces; soft unformed, dimpled, rounded faces. I looked down and since this is a warm day decided to wear shorts. My baby faces seemed to have wrinkles and a rather tired look. My knees and I have obviously gone through an aging process.

I know I feel more tired and though I don't admit, even to myself, there is sure to be a few more wrinkles, lines around the mouth and eyes than there were before my baby faces got older. All in all, aging is not my enemy but the accessories that come with age are most annoying. When your hair turns to "silver", clerks in the stores start treating you like you are either invisible or demented and senile. I am none of the above and neither is most of my peer group. They are wise, forgiving and have much to offer the ones who are following us in our march to our inevitable destiny. Again I look down at my knees and say "baby faces; you still look good to me".

BREAKFAST IN BED

I don't remember having breakfast in bed except in the hospital. I wouldn't call that a joyous occasion, just food that was put in front of you at a very early hour that you were expected to eat. I don't remember if it was good or bad; when you're sick, you re just waiting to get better.

It does sound so elegant though "breakfast in bed". We see it in the movies. Actually, it is very messy; crumbs falling all over and trying to balance a cup of coffee in a semi-reclining position. However, I have begun serving my cat "breakfast in bed". It is not actually breakfast—just a meal. It's not actually a bed—just a chaise lounge on the deck outside my living room. He has advanced to a resident senior citizen status and is reluctant to partake of his meals, unless it is something particularly tasteful. Otherwise, he glances casually at his plate and moves out to take his ease.

Since I am ever watchful of all members of my family and am concerned for his well being, I began offering him my services and brought his meal to this reclining creature who views me with a look of disdain tempered with "noblesse oblige" and daintily nibbles off the plate I hold carefully for him.

How did I become so servile to this animal that is years younger than me? I am not a push over and have stood my ground on many issues over the years. Yet here I am catering to a cat. How the mighty have fallen. The only excuse I can offer myself to this obsequious behavior is that I am a bigger person than he is. I can reason on all levels. He is totally selfish. I only hope that I will never need breakfast in bed. I would so much rather be benevolent than needy.

FLUENT IN CAT

Many people are bilingual, trilingual or multilingual. I, on the other hand, can speak English, American English. There are times I am at a loss for words. However, I do speak some "cat." Since my cat talks a lot (meows, howls) and since I've become accustomed to his voice now and then I do understand him. For instance, I just walked through the downstairs room and decided to replenish his water bowl in the bathroom. He has one upstairs in the kitchen and other is downstairs. He was reclining in the chair downstairs and he said "Water" or some cat word that means water. I perched gingerly on the floor and held the bowl for his comfort. He drank and drank and drank. I said, "Hey, are you are a camel preparing for a sojourn into the desert?" He didn't answer me, just kept drinking. I said, "Who was your maid this time last week?" He just kept drinking.

I said, "Am I your water boy?" He just kept drinking. O.K. I do perhaps go overboard a bit on spoiling this furry creature but how can you say "No" to a cat; a cat that understands English while I am so limited in "cat." This all reminds me of a song, a western cowboy kind of song "Cool, cool water." I don't remember the words but I know I have one cool cat.

This morning after a leisurely breakfast, my cat climbed up the side of my chair and proceeded to groom himself; to settle down for his morning nap. Hey, my cat doesn't sit in my lap in the morning. In fact, my cat hardly sits in my lap at all.

Come evening, if all things are in the right sequence, time, weather, dinner, sounds—he will accommodate me, so to speak, by sitting in my lap for perhaps thirty minutes. I have adjusted to his schedule and welcome his short-term interest.

Mornings now, that's another story. I like to peruse the newspaper and it is very difficult to turn the pages with a creature on your lap. Firstly, he gets annoyed as I try to carefully read without too much rustling and it is hard to concentrate. I give up. If my cat decides to perch on my lap in the a.m., the strains of the song "Love is where you find it" comes to mind. Never turn your back on love, any love.

FUNNY AS A
RUBBER CRUTCH

Yes, "funny as a rubber crutch". The trick is not to use a crutch and avoid any pitfalls. Laughing at myself is one of my favorite pastimes. At times I think I know all the answers but realistically I am just winging it. My ability to solve problems applies only to myself and if I land on my feet, I've will have resumed my upright stance for the moment.

We are always teetering and tottering. Why is it so important to be right? There is no such thing as "right" but there such a thing as "wrong". The word "wrong" to me should be defined as "insensitive, manipulative, cruel, self serving". "Right" is whatever makes us feel good, worthwhile, happy and content.

How in the world did I fall into a dictionary mode this morning? I guess I have nothing better to do and when I thought of the phrase "funny as a rubber crutch", I began to visualize the tilting and balancing act I have embarked upon in these past two years. I find myself smiling and am reminded of those "Have a Good Day" buttons with the big smile. O.K. "Have a Good Day".

As I was meandering along I saw a reflection of myself in a mirror. I looked a lot different than I remembered and I thought "Time Marches On". It's just a bromide of a statement that we all say from time to time. I have always been out of step or maybe I just wanted to saunter along sometimes faster and sometimes I guess you could call me a straggler. There was always so much to see, so much to do. Stopping and watching the world, my world was not to be hurried but to be relished, sampled and savored.

"Marches On" indeed, time moves, hurries, passes, speeds and sometimes for brief seconds stops. How phrases remain in the back room of our mind and wisps of airborne thoughts surround us. Like smoke blown by the wind, they move away and we continue our timely march or in my case, a slow walk, on and on and on.

FIREFLIES AND JUNE BUGS

How wonderful it was to be young, really young—grammar school young. As I have grown older, I've begun to remember all the little things that happened; funny, sad, precocious—all the evolving of the me. Whether anyone reads this or not, relates to it or not, doesn't matter because at sometime in your life you start to explore your beginning and sort out the fragments in the pockets of your mind.

You pull out an Indian head penny and a story emerges. You walk past a drug store, another story. You sit under a tree, another and then another. It's like spring-cleaning your mind. The days are numbered but I think I have such bounty in storage that I will have to live a very long time to sort it all out and if not, I will have certainly done a good job trying.

I am watching the sunrise. A broad orange band across the horizon is slowly moving up and reaching for the sky. As the darkness turns lighter and a sleeping city yawns and begins moving into the day, I contemplate the magnificence of life. To have been born and been able to observe this unbelievable miracle of beauty is something I want to hold close and cherish all the allotted days of my life.

Floating clouds intrude into the morning landscape smearing the colors to remind us that every thing changes, always changes and not to take anything for granted. I sit here quietly waiting for the day to begin; another day to add to the sum of the years of my life. There are so many unanswered questions in my mind. I only hope I can live my life in broad beautiful bands of color and as I grow older continue to appreciate all around me.

BURNING BRIDGES

I don't burn bridges, but bridges have burnt me. Sometimes, I feel like I am the only innocent moving in the world. I have never looked at people as enemies, rivals, conspirators or devious, manipulative minds. I walk among them and I confide, befriend and empathize with them re their innumerable problems. I've finally begun to realize the more problems people share with you, the bigger problem you are going to have with them.

We share with friends but we try very hard not to burden them. All of our backs are bowed with innumerable distressing events, which we have lived through. We come out of each tunnel of sadness to seek the light. Time and again, all through my life I have had to move away by burning bridges (people who would use you and if you allow them they will use you up). They are like hot embers snapping at your heels, whining chards, complaining sparks and once you feel the inferno about to consume you—run to the nearest exit.

I did burn a bridge once. I left the city where I had been born, went to school and spent my teen years. I was always the outsider. I was always different. I was ostracized by my peer group but never understood why. We had moved to the wrong side of the tracks during the depression, which obviously put me on a lower social level. I was smart, pretty, polite but virtually ignored at parties and gatherings. I urged my mother to let me move to another city. She promised that if I would work for one year to increase my chances of employment somewhere else, she would allow me to go. I was seventeen years old.

I did get a job for one year. In a general store, I was the secretary, bookkeeper, cashier, saleslady and part time driver. I did not know how to drive but to get this job I said I knew. Of course, I was found out. I was working for literally peanuts (48 hours@$10.00 a week). My boss's son was given the task of teaching me. It took about a week but I loved to drive and I did well enough. The excitement of a general store in those days delighted me. There was much doing; people milling about, my boss yelling at his wife and his son. I engaged in a conspiracy with his wife who took monies from the cash register and mark it "refund". She said her husband never gave her enough to run their home properly. The gentle salesmen; one large and funny—the other tall, thin and I believe an alcoholic. Both perfect gentlemen. I blossomed in their kindness. The three salesladies; one fat and motherly, one slim and gossipy who talked about her sex life with her husband (I listened quietly with perked up ears) and Mrs. Killough, tall, dark, elegant whom I admired. I felt great pleasure in her company and we often had lunch together.

Time does run on and it did. At the end of the year, my mother knew I was chomping at the bit. She asked if I would like to go to San Francisco. She had a sister there. Since WWII had started, jobs were plentiful. I was excited and thought it too good to be true; going to California was like a wonderful dream. My mother only put forth one obstacle; she said she was going with me. This was no hindrance in any way. She was and remained my best friend until she died.

Before we left, I was invited to a party by one of the girls. I went with bells on; I came in breezily, laughing and said, "Where's the wine?" My friend's mother was a very generous, warm woman who had befriended me years before. I thought of her as young aunt with a great sense of humor. I found a bottle of wine in the kitchen, where the boys were assembled, and preceded to pour small glasses of grape wine. They all looked at me shocked. You would think I had disrobed and was doing the dance of the seven veils. The girls were all gathered like a covey of geese in the living room. Teenagers in those days were introverted until enough time passed; then they began slowly making their way toward each other, first talking, playing party games and then perhaps dancing. Here I was the "shy, outcast" being totally out there, unrestricted, drinking, laughing. In retrospect, I was disrobing figuratively and I was for the first time in my life being *me*. I was glad I was me. The boys circled about me and I danced with most of them. The girls stayed in the living room and muttered. I had a marvelous time. I laughed, I danced—I had finally had my coming out party. It was now time to leave the party and the city. It was time to begin a new life with the new me who had been shunned and rejected.

I did start a new life. I had to do much backing and filling, but I never again became the lonely, rejected child whose role others thrust upon her. That is what I mean by my "burning my bridge". I separated myself from the past by a very innocent abandonment of the priggishness of the place I had spent my young life.

Years and years have passed but remembering that evening even now gives me time to pause and smile. When you have arrived at your moment of truth, nothing can equal the elation. Utter freedom of expression is compulsory for peace of mind. I just have to look over my shoulder once in a while and be sure that the unhappy, lonely girl is long gone and even in moments of sadness or illness never relinquish the spirit I acquired and developed and continue to hone. Take it from one who knows and I know it's a cliché "Be true to yourself" and no can every hurt you!

PARDON MY DUST

I often talk to myself when I go to bed in the late evenings. Living alone has turned me into an effective conversationalist with myself. During the day, there are friends to converse with, chores to do and then comes the night. The nights, alas, alack; I don't think I ever talked upon retiring when I had a companion. All the talk between us had been used up by bedtime.

Last night I said, "I'm going to hit the dust"; another dated phrase from my generation. Then I began to smile and thought of my final resting place. I, if all goes, as it should, be placed dust down in some sort of container (next to my husband who by now will have become even dustier than I). Why do I find this so amusing? "A gathering of dust". We, all of us, are so insignificant in the scheme of things—a few short years on a planet billions of years old—running madly around, trying to make do, living, loving, laughing, crying, creeping, calculating.

Then lo and behold, the end is approaching. I have thought and observed the question of the ages. "Why are we here, what was it all about, was it worth it?" I think I have the answers or maybe my answers. I am here because I am. In my case, it was about a myriad of things, wonderful, beautiful things, food for the eye, warmth for the soul, love for the heart. This doesn't mean that there were not desperate, painful, utterly horrific times of sadness that only a very small pit in my stomach vaguely remembers.

Was it worth it? You bet your bottom dollar, it was. You better believe it! It was a once in a lifetime experience. Here I go with another "in your face" remark. I can sit here, growing older, some days feeling like I'd like to chuck it all and then the overwhelming amazement that I have been born and have existed is like I won a zillion dollar lotto. "Hit the Dust"! That too will be included in my resume. If some small particle of me remains somewhere on this earth or even floating around and about and, if perhaps a drop of rain or a little moisture should fall upon this speck, I would like to think I'll be laughing and saying "Here's mud in your eye".

WIDDER WOMAN

A southern expression epitomizing the state of women left husbandless "widder women". Husbands, who have died and left these lonely, lost, unwanted species to wander the earth until they join their men.

I am one of these "widder women" and I have been lonely, lost and unwanted for the past two years. At least, I felt lonely, lost and unwanted. I feel for some unknown reason I have turned a sharp corner and if I allow myself to move forward, I will no longer be lonely, lost and unwanted. I think I have started to utilize the brains and savvy I was born with and have only to open my eyes and look around. Possibly I might have a profound effect in some way but mostly on myself. I feel like I still have the energy and capacity to do much and enjoy much. Even as I sit here writing enthusiastic utterances to myself, I know underneath this bravado is another "widder woman'. The whole point of this delusional diatribe is that I enjoy the delusion or illusion. So what difference does it make? If I make the effort to enjoy the pleasure of being for the moment, the hour or the day all is well. I see reality but it is no longer bleak or black. It embraces me, charms me and kindly nudges me on. "Widder woman" you're still here taste the air, smell the sky—You still have time.

BETTER THAN SEX

Writing is better than sex. There is no orgasm as such; it is just a pleasurable relationship between you and your words. In the usual conversation between two or more parties, there's a give or take, an opinion not really analyzed or given any real merit. Just talk. Talk words.

Writing is truly the most absolutely pure, blissful, enervating, exciting event you can possibly believe. It took me many long years of marching to different drums and drummers. I had to arrive alone, at my own place, to realize that I have utter contentment with my words, my thoughts, my dreams, undreamt or real. It doesn't matter whether I am ever published or read or even heard. I have the music of words in my ears. Of course, we all like to be noticed and if somewhere, someone reads or hears me that will be a big plus.

Meanwhile, whenever my imagination and memories become ignited, I eagerly reach for a notebook and pen; and the thrill begins again. How ignoble to compare sex with writing. Obviously, I was born with strong desires, to play, to love, to travel, to be useful and useless. The desire is still there. They are now channeled into another direction. Now they have become more circumscribed. Age has dealt me a few debilitating blows, nothing devastating. It just has given me the perspective to do what I want to do, when I want to do it. That is "write".

I'm still playing, still doing many other things but my priorities have changed. I sometimes feel I know all the answers to all the questions anyone would ask me. I know no answer, only my answer.

I have lived my life and played my role. If I don't know who I am by this time, I'd better look again. No doubt I am probably still hiding behind myself.

HOW DID THEY LOVE ME?

Sometimes in the night hours, I begin to think of the men who loved me and whom I loved. The first was a casual love with a casual man. I was young, virginal and tentative. He casually loved me, indifferent, charming but if there was any emotion contained in some deep pocket, it was never apparent or revealed. The light touch was not intimidating; in fact in some ways comfortable. Nothing was expected from me and in turn I expected very little from him.

The next man was respectful, appreciative and tactful. He endured my lightness, my lack of total commitment but I did love him and began to find a road into a depth of love I never knew existed. I became involved, I became interested but it was only a transition to a more passionate time.

I met the new one; the delight of my body and my life. We were young, smooth skinned, happy kittens/puppies playing with each other. We touched, we laughed; we thoroughly enjoyed springtime sexuality; no sweating, no heavy-duty emotions. We found pleasure both sexual, emotional and always anticipating each other's smile and laughter. Neither of us played a major role; only two joyous children reveling in the sunshine of our lives.

The last one, the fourth one, at last I met the conqueror. He needed to be the only one I ever knew or loved. He needed to feel that he was the master of my fate. He needed to take care of me, to nurture me and take control. I leaned easily against his strength; I loved his strength, I loved his compassion, I loved his mind. I loved him but I was not willing to be placed in a lesser role than an equal. This was difficult for us both. I was coming out of a life lived on the light side and he was coming out of a life lived in the dark. Slowly we began to mix the colors and appreciate the variations. Slowly, we evolved into a marriage, a marriage of souls, well beyond the casual, the respectful, and the playful. We became a solid unit. Each of us could depend, enjoy, and need the other. If I spent my days as well as I remember, I will always salute my last love. A true warrior who believed in people, a true soldier that fought other people's battles, a true dreamer who never had the time to dream his own dreams and enough compassion for the entire human race.

Enough of love; never enough of love. Here I am in a warm room, with my cat that is busy washing and grooming his elegant coat. We both know it has been grand, truly grand!

"AND THE TRUTH SHALL SET YOU FREE"

We are surrounded by phrases, poems, quotes, sayings and they all sound beneficial sometimes to someone. For the first time in my life, I truly know that "the truth shall set me free". I feel completely unshackled, completely euphoric, completely at ease. The truth is being sincere to your own nature. I thought I was.

At this time in my life, I have finally penetrated my core; I have finally begun to realize my self worth. I no longer need to be nice for niceness sake. It truly is o.k. to be me. I answer to no man/woman, only to myself. I guess you have to go through fire and pain, symbolically at least to reach yourself and find that you're the you that has been there all your life.

Many things, many people, many circumstances shaped you into this malleable person most people have seen but it was only a façade. I was afraid of rejection, afraid and was unaware of the fear. How odd, how very odd to have finally reached this miraculous plateau of freedom. I take nothing for granted but I will never be the same again, not better, just never the same. Hallelujah! Free at Last!

FLAT EARTH THEORY

Have you ever had the feeling that when you reached the corner, you couldn't go around it. Every corner has a corner and we go round in circles all our lives. Of course, there is another perspective—the so-called "flat earth theory". From the time we begin walking and thinking, we move forward—straight ahead, a stop here and there but we keep on moving. Day after day, year after year. We keep growing older, wiser, moving ahead on the road we have chosen but it is the "flat earth" perspective.

Corners don't start appearing like mirages until we have aged a bit. Then we want to know "What's around the corner?" Each time I seem to have reached a corner, it would move illusively out of view. I guess I'll never see around the bend anymore. Corners are like fake stage sets—while you're involved in the play, you forget it is only fantasy. The curtain comes down, the lights are turned on brightly and reality sets in.

How easy it is to dream, how easy it is to believe life goes on forever. There is really no down side to all of this, just reality. The world we reside in at the moment is beautiful, the sounds and smells are very real. It is just that sooner or later, others will be participating in the plays. We have used up our vouchers, played our roles and long, long past the time of our departure, someone else will be trying to look around the corner and the cycle continues.

HAIR, THE LONG
AND SHORT OF IT

I'm getting mixed messages. We have all read about Samson and Delilah. We all remember that when she convinced him to cut his hair and his strength retreated. This has nothing at all to do with Samson and Delilah, but it has to do with hair. I cut it often. I wear it short. I don't know how strong I am. I decided not to cut my hair a few weeks ago and it is growing. Actually, it looks quite nice. Full, feminine and fluffy, albeit a certain shade of silver. It blows in the wind; it lies around my head. I look in the mirror and I see a woman of a certain age with hair, not short, trim, tapered hair—but hair, glorious strands moving about covering a head.

Somehow I feel stronger, more in charge. I wonder, is it the possession of more hair? No, that couldn't be the reason or maybe it is. Possibly, just possibly like everything else in our lives, there are certain natural assets given to us to be appreciated. For instance, nice skin, pretty eyes, a symmetric nose and full lips, eyebrows and lashes that matches. One could keep adding, long legs, tapered waist, full bosoms, and graceful neck. Nobody gets it all but sometimes we get more than others.

Even hair; I have hair; I had hair—another color, another age. Now I think I will keep letting it grow. How far or for how long, I don't know. As long as I feel that like Samson, should I cut it, I will be reduced to less than I feel now—I will let it keep growing and growing and growing. And then one day, I will look in the mirror and say "Hey, I need a haircut."

ONE OF THE SADDEST DAYS OF MY LIFE

I loved fairy tales. I loved to read. Each week during the summer, I spent going to the Waco Public Library taking out four books each week (the maximum allowed) and began my journey into the magical land of Ali Baba and the Forty Thieves, 1001 Nights, Alice in Wonderland and Dorothy on her way to meet the Wizard of Oz. From age nine through age eleven, nothing could make me happier than to have this magical world at my fingertips.

There was a corner on the second floor of the library that contained all the fairy tales in the world (my world). I eagerly and selectively removed four books each time from the shelves. As time went on my selection dwindled and since the books were arranged alphabetically, I would pick those, which I had overlooked to be sure, I wasn't going to miss one juicy morsel of fantasy. On and on I read and slowly but much too fast, I finally in desperation reached the "Z's". The "Z's"; the end of my childhood. No more kings or queens, no more castles, no more flights of magic carpets, no more dragons, no more mysterious potions, no more! I had reached the end.

I asked one of my cousin's who was five years older than me what books I should read now. The shelves on the other side of the library were foreign to me. She suggested a few books. I went to those bookshelves and gingerly took out two books. I began to read. I had no interest in these girls who played tennis or rode horses. I could not identify with them at all. I had lived in the

Land of Oz. I had lived in Wonderland. I had stood in a tower with long flowing hair. I had seen the prince approach to rescue me on his sleek shining steed. I had spent years in faraway places with colorful bazaars and danger lurking down long dark cobblestone alleys. Now I found myself in this colorless world of rosy cheeked, well-mannered girls who if they had been real would have found me a very unwanted stranger among them.

I continued to read but I never went near those shelves again. I moved from shelf to shelf—a book here, a book there. There was life after fairytales but it would take some getting used to.

The day I reached the "Z's" stands out in my memory as day of despair. The "Z's" were not a small step into the future; it was a giant step out of the past.

SHOE SHINE BOY

"Shoeshine boy, got no time to play
Shoeshine boy, got no time to pray
Every nickel counts a lot
So shine, shine shoeshine boy".

This was one songs of the '30's, a song of the "Great Depression". I was too young to worry much about the Great Depression but I did want to play and sing, so I sang "Shoe Shine Boy". The melody was simple, the words were easy and my voice was only capable of handling a very limited range. Being a born entertainer with no obvious talent, but having no one to either encourage or discourage me, I took my life in my own hands and whenever an audience gathered, I would begin my "gig".

Singing "Shoeshine Boy: (the only song I knew); I can remember swaying back and forth singing, pleased by the sounds coming out of my small mouth. I must have been seven or eight years old. In time, my repertoire increased, I began tapping to the sound of myself singing "Anchors Away M' Boy, Anchors Away". I would tap and tap and move quickly side-to-side and away. I never had a full house. Actually, my most loyal audience was Mary, Martha and Joseph, the triplets who lived next door. They were about a year younger than me; the Merrill triplets, my fan club. They would sit stoically on a bench in front of me while I sang and danced enthusiastically. I don't think they ever clapped. They sat and sat until I tired and then we would go out into the yard to do something else. They were always waiting to see what I was going to do and see if they were to be included. What power to have at a young age. I would soon grow weary of entertaining—I needed audience participation and I still do.

I do remember a very bad thing I did to Mary, Martha and Joseph. I took grass and put it in a glass and squished it around; then I put water into the glass and a bit of soap. I shook the glass vigorously. It looked like a green ice cream soda. I urged them to taste my concoction; which they did. It must have tasted terrible. They said nothing; each one sipping the green frothy liquid and passing it to the next one. How odd and strange that someone can convince others to do almost anything.

How easy it was to make a green ice cream soda, how easy it was to have others taste my bad tasting brew. How glad I am and how sorry I am in retrospect that I caused my loyal group to drink a putrid drink. I hope Mary, Martha and Joseph have forgiven me.

THINGS ARE LOOKING UP

When we talk about the dead, we look up and say or think "They've gone to a better place" or "I hope they will look down and give me strength" or a lot of uplifting thoughts.

I did the same thing this morning.

There are a lot of dead people in my life; a lot of people I looked up to when they were alive. All of a sudden I wondered why do I have to look up to talk to them. If they are truly in my room, they can hear me or see me from any direction. They could very well be behind me—to the right—to the left—even in a corner or in the next room.

I must quit looking up. Outside of elevating my chin, there is no logical reason to continue this raising of the eyes. All of my loved ones would find this amusing or unnecessary. They knew me well. They knew I wasn't one to be demure and condescending. They knew that I tried to go "eyeball to eyeball" with anyone.

No longer will I look up when thinking or trying to communicate with those who have departed this world. I will go "eyeball to eyeball" with them or at least I hope I do. I will continue to look up though. I will look up at the sky and the clouds. I will look up at tall buildings and flagpoles. I will look up to see if my roof is leaking or if I hear strange sounds overhead. Every now and then I might peek up from the corner of my eyes to see if someone from the long gone just might be up there looking down.

I FORGOT TO GET OLD

CLEARING THE DECKS

There is a big advantage to a long life. You have experienced so many, many things. Sometimes, you feel wise beyond words. For example, you've met many people, some forgotten, some forgettable. You've tasted many foods from many lands. Your taste buds are not only educated; they have a doctorate in smells and tastes. You've read many books, some eloquent, some funny, some just books. This doesn't include cookbooks, magazines, newspapers and even junk mail. You know about pain and pills. You know about doctors, nurses and hospitals; if given a choice it would have been good not to know them so well. You know about houses, furniture, appliances, pots and pans.

You don't know all there is to know but enough for you to last the rest of your life. There is so much more, so very much more you know. You know about machinery (this includes automobiles, scissors, screw drivers, hammers pliers, electrical equipment (globes, switches, batteries, fuses and extension cords).

Oh my, how did I live so long and learn so much. Did I utilize my vast amount of knowledge? Yes and no; mostly when necessary. Now I sit here "clearing the decks". It is an old Navy term that I can't even find in my many, many dictionaries, Bartlett's quotations or Roget's Thesaurus. It means literally to clean an obstruction off the deck of a ship in preparation for what is to come. This long life I have been the recipient of has one downside; it won't go on forever and being realistic I am on the short end. This is not to be a sad story. Sad stories are about lost kittens, abandoned children, war, hunger and poverty.

This is just about how much you can acquire in your life if you live long enough. Here I am completely equipped to tackle many jobs; however, I am mostly retired and will let others do the heavy work. Yet, if pushed or prodded by necessity I do have the tools around me ready and willing to take care of most problems.

OLD WITCHES

"Old witches never die, they just fly away". My husband used to tease me and call me a "witch second class". My mother was given the honor of first class witch. She had the power to assess situations, size up people and she was never wrong. She never sat in judgment, just called them like she saw them. She never abused her power and I doubt whether she ever thought she had any power.

I, on the other hand, was not that astute at seeing the obvious; I had limited insight. I knew who, what and where I liked but if I turned out to be wrong, I did an about face and continued in another direction. After my mother died, I began to assume some of her powers. Unlike my mother, I am more aware of my prowess. I am a bit cautious and tentative about being a witch. I will use my powers at the present time to find parking spaces, get well faster than I get sick and generally not pursue my new role too strenuously.

How did I become a witch? It's very simple. My ancestry goes way, way back to Hungary, Rumania, and Transylvania. Both my parents were born and grew up in the foothills of the Carpathian Mountains. All my aunts and uncles came to this country and whether they wee witches or warlocks I never knew. Mostly, they were too busy putting down roots in a new country and bestowing whatever wisdom they had inherited to their children.

I am the lucky one. I am my mother's daughter and I also belong to my father. What a witch's brew they produced. I've had a long happy melancholy life. At this juncture, now that I have graduated to witch first class, I will be circumspect and try to use my powers for good, that is most of the time.

THE LOLA BOOTS

It was sort of raining today. The forecast called for showers, rain, and wind—all in all stormy weather. I needed to do my grocery shopping and a little rain never stopped me. To be on the prudent side, I decided to wear my rubber boots—they still fit, they still look good after sitting in my closet for almost thirty years. I pulled them on, barely used and remembered when I went with a friend and neighbor downtown. I think we both bought boots that day. Lola moved long ago. She divorced, moved to another city, moved back; I saw her briefly but she had changed. She was no longer the fun loving, free spirited, sloppy housekeeper I enjoyed. And her housekeeping is a story unto itself. She always started to clean, took out the vacuum cleaner, or started washing dishes but someone or something would interrupt and Lola left everything. The vacuum would stand for days leaning against the wall. The dishes were waiting in water long cold. It didn't really matter with Lola and or with anyone that knew her; we all knew she had found something more exciting, which needed her attention.

In my Lola days that lasted only about three years, she was always involved in a new adventure. Mostly, I didn't partake in them. Lola had energy to burn and my flame was only flickering. She encouraged me to join her in a ballet class. Here we were, women in our thirties but Lola knew a retired ballet teacher who was well into her sixties or maybe beyond. I loved to dance and thought it might be good exercise plus fun. The teacher owned a huge home on a cobblestone street. The house had a ballroom in which she had installed the bars for us ballerinas to use for practice.

The music began, possibly Swan Lake and with one leg on the bar, she proceeded to say "Bend, bend, bend". I'm not very bendable but tried.

We were taught the first position, the second position. I liked it well enough but I was way past becoming a ballerina. Lola was good; she was agile. We returned once or twice a week for about a month. On my last lesson with one leg on the bar and with this small, taut bodied teacher calling "Bend, bend, bend"; she gave my back a forceful push and I bent. I left there in the "bent" position and with the help of a heating pad it was a long time before I unbent. Lola continued to go until another new adventure took her elsewhere.

Then she began making colored mosaics; colored chips of glass were scattered all over her house. She used some kind of tool to cut the different colored glass. I don't know whether she ever finished this project before she moved. Lola and her husband moved across the bay to a glorious house with a pool and she began teaching Speed Reading. Next thing I heard they were getting a divorce. Like a lot of people in our lives, she faded away and until this morning when I put on my rain boots, I hadn't thought about her in years. "Lola" boots—I think I've given them a good name. She has probably endured as well as my boots and is still involved in some exotic new age adventure.

PRIVATE PROPERTY, KEEP OUT

My cat has his own private deck; right outside the living room with a smashing view of the city, the deck extends all across the back of my house. The "resident, occupant" hasn't put it to much use. The weather here is mostly cool and foggy. The word "deck" denotes laying on a chaise lounge, sipping cold drinks and generally hanging out in the warmth and sunlight which hovers overhead; this does not hold true if you live in San Francisco. There are other parts of the city that are warmer, but I live in the Middle Kingdom.

However, for all intents and purposes, this should be called "Finian's deck". He usually chooses to go outside and loll about on the lower deck, which is large and holds a large assortment of the cats from next door. There is Molly, the only female, and a brown tabby that resembles Finian in coloring and she usually spends hours gazing at his princely presence but never approaches him, though I don't think he would mind. Then, of course, Fuzz Ball a big gray clumsy cat with a low I.Q. We have Fluffy who is between sixteen and eighteen and just lies at the nearest and most convenient spot. Pretty Boy Floyd who wandered in from somewhere a few years ago and now looks like a stuffed capon; blue eyes, part Siamese, weighs about twenty pounds. He loves everybody that passes his way. There are two other cats but they usually don't venture to the deck. Maybe Finian hasn't given them permission.

So you see, he sits among his admiring throng; taking catnaps but always-on guard in case one of these cats should displease him. Today, he chose to remain upstairs on his private deck. He had looked down and decided he needed a bit of privacy. He stretched out taking his ease in the sun.

Is this what we are all about? We move about in the world of people; standing in line, navigating our way through crowds and wend our way home and breathe a sigh of relief. We are in our own space away from the hustle and bustle. It's good to go out, move about, talk to others, break bread and join the human race. At the end of the day or whenever we are surfeited by our comings and goings, how good it is to return to our private property.

I looked out at Finian on his private deck this morning. He's not quite asleep, just relaxing. That's how I feel today not quite asleep, just relaxing. How good it is, how peaceful, how private.

SLEEPING HABITS

My cat, Finian, has always been super independent. I know this is a cat thing but I think he carries it to extremes. For instance, regarding his sleeping quarters—early on we purchased a small wicker bed with accompanying cushion. As I remember, he played in it occasionally. We then bought a large size wicker bed, again with larger cushion—this he ignored completely.

Over the year, there have been very few places he hasn't slept; high, high on bookshelves at least nine feet from the floor; high, high on window ledges at least ten feet from the floor. Every chair in the house has been granted a few nights of his life. The couch in the den was his preference for at least a year. However, he only wanted a certain corner and would come in late at night, give us dirty looks for not getting up. If we stayed up later, which we did much of the time, he would go in and out of the room in total exasperation. Eventually, we relinquished the couch.

Our bed became his favorite now and then. First one side, then the other side and the most annoying thing of all, he wanted to sleep on my pillow. I don't relish fleas or cat hair in my face. I put a towel on half of the pillow for a short while as this stubborn creature was going to have his way with me. For a short period he spent time on the living room couch, but when we stopped reprimanding him about this, he left the couch.

Occasionally, he jumped up on a chest but this was rare. He found the green room with the green bedspread. It was only painted green last year (Finian's favorite color). This is our guest room and

he's welcome to it. The room is downstairs with its own bath—
not bad accommodations for a pussycat.

Once I found him on the dining room table and this really
made me mad, very mad and I told him "You're for it" (whatever
that means) and he never set foot on the table again!

Recently, I found him sleeping on the bottom shelf of a small
bookcase in the garage, which is adjacent to the house; thusly he
has entrance any time he chooses. He's curled snuggly along the
shelf, his tail trailing on the floor of the garage. I've checked on
him periodically during the evening hours and he looks dreamingly
at me through his beautiful green eyes.

Maybe he is absorbing the energy contained in the books that
were once on that shelf; maybe he likes to be in the garage, near
the car, washing machine or dryer, or maybe and this is probably
closer to the truth, in case of fire or earthquake, he can reach the
back door and be long gone before disaster strikes. That's pretty
smart, in fact it's brilliant.

I think there is a Boy Scout pledge "always be prepared"; in
battle "Always on the ready"; and in life "Never give a sucker an
ever break" or is it "Watch your back". I don't really know. There
are so many bromides in the worlds. Finian, and only Finian knows
why he moves about so much and why he picks and chooses where
to spend his nights. Like any independent thinker, he has a right
to keep his own counsel but we both know where each other is and
that's the only thing of importance.

HANDMADE

A machine is a machine and whatever and however it is programmed, the finished product be it a car or a pair of shoes will all look alike. Even the defects are the same.

I think of myself as handmade. My parents did the best they could to shape me but times being what they were, their lives were busy providing food and shelter. No one told me to study; no one encouraged or discouraged me in my comings and goings. To me, this was a perfectly natural state. I was well fed and well clothed. On to education; I liked pencils and notebooks; I liked blackboards and desks; I liked most of my teachers; I liked pushing through the crowded halls among other students and especially I liked learning.

As soon as school was over, I forgot subjects that were not worth remembering. That is when the person I've become showed the flaws of a handmade garment.

I moved out into the world and changed jobs frequently, perfecting my imperfection. Many people have had an influence on me. Those who loved me hugged me and praised me; wove the strands of lovely blended colors that are part of my makeup into the fabric of my being.

The sharp angry colors that show up under certain lights or conditions were created by the cruelty or lack of compassion I encountered.

Anything handmade has a few loose threads and a little unevenness of pattern here and there. That is how life molded me—a lot of happiness, a lot of sadness, but the finished product is quite remarkable, even if I say so myself.

AQUI, AQUI

We were taking a trip to Mexico. I bought a Spanish language record but we took our trip a month early leaving me no time to even get any rudimentary skill in Spanish. I had been listening to the first part of the lesson, had learned to count to "ten" and how to pronounce the "g" before an "e" and an "i" and very little else.

We went to Mexico; my first trip out of the United States—a wonderful trip. I could use my newfound language in the hotel and tell the operator our floor "Dos", "Tress", Quattro". We went to the Anthropological Museum, the Folkloric Ballet and many great restaurants. We took cabs, buses, anything that moved. I learned how to take the one peso cab (stand in front of your hotel with your hand out showing one finger—cabs would stop if there was room for more passengers).

We boarded a public bus on our way to see a bazaar or something I read about in my travel guide. As the bus moved through crowded streets, I saw a large red brick building and as we stopped in front there was a big sign that read "MOMIAS". I wanted to investigate this interesting place and I foolishly remarked, "I want to see the mommies". I quickly moved to the front of the bus and wanted desperately to get off at the next stop. I could not think of the word for "Stop" but I remembered "Aqui" (here) so I loudly said "Aqui, aqui" and the bus stopped. We got off, walked back a block or so and entered the building, which turned out to be an old monastery. We wandered around and saw Mexican families milling about; no "gringos" in sight. We followed the people who were headed down the stone steps into a huge well lit chamber and as I looked around I instantly knew what the word "Momias" meant; not mommies but mummies. Standing, sitting and lying all around the room dressed in garments threadbare with age barely covering the bones were skeletons. These were the priests, nuns or whoever resided in this place many, many years ago. This was the Mexican holiday "Day of the Dead". The children were sitting on the steps or near these long dead people, eating, drinking and laughing. I felt uneasy. I had never been to a graveyard of unburied dead people.

The memory still lingers. We bury our dead in this country. We cremate our dead. They do the same in many countries but since I couldn't ask questions at that place at that time; I thought probably it was considered an honor to die and remain above ground. I mostly remember the children being at ease among the long dead.

We have Halloween where we use costumes of skeletons; and in horror films there could be one or two skeletons. Here in front of so many people were probably a dozen skeletons in tattered, aged clothing with children enjoying themselves at their feet.

My attitude toward death never had a clear meaning but I think the Mexicans" "Day of the Dead" serves a good purpose. We shouldn't treat death, as only a tragedy. We should rejoice that we were given life. Aqui, Aqui . . . ."Here, here, here"!

BEHIND GOD'S BACK

My mother used to say that she grew up behind God's back. She was born and spent her early years in the northern part of Hungary. I would ask her to tell me stories about "the old country". She told me stories about her mother who would gather with other women of the village in the evening and pluck down from the geese. I could almost hear the women laughing as they worked making the wonderful feather beds. Her mother made one for each of her daughters as part of their dowry, which they each brought to America. I remember sleeping under the big fluffy pillow like comforter, which was not to my liking. It moved about above me hovering as I slept but now I own one and am constantly delighted by the lightness and warmth.

Her father was often unemployed; a cabinetmaker by trade and a part time bookkeeper for the Count who owned the forest lands which were logged. My mother said that her father never received much of the salary he earned, but he encouraged the peasants to take the scrap lumber for firewood. Her father was the village storyteller; he would go down to the saloon, play the zither and tell stories.

Her mother had nine children; three died when very small and her life consisted of trying to provide food for her children. They lived on potatoes, noodles and whatever fruit or vegetables were in season. Dairy products were available from the cow they owned and somehow or other, she always managed to get a chicken for the Sabbath meal. I asked my mother whether she liked dark or light meat. She laughed and said the men had first choice (her father and grandfather who lived with them) and all the children shared the remainder. She said that mostly she got whatever went over the fence last and then she would laugh. There was no bitterness in my mother. She loved her parents, her sisters and brothers. She loved her grandfather. She felt family was the most important thing in the world.

As she grew older and found there was no opportunity for young people in Hungary, plans were made for her to come to America. Her older sister had already emigrated and was saving money to enable the next one to come to the "promised land". This was my mother. She left Hungary and did come to America at the age of 15. She endured all of the hardships of the early immigrants, menial jobs, low pay and long hours. I think that is when she became aware and told me she grew up "behind God's back".

Life was very hard; life was very cruel. Eventually, the next sister was sent for and then the rest of the family (her mother, father and two younger brothers). Her mother died six months after they arrived. If there was a God, he certainly was not looking her way. She maintained her dignity and sense of humor all her life. She might have grown up behind God's back but even if he didn't see her, He must have felt her presence, as I still do.

HOLD MY HAND

Tonight we turn our clocks back. By morning I will see the sun, if it deigns to rise, i.e. not be dimmed by clouds or fog. Another time change. "Fall back, spring forward". I guess I've fallen back a little this evening. I've been moving forward but as I turned the clocks back an hour, I seem to be diminished by the time change. Sadness seems to have descended on my shoulders. I want to reach out and touch someone. I want someone to say, "I care about you". I want to be wanted. I have worth and I am worthwhile but that thought gives me little pleasure as the hour is moved back.

How odd, how very odd to sit here in warmth and comfort and find my life so wanting. Tomorrow is not far away and I will again relish the world around me but tonight I need someone to hold my hand. I extend my hand into the emptiness and I feel nothing. I would like to weep for all the lonely people; I would like to tell them that there are so many of us but that gives me little solace.

Was I ever happy as I think I was? Was I ever content, as I prefer to remember? The answer probably lies somewhere in between. Being alone clears out all the cobwebs and you see yourself and can define your emotions more clearly than any other time in your life. I would prefer to turn back like my clocks and never face the stark reality which I now face daily. I have learned much about myself. Mostly positive but tonight, at least for tonight, I wish someone would hold my hand.

HALLOWEEN

("Hold my Hand")

It is 8:00 PM. No trick or treaters at my door. Parents escort most children, if they go out at all and most don't go to strange doors. I still need someone to hold my hand. Tonight seems to be a needy night. I start remembering Halloweens. The older one gets, holidays seem to have piled up somewhere back in our memories. Our memories have a large cast of characters. As people fall away from our lives like leaves from a tree in autumn; I feel like I, too, am a tree still alive but the largest most luxuriant leaves are gone. So here I am again, another holiday and no one to hold my hand

CAT WHO WALKS
IN THE SNOW

Outside it's raining, the wind is blowing and all in all, it's a good day to stay inside by the fire or read a good book. My cat has been outside all day except for short period to have his meals. Every time I try to seduce him in, he gives me his nonchalant look and if I try to touch him, he runs down the stairs into the damp yard.

I always thought cats liked warm, cozy places but not this fellow. I don't know his ancestry but people have looked at him and said, "He's a Maine Coon". I bought a Cat Book and sure enough he has the features described as a "Maine Coon"; short sleek hair on his back and thick fur on his belly. Apparently, these cats started out in Maine and eventually over the years made their long journey across the country. Here I am in mostly sunny California with a Maine Coon cat. It is really rather nice to have an all-weather cat. I could move anywhere and he would be right at home. If I could give him an Indian name, it would be "Cat Who Walks in the Snow".

Unfortunately, Finian will probably never have a chance to try out his Indian name. I have a feeling if it every really snowed here a substantial amount, this so-called Maine Coon would probably be delighted to warm his bones on a soft couch or a warm rug. So it goes, we have all moved away from our ancient roots and have adapted to foreign lands. I am so glad I ended up here. If I had an Indian name it would be "Woman Who Moves Slowly", especially next to my "Cat That Walks in The Snow".

ACHES & PAINS

I have a backache you wouldn't believe. I spent the evening at a charitable dinner at a hotel that is older than I am. The hotel seems to be in better shape than me and that is well and good. Old elegant buildings should be maintained. Each generation should have the opportunity to enter marble lobbies with polished walnut walls and high ceilings that rise majestically. I, on the other hand, will be long gone and so will all the other people who were moving about me this evening. Beautifully groomed people, all talking, eating, drinking and yet I was surrounded by so many aches and pains.

The woman next to me at dinner had almost no vision, another was moving into the high 90's, still eating, talking but as I looked at her parchment skin, I felt so sad. All of these people were once young and handsome and now and now . . . I am one of them too. Aches and pains have not evaded me. I am very familiar with these two nouns. How sad, how very sad to get old; on the other hand, the alternative is not very palatable. There is no remedy for old age. Today, I might feel the sadness of death creeping closer but by morning, I will push it back where it belongs.

Death comes to everyone. Dwelling on the inevitable is a very foolish waste of time. It's just when your aches and pains get a foot in the door of your mind, you let your guard down and realize how vulnerable we are "Pain, pain, go away, come again another day."

IN THE WET

Well, you see it's like this. I had a flood. Around midnight a few weeks ago, I turned on the faucet and no hot water. Going downstairs to see if the pilot light on the hot water heater had blown out, I opened the door into my garage and lo and behold, there was a flood.

The hot water heater had apparently disintegrated though it was still in one piece, but the water was flowing and flowing and the garage and laundry room were small lakes. I went upstairs, looked in the Yellow Pages under hot water heaters and called a 24-hour "at your service line". The first two numbers rang and rang; the third number was answered by a sleepy voice. "Turn off the pilot light" the voice, said. "Where is the light?" "You'll see it at the base of the heater." I said, "O.K. don't go away, I am going to call you back." Sure enough I found the pilot light and turned it to the off position, but the water was still gushing merrily along the floor. I turned the knob on the heater and turned and turned and it seemed to never end.

I finally made my way across the creek and turned off the knob that controls all the water in the house. I hurried back upstairs and called again. "What do I do now?" "Nothing, we will be out tomorrow afternoon; there is nothing that can done tonight." "O.K. I'll see you tomorrow."

I went back downstairs and this time I finally turned the water off at the heater. The water was moving stealthily into the downstairs bedroom. I grabbed towels, bathmats placing them at the door to the bedroom, trying to stem the tide and then proceeded to try to get a handle on the ongoing flood.

I went back upstairs, put on a jacket over my gown, put on my rubber boots and descended into the cold, dank garage. Taking a broom, I began sweeping water out the backdoor, out the backdoor; opened the garage door, swept more water out the front, out the front—then back to the back door, then out again to the garage door. For almost four hours, I worked to salvage my home from its watery grave.

My cat came down and looked up at me "Meow . . . . meow, meow . . ."

"What in the world do you want, its 2:00 AM?" "Meow, meow." I know he wants to go out the back door. I picked him up and carried him over the water and out the back door. "Meow, meow." Now what, oh . . . he wants to come back in, actually he really didn't want to go out. Maybe he just wants to keep me company. I walked through the water to the back door, picked him up and put him on dry land. He proceeded to walk around the edges of the water and seemingly enjoyed the excitement of his mistress sweeping water back and forth. Alas, I gave up and went upstairs . . . to sleep perhaps to dream?

The next day, I called people who came to pump out the water and they turned on big units to dry out the walls. Three big machines were plugged into my electrical sockets and the throbbing of the engines was pulsating through the night and into the next day. Clear plastic hoses were placed into the basin of the downstairs bathroom; also into the basin in the laundry room. My house looked like it was in an intensive care ward.

However, my cat's litter box was moved from the garage into the lobby. Finian, my cat, found this quite unremarkable. Nothing really fazes him. I soon found small gray footprints all over my house. My cat with his damp paws encased in the clay dirt from the litter box was leaving his mark all over the house. I examined his feet and found the clay had hardened like cement. Now I was the owner of a "tagger", like one of those people that paint graffiti and sneak off into the night. I tried to remove the clay but at the risk of being bitten or scratched decided to call a pet groomer and present my problem. I was told the only solution was to soak his feet. "How?" "Run a little water in the tub and put him in." "Oh yeah, well I'll try."

I ran about an inch or so of warm water in the tub and called out "Finian how about a little bath?" He came uneasily into the bathroom. I picked him up and placed him in the tub. He stood quietly and then began moving back and forth, reaching down and drinking the water. I stayed in the bathroom and talked to him. "How do you like the tub, looks to me like you're having a good time." He didn't even lift his head, just kept looking at the water luxuriating in this new experience.

A week has past and at least twice a day; he calls out and jumps into the tub. He stays in for ten, fifteen minutes and then jumps out. His feet are slowly showing signs of his original paws. This has been a learning experience for both of us. I learned I could survive a flood; at least a minor one and Finian has shown me that even though it is said, "You can't teach an old dog new tricks", I have an old cat that is pretty damn smart.

THE SAVAGE BEAST

Finian, my cat, and I are sitting quietly together listening to a concert; a very unusual concert. It is a combination of original string music with the beating of drums in the background—a concert at the Acropolis in Athens. The piano becomes the star of the music and then the rest of the orchestra gives added brilliance to the galaxy of sounds. Oh, to be a maker of such beautiful music; music does calm the savage beast. I am the savage, thousands of years removed from my early ancestors. The beast, Finian, sits contentedly on my lap; he too is thousands of years removed from his beginnings.

Primitive sounds are captured in the drumbeats, which are singled out now and then from the other instruments. Where will our descendants be a thousand years from now? For the now, I am listening to heavenly unearthly music and that will have to soothe the savage best for the present.

I just looked down and saw that my cat is beginning to get gray hair. Only a little but it is a sign, he is beginning to join me as a senior. My hair started aging long before I did. I managed to conceal the evidence for many years. Eventually I retreated from the concept of being young forever and allowed my gray hair to see the light of day. Not only was I gray, I was (as I like to think) platinum sliver. I still don't recognize myself in the mirror at first glance but there is no question it is me.

Of course, now that my cat is beginning to gray, I would hope his companionship would enable me to accept my own hair. I hate those cute sayings re hair "Just because there's snow on the roof, doesn't mean there's no fire in the basement". This is not snow on my head; it is perfectly good hair. Like it or not, the two of us are getting older. I'll accept another cliché I just remembered, "We are not getting older, we are getting better".

STAND BY ME

I never think of myself as courageous but I think everyone at some time or times during their life goes one step beyond. On my trip to Italy, it became apparent to me that crossing the Via Veneto in Rome was for the young and brave. There were no stop signs, or traffic control policemen. A few people from our tour stood watching the traffic frozen in terror. I grabbed my husband's cane walked resolutely into the street waving it madly like an orchestra leader out of control. The cars came to a screeching halt and I motioned for our group to walk, which they did hesitatingly, and then this not so "chicken" woman crossed to the other side.

On this same trip, we spent a few days in Venice. To me Venice was a magical kingdom, a city floating on a sea. The magic did not extend to the meals in our hotel where we all gathered to eat in the evening. Our dinner was a total disaster. I have no idea what kind of meat we were served but between the smell and the taste, I for one was not going to eat it. There were perhaps twenty people at our table. We occupied two tables; our tour group was approximately forty people. Everyone was examining their food. I casually walked over to the small table where our guide and driver were eating. I glanced down and saw large bowls of some kind of pasta. When I returned to the table, all the faces were looking to me for guidance. I remarked, "We will not eat this food, we will have a food strike". I remembered in movies when prisoners are dissatisfied with their food, they all start hitting their glasses or a plate until the din becomes the sound of a rebellion. I told them to do what I did and I took a spoon and began clanging on my glass; soon the other joined me and we made our presence known in a dining room in Venice.

The manager or whatever title was bestowed on the man who ran the dining room came over and asked me "Senora, what is the problem?" I conveyed to him our dissatisfaction with the food. He tried to placate me but I stood firm. I then asked, "What is our guide and driver eating?" He went over to look and then said "Only pasta carbonara". I said, "That sounds good". The guide came over to investigate and I told him our complaint. The manager said, "If you like, we will prepare the pasta carbonara for your table." I replied, "That would be satisfactory".

We were served large bowls of the most delicious pasta I have ever eaten. Our tour mates watched from the other table and wanted to know what happened. They were told that I had initiated a strike. They all looked crestfallen as they had eaten or partially eaten the mystery meat.

True, the act I performed was not particularly heroic or challenging and my table companions have probably forgotten how I stood up for the right to eat the right stuff but I remember and feel pleased that I acted out of my convictions and I continue to do so in small ways. If push comes to shove on some issue in the future, I will be waiting in the wings to stand up for what I believe.

SAMO-SAME-O

On the night before Christmas, nothing is stirring in my house. My cat is lying delightfully on the rug next to me and I am watching television sporadically without sound. Today I walked through a shopping mall and saw a majestic Christmas tree dressed to the nines i.e. decorated within an inch of its life. Beautiful colored balls and dangling angels; it was truly a splendid tree. Near sat Santa Claus with the perennial child on his lap, asking the perennial question "What do you want for Christmas?" Children were lined up to have their turn in Santa's lap and a photo opportunity.

I have seen this scene before many, many times. The years go around and 'round; every year another Christmas, Christmas trees and Santas. Life is repetitious but as dull as this sounds, there is great comfort in order. We know Tuesday follows Monday and January starts the year; each month is as familiar to us as our own names. I guess I am trying to rationalize my inner restlessness and appreciate the every day routine, which is what keeps us to the course and our feet on the ground. My mind can float, moving up and down with the wind currents of my thoughts but coming down to earth and going through our every days is our destiny; every minute is different just as every month, every Christmas and every Santa Claus.

A WOMAN OF LETTERS

It occurred to me that I am full of words, ordinary words, thoughtful words, existential words, and humorous words and given half a chance, they come dancing out on paper. Not being a science fiction writer but nonetheless having an imaginative mind, I thought by some strange circumstance someone should make an incision on any part of my body, they would probably find intermingled with my internal workings thousands of words hidden in every crevice. Many, many words waiting to take their turn and become a story.

Tucked away at the very tips of my fingers are letters to be put together to form words. Each toe has its own storage house of letters, each ear lobe and eyelid. In the elbows and knees are larger storehouses and all through this body I inhabit at the moment is a tremendous treasure trove of words and letters.

I am writing and using as many as I find necessary to say what I have to say, but there is no way I could possibly utilize this bounty of words and letters that are so cleverly concealed. Since we all die and surely I will die some day, it is my wish to be cremated and turned to ash and dust. I thought wouldn't it be amusing when that time comes, some ash will float away into the atmosphere and if by chance it should fall upon the earth, someone with microscopic vision would look down and see not a bit of ash, but a charred letter.

ARIGATO

On our way to Japan, we went to Canada. My husband was entitled to travel Space Available through the military. He was a retired Army wartime officer. His whole military career is another story but that will have to wait for another time. We had just found out of our eligibility for "space available". This is a flight to anywhere a military plane is going from certain designated airbases. We live about forty miles from one and drove up to find out the details. Living on the west coast all military planes were flying west. We inquired about a flight to Japan. No problem. There were flights to Japan daily. We only needed to get certain shots and bring our passports and identification and off we would fly. Drive our car to the airbase; park it; no problem. Two weeks in Japan. What a trip, what excitement stirred in my adventurous heart.

We went home; we got our shots; we got all the necessary papers. My husband requested a three-week vacation. Japan, a trip of a lifetime! I bought travel books. I learned about the weather and customs. I learned to say "thank you" and a few necessary phrases. I read about Japanese inns and the beauty of Kyoto. We planned very carefully; it would be summer in Japan. We took warm weather clothes. How exciting, how grand!

The day came and we drove to the airbase, suitcases packed, ready to go. We entered the airport and proceeded to the desk fully equipped with all details complete. The sergeant at the desk said "All planes to Japan are full for this week; there are fewer flights at this time of the year.

That was the end. No Japan. No vacation. I was devastated. My husband said, "You've always wanted to go to Canada, didn't you?" I said, "Yes, of course". He said, "I've taken time off, the car is packed, we'll just head north". We did, we headed north. Northern California was beautiful. Oregon was greener than I could believe. Crater Lake was a mile deep. When we got to Portland, Oregon our summer clothes were too summery. We bought sweaters in Portland. We continued driving north to Seattle, a beautiful city; on north to Canada. Over the border to Vancouver, a truly beautiful city and then took the ferry to Victoria, on an island . . . . another delight. Back we went on another ferry to the U.S.A. and the state of Washington. We drove through the Olympic peninsula, down the coast, the magnificent northwest coast of this country.

I never got to Japan. It really doesn't matter. The surprise alternative was one of the most joyous trips I ever took. Sayonara!

LOVER'S LEAP

There is an Indian legend that two people from different tribes were not given permission to marry. They went to a cliff overlooking the Brazos River and jumped to their death; not able to be together in life, they chose to be together in death. This story has many similarities to the Romeo and Juliet tragedy but as a child when I first went up to Lover's Leap in Cameron Park in Waco, I only knew of the Indian legend. I went up often and looked down at the broad rust colored river. The winding road up to the cliff was wall-to-wall honeysuckle growing along the side. The scent was the sweetest in the world and the sound of hundreds of bees still rings in my ears.

As teenagers, we would go up in the summertime and have weenie roasts. The smell of blackened hot dogs on the fire and the taste that to this day has never been repeated still lingers in my memory. We were in our mid teens between childhood and adulthood; self-conscious, giggly, embarrassed and full of bravado. In the early summer evening surrounded by the sweet smell of honeysuckle, crisp hot dogs, we were not in a hurry to grow up. Lover's Leap seemed to have a very romantic meaning in my life during those years. I cannot even remember the names of the other kids that were milling about laughing, eating and probably teasing each other.

I went back to Lover's Leap about eight years ago and looked down at the river. Nothing had changed but me. How odd it seemed, the legend lived on, the honeysuckle was still blooming, the bees were still buzzing and I had long reached adulthood. It all seemed sad somehow but I could still close my mind's eye and see two young Indians hand in hand jump from the high cliff.

THE DAY INFAMY ENDED

It was summer 1945; I was on the train en route to San Francisco. The train was rolling along the coast of California. Now and then, the Pacific Ocean appeared and disappeared from view. Many men in uniform surrounded me, including my husband. There were no sounds but the clacking of the wheels and the murmur of voices. Suddenly, a loud voice came over the loud speaker. "I have a bulletin of utmost importance. The Japanese have surrendered!"

Stillness settled upon the coach and then cries of jubilation, shouts and deep sighs were heard. As if moving in slow motion, we all arose and began singing "the Star Spangled Banner". We were all Americans, our country had won the war—but mostly the WAR was over. Goose bumps crept up my arms as I was singing and trying to remember all the words. It really didn't matter. All I could think of was "the war is over".

We arrived in San Francisco to a scene of frantic hilarity. I wanted so much to join in. I wanted to be a part of this celebration. This was not to be. My husband asked the porter to drive us to my parents home. We arrived but I was still bursting with excitement. I wanted to go downtown. My husband had only recently returned from two years in a German prison camp and he had had his war. This was August 15, 1945 and when I think about it now, I am still elated. I was and still am proud to be an American. Patriotism has been used and abused but being a part of that moment is still one of the highlights of my life.

I'VE BEEN HERE

Having lived several lives and having heard hundreds of stories, I often wonder if I will have time enough to sort out my lives and review the stories. Each life and each story is noteworthy and if I had all the time in the world, I suppose I would like to put them all on paper for posterity.

Flipping through the pages of my mind, I stop now and then to reexamine my memories. All of us have so many memories, some dramatic, some charming and some mundane. I would so much like to climb on a mountaintop and scream at the top of my lungs "I've been here!" Down here on the flatlands, I can only write the words "I've been here" by recanting experiences to limited audiences.

I deeply resent the limits life sets for us. We are all so much more and I cannot add or subtract a second from each lifetime. This is not a story; this is only the truth and it does not set me free. I am a prisoner of my truth.

MY ETERNAL SPRING

Now I lay me down to sleep. I don't think so! I've been sleeping on the same mattress past its Silver Anniversary. It is very hard to give up a good companion after all these years. Besides since so much of your time is spent in bed, change can become a dilemma and it did.

I had noticed my box spring had a hernia; bulging out at the end. The top looked pretty good, a bit like an unpaved street but the potholes were multiplying. I gave in and I almost gave up. Going for a new mattress is one of the most difficult trips I could possibly make. All mattresses look more or less alike. I decided to go to the one and only place in the city that makes their mattresses from scratch guaranteed to be pure cotton, the best innersprings available, guaranteed for twenty years.

I chose one that seemed pleasant and when it arrived I spent several pleasant nights on a very, very soft surface. I felt like I was in a hammock, swinging in the breeze. This was not going to do and I exchanged it for a medium top and a double-decker soft bottom. You guessed it. It, too, was pleasant but in a much more independent way. Once I was ensconced it molded around me and when I turned over, it followed me from one side of the bed to the other. I called it my "trampoline".

I then asked them to make one up for me as follows, medium density top and medium density bottom. I thought now I am playing it safe; really safe didn't begin to describe this new arrival. I spent the first night on a seemingly soft surface but underneath it had a stern and solid feel. No one was going to get the better of this bed. Slowly and insidiously a very overpowering chemical scent enveloped me. I changed sheets in the middle of the night thinking maybe the soap used in the washer had left a strange residue. No luck. The smell hovered and descended on my arms and legs that began burning. I was not only to be sent from my room; I was left with a minor rash and verging on a nervous breakdown. In fact, I closed the door to the bedroom to contain the smell that was seeping into the rest of the house.

I spent the night luxuriously on my living room couch, a bit narrow but still user friendly. I called early and told my sad story and was told they would pick up this demon; return mattress #2 since my options were not limitless and they had long ago picked up my lovely old mattress, which had been discarded.

I carefully remade the "trampoline" and look forward to "springtime sleep" for many nights. I compromised and decided that sleeping on a "trampoline" is better than a "hammock" and the last straw of the "bed from hell" pushed me into accepting the least offensive and again reminding me, nothing is perfect.

P.S. I should mention the energy involved in making and remaking this king size bed. Off and on, fitted sheets, mattress pad, top sheet, blankets, and comforters—the exercise I got was incredible. I am completely totaled after my bout with the mattresses. Hey, no one said life was easy.

AT THE END OF THE DAY

At the end of the day, my life comes to a halt, i.e. the house, the television, the phone become my companions. During the daylight hours, I am free to pursue anything my heart desires. The entire world is outside and I breath in the fresh air and then comes dusk.

I scurry in and leave my energy behind to be recharged come morning. The sky darkens; I turn on the news; I feed my cat, Finian and my life stops. Sometimes I talk to friends on the phone, I do watch television but going to sleep is the only goal in sight. "Sleep, to sleep—Shakespeare said it best. "Sleep that knits up the ravell'd sleeve of care". I welcome the soft mattress and the dreams that accompany me through the night.

Most of my life has been shared. First with my parents, then marriage consumed the rest of it. Though I thought of myself as independent, making decisions was never a one-person job. There was always someone else to consider, to talk with, and to argue with, to compromise with and ultimately plans were made, problems assessed and solved. There were days, hours and years that now seem to be compressed into a very tight ball of memory yarn.

Now I, alone, make decisions. I make plans; I solve problems. At the beginning, I moved blindly into this new world but slowly I began viewing life from my very own perspective. It is almost like watching the fog over the city burn off with objects appearing one by one, then a whole scene becomes visible. This time of my life, I am coming out and trying to move slowly and cautiously, trying not to stumble.

SWAN LAKE

I finally sat myself down and began the tortuous job of doing my income taxes. I've been doing it all these years and having no extra curricular investments or properties, my tax chore should be a "piece of cake".

Begin, fill in small boxes, next to small lines; numbers, numbers, and numbers—it's very hard to befriend them. Still and all, it must be done. I hit a snag. Only one? I called the IRS for information. I followed instructions, push four or five and then after the next announcement, another push. Then the wait begins.

I was lucky this time. They were playing Tchaikosky's Swan Lake. I could hum along and mentally watch the ballet dancers. Interruption. "All the lines are busy, etc"—back to the ballet. I could feel my body sway to the music. Interruption "All the lines are still busy". Again the lovely, melodious tones—again I was a swan and soon disaster seemed imminent. Just as I was beginning to become a very anxious swan; I was connected to a well-informed woman. I asked my questions and was answered quickly and politely.

I returned to my tax form. No problem, just add, subtract and percentage here and there; sign, check enclosed and thus ended my 1994 IRS form. (What happened to the swan in Swan Lake?) I know what happened but I was cut off from the music at a crucial crescendo. How can such a mundane task be compared to Swan Lake? Possibly there is a common denominator if I choose to observe it as such. Reality and imagery—or to stretch this a little further "Pay your taxes or you'll be a dead duck"!

TRIALS AND TRIBULATIONS

We are caught up in "The Trial of the Century". A celebrity is on the hot seat, so to speak. Television, tabloids, newspapers all report in depth about a very unordinary man who may or may not be guilty. I feel we all are on trial somehow. This voyeuristic viewing and delving into the sordid world of spousal abuse, racism, violent crimes and possible drug use leaves us all tarnished which diminishes our persona. All of us at some time have slowed down to look at an accident on the road or gathered to watch a fire reduce a building to ashes. None of us are guiltless; tragedy in one form or the other peeks our interest. Perhaps, it's the inner satisfaction "It isn't happening to me".

I believe over the years we have been inundated with horrors. We turn on our television and watch "live" wars where the dead are casually laying here and there like scattered leaves. We open our newspaper and see the wreckage of a plane; the results of an earthquake, houses thrown around by a tornado having no semblance to their original structure. We are drowning in a sea of others misery and I, for one, who has no power to change the media feel I have to speak out from time to time and say "Enough".

I feel shame when I become engrossed in this trial and forget the real issues. People are being killed, murdered all over the world and the most we can do is watch or read about it. We continue our daily lives but subliminally, I feel we are reduced to a non-caring, non-feeling homo sapiens who have not advanced far from our primitive ancestors.

A soapbox would not be appropriate for my voice. The outrage
I feel at time has no sound and that is the saddest part. The silence
around me is deafening.

TODAY, I AM

"How goodly are they tents, oh Jacob". Standing at the lectern in a small synagogue in Texas, I proudly read these words in Hebrew and English. I cannot remember the rest of the text but how glorious it was to be standing in front of a small congregation including my mother and father.

As I glance over at the picture of my confirmation class, which sits on the library table, many memories return to me. There were five girls, including myself; all dressed in long white organza dresses. Our Rabbi originated the idea of the group confirmation after we had completed our Hebrew education. We were all twelve years old and were entering womanhood. I was the first to address the congregation and after reading from the Torah, each of us gave a speech depicting a virtue. I remember my speech was entitled "Modesty". We were given a small white prayer book with our name engraved in gold. As I look at the picture, I see my unsmiling face. This was a very important day and I was not to take it lightly.

My parents took me out for ice cream and a movie still elegantly wearing my long white dress. The movie was "San Francisco" starring Jeanette McDonald and Clark Gable. Could this have been a foretelling of my coming to San Francisco only a few years later? Again, I look at the picture; we all had gardenias in our hair and carried bouquets of white carnations. Where did all the years go? Every time I enter a synagogue, the overwhelming feeling of pride in who I am and my ancient heritage surrounds me. Again, the words "How goodly are they tents, Oh Jacob" enters my mind; the words in Hebrew *Mah tovu ohlehu Yaacov;* yes, how goodly that we are still here.

TIME STOOD STILL

Time stood still when I began to make arrangements for my husband's funeral. The doctors told me his death was imminent and I began the most amazing task of my life. I was not prepared for a death or a dying. I had been through this a few years before when my mother died. I had a husband then; I had a companion in my sorrow. I wanted my mother buried in Texas next to my father and brother.

There were a multitude of assorted jobs; funeral home in San Francisco and Waco; calls to relatives; planes tickets; hotel reservation, informing the congregation and a rabbi 2,000 miles away. It was completed and everything was arranged. I did not want to leave my mother's grave in Waco. I felt I was deserting her and would never see her again.

Now I am truly alone with a clock that has no hands. There is no one left to bury anymore. Time is running out and I am truly abandoned.

AMERICA, THE BEAUTIFUL

I have been reading in the paper about legal and illegal immigrants and motor voter registration laws. It seems more people want to vote, just haven't got around to registering. Legal immigrants want to become citizens but have neglected taking the test for a variety of reasons.

My parents were also immigrants, entering this country in New York in the early 1900's. My mother told me I was very effective in helping her become a citizen. She told me she studied for her test and a judge was the deciding factor in the small city where she resided. I can imagine my small, shy mother entering a courtroom in this country, perhaps seated beside others who were waiting their turn to be questioned.

Back in those days, the word baby sitter was unknown so my mother sat tentatively with her six month infant daughter, nervously waiting for the judge to begin his interrogation. When her name was called, the questions began, and I (the baby) began to cry. My continued wailing interrupted each question. My mother tried desperately to quiet me but to no avail. The judge was exasperated and said, "You are granted your citizenship. Please remove that child from the courtroom".

Over the years, my mother said that was one of the happiest days of her life. She became an American citizen. I asked her years later if she would like to visit Hungary, her place of origin. She looked at me perplexed and said "America is my home, I have no wish to return". I wonder if the new immigrants feel this deep patriotism that both my parents felt. I remember a quote from somewhere "My country, right or wrong". I was the lucky one. I did not have to immigrate or learn a new language or culture. I grew up with this wonderful sense of freedom that Americans share with each other. So again "My country, right or wrong".

A JOB IS A JOB IS A JOB

Once upon a time I had a job; and then another job; and then another. I think I must have set the record for holding the most jobs in the shortest period of time.

#1 Job—I was seventeen, long term employment—one year—general store.

I was a combination secretary, bookkeeper, casher, saleslady and sometime driver. Then I moved to another city.

#2—Garwood Industries—boring, boring—one month.

#3—Cleveland Tractor—despised typing the words "nuts & bolts" many times, in many letters—one month.

#4—Immigration and Naturalization—long term (nine months)—sorta liked the job but was considered too high spirited (a very long story but interesting).

#5—Food Broker—this time the words I had to type over and over were "peanut butter and mayonnaise"—got very upset stomach—two months.

#6—Decided to try sales—Children's clothes—Forget it—Two weeks, didn't relate to children well and visa versa.

#7—Dental Lab—View from office excellent—View of drawers with rows of false teeth, too distracting—one week. (Did see a fantastic parade from window).

#8—Paper Box Company—Old Building, too dark and cage elevators very unreliable—three days.

#9—Office of Rehabilitation (They took pity on me)—Hired me and fired me—I wasn't disabled enough (another story)—one month.

#10—War Housing 1944—Another long term (nine months)—Became discouraged since we had no housing to offer and placed a sign on my receptionist's desk "NO HOUSES, NO APARTMENTS, NO ROOMS' (and I should add, no job) plus another long story; and this one has a lot of drama).

#11—Army Housing (Same office as previous job)—Two weeks—Thank God, somebody took me away from all this—I got married.

Eventually, ten years later I resumed my career.

#12—Temple Beth Israel—Long term—one year—No comment.

#13—Can Do Industries—I didn't *do* at all—one month.

Left town and began anew.

#14—Mutual of New York—Long term—one year—Great boss (He really liked me)—Lousy pay.

#15—Reinsurance Company—Long term—one year—Office closed, oh well I was thinking about leaving anyway. English boss did a great job of imitating Churchill, also doing his bulldog impressions.

#16—Import/Export—One month—Atmosphere not conducive to happiness—Stupid bosses gave dictation all day and expected work to be typed up by nightfall—I told them they needed more help—After I left, they hired three people to take my place, hah—I told them.

#17—Jewish Federation—Long term—1 ½ years—Might have lasted but luckily I was whisked away into marriage again but I did venture out briefly.

#18—Temple Emanuel—one month—no comment.

#19—Insurance (Mr. Duncan)—Two weeks—I was accused of being a Communist; (I made favorable remarks about unions) this was 1960 (The Red Menace Years).

#20—Fromm and Sichel—Brokers for Christian Brothers wine—Great boss—Almost three months—Got sick, quite sick, recovered but never to work again.

I will now try to add up my working time: 1 year + 1 mo. + 1 mo. + 9 mo. + 2 mo. + 2 weeks + 1 week + 3 days + 1 mo. + 9 mo. + 2 weeks. Add the remainder: 1 year + 1 mo. + 1 year + 1 Year + 1 mo. + 1 ½ years + 1 mo. + 2 weeks + 3 mo.

The grand total of 7 years, 4 months, three weeks and 3 days during my work related life of about 8 years of so.

P.S. I just remembered Job #21—It would be between #10 and #11. It was April 1945. I had just started to work at the Union League Club. When I got off the streetcar, the newsstands were stacked with papers announcing President Roosevelt's death. I was overcome with grief. He had died the day before April 12, 1945. He had stood for social justice through my formative years and I walked into the office and said "Isn't this a sad day?" The office manager turned to me and said, "The dictator's dead, I am glad!" I hastily cleaned out my few personal belongings and said loudly "I QUIT!" As I walked the empty streets of San Francisco that April morning, the air was heavy with the nation's grief. Another job I walked away from but I've never walked away from my beliefs.

Oh yes; somewhere between #16 and #17—Job #22—Fiberboard Corporation—I was confronted with a very involved situation about the desk I was to occupy. There was no typewriter on the desk and there had never been one; so what shall be done? It took the better part of my first day to sort this out. Then the bells started ringing. Bells were rung at 10:00 AM (coffee break in the cafeteria upstairs); 10:15 AM (return to desk): 12:00 Noon—Lunch—(Return at 1:00 PM)—3:00 PM (Afternoon coffee break)—3:15 PM (Return to desk)—5:00 PM—End of Day—Cover typewriter, close drawers of desk, depart until 8:30 AM next day. Enter building and begin identical routine. After several days of bells, I couldn't take it anymore. If I was in the middle of a project—you had to STOP! The bells regulated the whole day. I have walked to the sound of another drum but I'll be damned if I'm going to become a ding-a-ling.

As Thoreau said, "*If a man does not keep pace with his companions, perhaps it is because he hears a different drummer. Let him step to the music he hears, however measured or far away*". I have always stepped to the music I've heard but that doesn't mean I am tone deaf.

   # 23—Again a job in my memory. Listening to a conversation about sexual harassment reminded me of this job which I believe was between #8 and #9—but the important thing was how I handled what we called men who "got fresh". There I was starting another new job, San Francisco Financial District, one girl office, insurance broker. I must have been on the job about a week or so. My boss asked me out for lunch and I refused. As the days passed he made suggestive remarks. I don't remember the "moment of truth", but one day his behavior became aggressive. I coolly picked up my typewriter, remember this was before the electrics, and they were moveable. I approached the window, swinging the typewriter and declared "One more step toward me and I will throw this machine out the window". Mr. P. protested, "We are on the twelfth floor, you could kill someone". My reply was "True and you will be responsible". He quickly backed off. I knew this job was over and found out from a fellow worker that he was interviewing new applicants in her boss's office. To save him further embarrassment and hopefully to leave him temporarily stranded with no secretary, I typed up my resignation left it in the typewriter and left.

   Ee Gads! Job #24 I've just remembered another job. I went to work for the ADL, Anti Defamation League. I was and still am a believer in defamation that is anti-defamation. This was another bummer and another long story. I think but I'm not sure that this is the last job I will remember. Needless to say, this job lasted a few weeks, maybe a month—No comment.

   What is wrong with me, I'm a great worker or I was. I seem to resent authority and of course, I was a restless soul; short interest span and other things. One of my nicer employer's probably summed it up best. "I would much prefer to have you as a friend than as my secretary. You make me feel apologetic when I ask you to do something". As a worker I believe a modicum of subservience is necessary and even when I tried to keep my independent nature under cover, the hot air emanating from pompous authority figures always blew it off and there I was again revealed as my own self.

To work or not to work, that is the question, whether *'tis nobler in the mind to suffer the slings and arrows of outrageous fortune*—with gratitude to Shakespeare's eloquent words, I would add my own "a restless soul is ever restless and I can vouch for that".

BEDTIME STORIES

I do believe there is some mysterious spell that was placed on me early on. I have never taken a trip that didn't have its share of odd incidents—nothing tragic, but just a deviation from the norm especially when it came to hotels.

One of the trips was to Mexico. Having no idea about hotels except what I read in the travel books, I picked a beautiful name; the Maria Isabel in Mexico City. We arrived and the hotel lobby was elegant, beautiful, tile floors, circular staircase, and lovely garden. We took the elevator up to our room, a very small room with two very narrow beds wedged against opposite walls. I was reconciled to make the best of it until I went into take a shower. This was my first experience with a shower where the water was directed at the ceiling and no adjustments could be made. Water falling from the ceiling doesn't do it for me when it comes to bathing. The next day, we started on a search and destroy mission of the hotels in Mexico City.

We finally settled on a building that seemed equipped with modern plumbing. The room was large, very large. The windows had a large crack from the last earthquake, but it looked secure enough. At last to relax; but it seemed we had no hot water and called downstairs. They sent up a very pleasant man with a hammer who began systematically knocking on any pipes that were visible in the bathroom. We said, "No, the pipes are not the problem. The hot water heater in your basement must not be working". After much talking and using sign language, he retreated and eventually we had hot water. Darkness descended upon the evening and we were cold. We turned on the thermostat. No heat. First no hot water and now no heat. We called downstairs again and were told they didn't turn on the furnace until winter and since this was September, technically it was fall. As we shivered, we suggested a space heater. Here again, our request was granted. The heater was delivered and turned on but for whatever reason, water began seeping out and covering the floor. We placed bath towels around it and decided it would do. Approximately, around five o'clock in the morning, we were awakened by the sound of jackhammers; they were constructing a building across the street. Except for Sunday, they worked around the clock. Actually, the evenings were quite scenic—the sparks from the welder's tools high on the beams looked like the fourth of July and we did enjoy the light show.

We moved on the Taxco, the town high in the hills famous for its silver. The hotel was an elegant large wooden rustic building. We went to town; saw the cathedral, truly one of the most gold plated interiors I have ever seen. Back to the hotel and to bed. A dog started to bark, then another dog, then another and all the dogs in Taxco were communicating with each other all night. Maybe there is something in the night air that brings out their urge to harmonize.

Wearily, we moved on to Acapulco. Lovely high-rise hotel; our room overlooked the bay; to sleep, to dream, or just to sleep. I lay down and then I heard it—a tremendous slapping sound. Roar—slap! Roar—slap! I looked out the window at the water. As the waves came ashore, they threw their hands up, so to speak, and wham, bam—hit the shore. I covered my head with a pillow but you can't fight Mother Nature.

Back to Mexico City for a few days. We took Aeronaves back and the pilot had a few tequilas. We landed at the airport with all the bathroom doers swinging madly, the overhead storage bins disgorging their contents—but we landed. A few more days in our no heat hotel but this time, our room was like the Sahara. We were told that the heat was on but it couldn't be adjusted. We spent the last several days in the tropics wearing shorts and very little else.

All in all Mexico was truly an experience even through sleep-deprived eyes. I can ramble on and on about the Anthropological Museum, the Ballet Folklorico, the Argentine restaurant where I first ate carne asada and the band played "Granada" with such gusto we got up and sang; the one peso cabs; churros and chocolata; Chapultapec Park; the upscale residential area in Mexico City built on centuries old lava rock; the enormous marketplace in Toluca on Fridays (where I ended up with a magnificent blanket that still hangs on my wall) and the beautiful dark eyed children along the road trying to sell us iguanas.

We boarded the plane on our return looking like the perennial tourist; straw hats perched precariously on our head and colorful straw baskets hanging from each arm. I couldn't pass up a basket I didn't like and they are still scattered here and there through my house and I still like them!

JERUSALEM ARTICHOKE

(Carciofi all giuda; artichoke of the Jews)

I love artichokes. I had read about artichokes prepared the Jewish way that had originated in Venice in the old ghetto district. The artichokes are partially flattened and fried until all the leaves are crisp. Arriving in Italy, I was looking forward to sample these artichokes. Like so many things in my life, I am compulsive in wanting to find or see something that has peaked my interest and I become unstoppable.

It is so difficult to move around in a foreign country without knowledge of the language but if you persevere, it can be done. I finally was told about a certain restaurant that served these delicacies but the location wasn't exactly precise or perhaps I didn't understand the directions. Needless to say, I found the general area and began asking several people but everyone threw up their hands, shaking their heads. At last, a man not only threw his hand in the air, he made a whooshing sound "Whoosh, whoosh". I thought I was getting somewhere. Up and down the street, around the corner and then I saw it—a fountain, long without water, but it made sense—*whoosh, whoosh* and sure enough just a few feet away for the restaurant.

We went in and found *carciofi all guida* on the menu. By translating lira into dollars—one artichoke was $8.00. O.K. when you're in Rome—also ordered gnocchi—$8.00. No one was in the restaurant but us. Out came a large artichoke, cut in half (not very good). Out came gnocchi (very small portion). I asked for bread—

no bread—if bread is ordered another $8.00. Forgot the bread. Can you imagine how much butter would have cost?

As it was nearing siesta that starts at 1:00 PM, the local crowd came pouring in and ordering; it seemed to me a bounty of food. Tables were covered with dishes. We found out later that there is a menu for tourists and one for Romans.

I did get to taste Jerusalem artichokes, which was my goal but encountering the prejudice against us tourists was disappointing. I guess that is one of the good things about Americans; if we overcharge—we do it to everyone!

A STRANGE THING
HAPPENED

When in Venice, we missed our walking tour to St. Mark's Square and the Doges Palace. Being a late riser has its downside, especially when traveling with groups. We asked the desk clerk at the hotel how to get to St. Mark's Square. He directed us outside and pointed to a large yellow arrow on the side of a building clearly marked "St. Mark's."

Off we went, follow the arrow—one block, two blocks, three blocks—what happened to the arrows? Venice has no cars and as I found out, all streets and bridges lead to St. Mark's Square—over to the Doge's Palace. We bought tickets and followed another tour tagging at the rear so not to be too noticeable. The guide was talking in English but several people turned and gave us hard looks. We were intruders but we did try to be as inconspicuous at possible. I over heard a word spoken and thought it sounded like Hebrew. With this knowledge under my belt, I ventured forth and said "Shalom" and before you know it, we were being surrounded by smiling faces saying "You're Jewish". Most of them spoke English and now we were welcome guests.

We walked through the Palace, over the Bridge of Sighs with the Israeli tour. We were asked why didn't we go to Israel? We said "Next time". We exchanged addresses and good wishes.

I've never gotten over Venice, a city floating in the sea connected by three hundred small bridges. I remained in a state of animated suspension during our brief time there. It is still dreamlike in my memory and how fortunate to have met members of our extended family of Israelis in this magical place. As we walked in the evening and watched the gondolas and heard the singing, I felt I was in a trance; never wanting to leave but there was still Israel waiting to be explored.

VOICES

I live alone. This is something comparatively new. I have lived with someone or some ones most of my life. As I have slowly settled into my solitaire life, I am aware of voices. The television has a voice; many voices but it comes in box form—I look at the faces talking and I have a very strange feeling that they are talking to me, through me and around me but since I cannot respond, I become this silent viewer surrounded by sound.

This makes me more aware of how unimportant my voice has become. Then, the telephone rings. Again, a voice but this time I am involved in a two-way conversation. I talk—the person at the other end of the line talks. For a period of time, we are connected. The call ends; we both hang up. The line is broken and I cease to exist in the world of sound. The silence around me is deafening. I look out my window.

There is a world of houses; now and then a car's engine roars into the air. It is quiet, so very quiet. I know this is a foolish thought but sometimes I don't think anyone lives in all those houses. I look over at my sleeping cat. My world is asleep except for a few muffled distant noises. I will soon go out and again be surrounded by voices and forget briefly about my silent world.

At times I embrace the silence but lately the quiet has become ominous—like an animal stalking its prey stealthily moving closer and closer. Am I about to be devoured?

WHERE THE HEART IS

Some years ago on a trip to New York, I felt compelled to find my mother's footsteps. She had left Hungary, sailed to America, and entered Ellis Island in 1908 at the age of sixteen. She entered this bewildering world, which must have enveloped her in confusion. Now, I, her daughter born in this country was visiting New York for the first time.

I wanted to see the area where she had lived, the street where she had shopped and maybe even the place where she had worked. I took a bus and went to the east side. She had talked about Avenue A and Orchard Street. I walked along Orchard Street and Avenue A and I couldn't find her imprint anywhere. It was not the busy, peopled streets she had told me about. It was just ordinary city streets with nothing to distinguish them from any other city. She had told me about the bedlam of sounds that surrounded her, the street peddlers who sold sandwiches and pickles, the sewing factories where she worked but mostly she told me how happy she felt when she left New York and embarked on a life in a small city in Texas.

She said she could again breathe fresh air, again have a garden of flowers and vegetables; especially she could hear the sound of quiet nights. I realized why I could not find my mother's footprints in New York. She had taken them with her and placed them carefully where she had found her home again in Texas. New York was never her home. It was just a transfer point between one home and then another.

I made that transition myself. I left Texas where I was born and now in San Francisco I feel I belong. I look out over the city at night and quietly rejoice that I, too, have come home.

My mother in the Catsckill Mountains—1914

DEATH,
THE GREAT LIBERATOR

I was gazing out the window. It's a beautiful cool morning with assorted white clouds as the sun rises. I feel free, I feel liberated. How ironic, that it takes a death to feel free. Not good, not happy, just free!

I did not realize during all the years of illness, pain, doctor visits and more pain that I would eventually move into the free zone. Our calendar is filled with dates; dates with doctors, labs, dentists, hospitals and on it goes. Pharmacies, back and forth, medicines, more pills for pain, the back and forth of illness.

Now death has liberated me. My husband is liberated, too. Death took away his pain. Death took away the endless days of worry and anxiety he endured. The days of continual suffering; he didn't complain, but just said, "I hope you never have to live this way, it would be better to be dead."

At which I would get angry and say, "Okay, if that's what you want."

He said, "Of course, that's not what I want. I want to be with you but not this way".

He got his wish, but I didn't get mine. I would want him here with me forever.

But I'm free. To go to sleep when I'm sleepy, to eat when I'm hungry at anytime. No schedules, no guidelines. I'm a little drunk on this freedom, like a prisoner-of-war released after years of imprisonment. I'm giddy on this freedom. I don't really know how to deal with it. I can come and go freely. No one needs me, no one.

At times, I'm breathless, too much fresh air after being interned. Did I feel like I was imprisoned? No, never—when you are with the one you love, there is no confinement, only companionship. How do you deal with this newfound freedom? Slowly, I'm doing whatever I want to do whenever I want to do it. I buy whatever I want to buy. I go wherever I want to go.

If only my heart would quit aching, if only I could feel as joyful as I'm acting. I'm laughing and joining the human race. I'm not really part of the scene but at times, I seem to melt into the big picture. I am alive and I'm free and I'm liberated. I guess that's the sum of it. One way or the other, we both are free.

DAMN

Too damn smart to die
Than how did it happen?
You knew everything and more
Dying did not have a reason.

Death has no place
There is no file, no program
No record, no tape, no C.D.
Called Death.

Death has no color, no scent
A container with no contents
A tree with no leaves
A garden without flowers
I refuse to acknowledge you.

Am I too damn smart to die?
I don't know
Don't think so
But I'll be damned if I do.

WHOSE LIFE IS IT ANY WAY?

Today gurus, well educated, articulate, non-stop talkers surround us offering enlightenment into our spiritual selves. The more I hear, the more amazed and saddened I am by the huge audience which sits in wide eyed wonder at the feet of these "holy people".

My reality is very simplistic. My life belongs to me! It is problematic enough without constant examination of one's navel. When I do soul searching, I am my own guru. Others metaphysical utterances are only sound bites designed to mesmerize and in the end, confuse and cloud whatever troubling issues we all have from time to time.

My life has been lived on a "need to know" and a "need to do" basis. I keep turning the pages of life and by and large it has been a pretty good read. My "Ageless Body and Timeless Mind" has never "Run with the Wolves". I was given one magnificent life and I do not intend to waste it searching for ephemeral answers to questions, I haven't yet asked.

JAVA JIVE

I like coffee, I like tea, I live the java jive and it likes me, a cuppa, cuppa, and cup of coffee. Hey, this brings back memories of my USO days. Artie Shaw playing "Stardust", Glenn Miller "Moonlight Cocktail", The Mills Brothers 'Till Then", Woody Herman "Blues in the Night", Harry James "I Don't' Want to Walk Without You" and Nat "King" Cole "Straighten Up and Fly Right".

Once I knew al the words to all these songs. These belonged to my generation and me. All the men we knew were in uniform. There was a war to the right of us and a war to the left of us. We were indestructible. Death was a word but only a word. We were dancing, laughing, singing and tomorrow was just another day.

We heard about island in the Pacific "The Marianas", the "Solomon Islands, the "Marshall Islands". We heard that London had blitzkrieg raids. We heard about the Maginot Line and yet, and yet, we continued to dance all those years to all this music. The music embraced us as we held each other and we felt safe.

What else should we have done? We could not have stopped the war; we could only console ourselves and enjoy the moment. Life is only a sum of moments. Each generation has its songs and it has its wars. I would settle for no more wars and just recycle the songs.

OH, JOY!

I have written much about my cat that has a silent purr. Only last night I heard a coughing sound coming from behind my chair. I looked around and saw *himself,* Finian, trying to purr. I encouraged him to give it the good old college try. "You can purr just as good as the other cats".

I started to think, what has made me purr? GOING FOR A RIDE! My Uncle Willie would pick us up in the big car every Sunday and I would scamper aboard. I was filled with utter joy. He would let me drive, seated in his lap, my hands on the steering wheel. I drove all the way out to the lake. The sheer pleasure of the road, as driver or passenger and the sound of the wind whipping past the windows, the speeding wheels taking me anywhere was pure ecstasy. Down country roads, over mountains, there was always an element of magic and mystery. *What else would I see?*

Everybody has a history and mine has been filled with cars. The white Pontiac and the blue Chevrolet showed me Lubbock, Texas and the Plainsmen Inn. We ate large T-bone steaks at a restaurant along a river. Clovis, New Mexico where a huge golden tarantula just about scared me witless. Albuquerque, New Mexico where I first tasted sopapillas in Old Town never to taste as good again. The big green Oldsmobile showed me the California 49er country—Sonora, Sutter Creek, Nevada City and on up through a "green" highway lined with trees to the Feather River. The small tan Olds took me to the Grand Canyon and down into Sedona Oak Creek Canyon, Arizona to the ghost town of Jerome. We stopped over night in Blythe, California where I befriended a beautiful mountain lion (in a large cage behind the hotel.) This cat really had a purr. The old Cadillac went north to the Avenue of the Giants, the city of roses (Portland), Seattle and over the border to Canada. In Vancouver, we ate the biggest and best blueberries in the world. By ferry over to Victoria; the car decided to have a flat tire during the crossing but we continued to have high tea at the Princess Hotel and get a taste of merry old England. Across the Juan de Fuca Straits to land at Port Angeles, Washington. The church bells rang on the hour all night either greeting us or encouraging our departure.

Drove down the Olympic Peninsula through a rain forest to emerge along the northern coast. We stopped to collect driftwood along a beach in Oregon. The big Copper Buick that went all the way to Tucson, Arizona and showed me the Desert Museum and Mt. Lemon. The Chevrolet Impala, I called "Big Red" that went to El Paso and Juarez and wandered up the California coast to the Hearst Castle and Big Sur. The Burgundy Wagon that rolled merrily back and forth to Palm Springs and the San Diego Zoo once, to change the scene. "Old Blue", the Ford Wagon didn't make too many trips. It meandered up to Tahoe and around the wine country; Sonoma, St. Helena and Napa. It would seem there has never been a car or a trip I didn't like. I guess I would have to give those cars a giant "Thumbs up" purr! If I had an Indian name it would have been *"Helen, want to go for a ride"*.

COBWEBS

I find cobwebs in my memory closet. Brushing them aside I begin to identify what was important. I find absolutely nothing that wasn't worth being or doing. My mind is a labyrinth with roads, alleys and places I've been and people I have known. They are cluttered together waiting for me to sort them out. Eventually I will write about some of the events and characters but I doubt whether I can do them justice. There are so many years crammed into my mind but I know life was good yes life was good!

If I had my life to live over again, I think the one place I would like to return to would be Venice. Walking down the streets, inhaling the sounds, smelling the past in the flowing present. The overwhelming emotion that drew me down one street, up another as I wandered endlessly in the city where the original "ghetto" had been created. All the dogs wore muzzles as they ran playfully down the streets bumping into each other. I stopped and talked to the cats of Venice. They live in communes, beautiful black fur with frosted streaks and almond shaped green eyes. Venice, a city built on piles from the cedars of Lebanon long ago turned into petrified wood standing in the sea, which churns, unceasing under the streets. Each street, each corridor pulled at me magnetically.

My love affair with Venice was not to be consummated, as my stay was brief. The night before leaving I watched a Venetian family at their dinner table through a window. Did they not know they were living in an enchanted place? The ordinary became the unordinary to me. Even now when I think about Venice, I am not sure if I was there . . . . perhaps it was a dream.

THOUGHTFUL THOUGHTS

The velvet of silence/no ears
Only eyes narrowed drawing
Inward/silence/the sound
Of nothing/the isolation
Hibernation/smooth water
Cool unmoving/cloudless sky/
Ring/ring/answer the phone
Talk/talk/retreat slowly
Retreat quietly/fall back/
Falling into silence. Sh . . . sh . . . sh.

Eternal waiting/for tomorrow/
Yesterday is gone/next week
Incoming/still waiting?
For what/for nothing.

HUNGER

The thin blond boy knocked at our door. My mother had become used to the appearance of gaunt faced young men during those desperate depression days. She always gave them a peanut butter sandwich and a cold drink. I would sit next to them on a bench under the large pecan tree, asking questions. Being only ten, my curiosity was intense. I had never been anywhere and their tales of wandering were adventures to my young mind.

I, myself, have never experienced hunger and today, it is hard for me to understand a time in this country when people were starving. This is a rich country with an abundance of foodstuff which is now stored in warehouses; surplus food not to feed the needy but to accommodate the growers and maintain a profit. By not sharing the tremendous harvest the market price remains high. Now and then, some of the surplus is distributed; thereby showing the goodwill of charitable hearts.

It is hard not to be bitter; people are still hungry in this land of the free and home of the brave. Would that I had the power to distribute to all the needy; there should never be an aching, empty stomach in this country. Now that I have written this diatribe, to get back to the good old, bad old days, I do think most people would share with others. Coming home from school, my mother always had a peanut butter sandwich waiting for me. The sandwich symbolized my mother's love and each sandwich she handed out to the wanderers those many years ago symbolized her compassion.

GRANDMA

I called her grandma. She really wasn't even related to me except; she was my cousins' grandma. My mother told me the story of Hannahnanee, who was a distant cousin. She had been orphaned when in her early teens and sent to work in the house of a Count in Budapest; a very young beautiful girl with blue eyes and thick blond hair. She became pregnant and the local community found her a husband to give the child a proper name. She left him and began making her own life with her daughter. She opened a stall in a large marketplace in Budapest. During this time, my mother visited them in Budapest and was enthralled by the big city. She laughingly called their living space "the hot bed"; a bed that had continuous occupancy in a room, which was rented only for sleeping.

My uncle met the beauteous daughter who had inherited the blue eyes and the blond hair. He fell instantly in love. He pleaded with her to marry him and offered to take both her and her mother to America. America, the most revered word and place during the turn of the century. She succumbed, married; they set sail. America, America far away from the grinding poverty of the European cities that devoured the poor, uneducated masses.

Four children and many years later, truly a grandma Hannahnanee entered my life. Grandma would visit and my mother would listen delighted at her Hungarian stories; I think they were risqué jokes but I am only guessing. I would sit with them and join in the laughter never understanding a word. Grandma always had a wicked gleam in her eyes and a smile on her face. She was a remarkable woman, taking care of the children, cooking which I understand was barely edible. She was too impatient so her food suffered from being tough, poorly cooked or probably downright bad. Grandma represented strength and joy. These are the women I subliminally tried to copy. My mother, my "grandma" were my role models and it is my wish that the carbon copy I became is recognizable.

P.S. I talked to my cousin, Margaret in Dallas. She is, of course, a real grand daughter. She said that they were terrible kids, her brother and sisters. They were always making fun of her accent and she would yell something in Hungarian and say in English "I'll slam you till you die". The kids would then fall over each other laughing.

THE VELCRO MIND

Self-analysis leaves much to be desired. However getting to know one's self and becoming acquainted with this strange creature, which is you can be rewarding. I have just recently become aware of the bits and pieces of trivia stored somewhere in the backroom of my mind. There is a lot of dust in a storehouse. Facts and figures pop into my head when discussing things of no real importance and I feel as if this strange substance in my brain has been attracting information all my life. All it needs is a little prompting and off it peels and there is a fact. I remember the large gypsy encased in a glass booth at county fairs. For a nickel deposited into a slot, out came your fortune or words of wisdom. I do not tell fortunes but I do give answers as if by rote.

Velcro mind are certainly no handicap but it would be nice to have retained more than snippets. It seems mine at this point only fit on a small card about the size that were dispended from the gypsy's enclosure. Oh well, I've always said I was a gypsy in a former life, so possibly this is some leftover talent which makes me seem glib even to myself. I wonder what I meant by that. Only the gypsy knows.

A HOUSE IS NOT A HOME

Once long ago we were house hunting; looking for a larger house in a warmer climate with no stairs; a house to grow older in; a house that demanded very little effort to move about and yet, it had to feel like home. Among the "I wannabe your home", one stands out. Walking in, a slow warm feeling overwhelmed me as I walked into a largish, yet smallish house cloaked in redwood shingles on a corner lot. It had a living room with window seats, conjuring up images of being cozily curled up with a book, looking out the huge bay windows, watching rain, leaves blowing across the yard, sunlight dancing off distant roofs; and in the second window seat a large tabby cat carefully washing up after a late lunch. This house had window seats, wonderful window seats.

The dining room was only a large enclosure with walls on three sides looking more like a chapel than a place to eat. There was room for only a table and four chairs; I thought perfect . . . . no formal dinner parties. Actually, it would be a perfect library; install shelves and a well-lighted spot. It could hold all the books you would want to read and those you've read.

The kitchen, a large long shiny counter made for cooking and high stools for eating. No wandering in circles while cooking; you only had to reach horizontally and everything was at your fingertips. The open counter looked out into a large sunny family room with television, comfortable chairs and colorful throw rugs. To continue, a large deck overlooking a low maintenance yard; pebbles, plants and trees—no grass to mow.

The bedrooms down a short hall—one to the right—one to

the left—both large and sunny. Almost a perfect house, almost. The real estate agent said, "Why don't you spend the night—it's furnished and the owners have given their permission after hearing how delighted you folks were with their home." We decided to spend the night.

Early evening, I sat in the window seat. It was good; it was great . . . . only waiting for me to curl up and read a book and of course, get a cat. The kitchen was fun. Eating at the counter I felt like I did as a teenager in a drugstore. Not quite like eating out but easy living, just relax and swing your legs from the high stools. The dining room—I don't do dinner parties—but it was there for me if I changed my mind. At last to sleep; the bed was comfortable and then it began. Cars began speeding past and around the bend; zoom, screech and again zoom, screech, and again and again. I got up and walked to the other side of the house, watching as they came around the curve. This lovely, gentle house was on a sharp curve and each car that came too fast or was unaware of the bend, braked and continued on its way. We had been too enchanted during our waking hours to notice the noise. The night was not filled with music, just the sound and fury of startled cars. We packed our belongings early and scurried away like guilty parents leaving their children with strangers.

I don't know who bought the house or if it was sold. We tried to get the blueprints and have the house built on another more sedate spot. No luck either way. I still love window seats. I still like eating at a counter. I really love the house I live in now. I just have to give it room for error. Warmer climate is an illusion that can quickly become *hot weather*. I did get a cat that seems perfectly comfortable on every seat in my house. Since my kitchen is small, it can be ignored or thought of as a take-out window. A house is not a home until you spend years living in it.

OUT IN THE COLD

The door slammed. There I was standing in front of my house at 8:00 AM. Cars whizzing by on their way to work and here I was in pajamas, short flimsy robe and slippers—locked out. The night before the scavenger trucks are due I always leave my iron gate ajar, held partially open by the garbage can. The incessant sound of my doorbell and the clanging of cans had rudely awakened me. Half asleep, I threw on the robe and rushed down the stairs. On opening the door, there sat my garbage can still heavily loaded and the gate was shut.

Unable the retrieve the green monsters contents (my can), the men had tried to alert me and now I was looking down the street at the departing truck. A gust of wind blew through my house and "bang", the front door closed locked securely. I could feel my face freeze in a "What do I do now look?" O.K., you're more or less dressed, ring a neighbor's bell and get help. Where should I start; went next door, ring #1 house—no answer. An Asian couple who haven't acknowledged my existence in years, but I keep ringing. Are they home, ring, ring. Do they answer doorbells? I hate to make snide remarks but I live in a non-existential type neighborhood. No pun intended. People on my street drive hurriedly into their garages, close the doors or scurry into their homes without looking around. Sometimes I have felt I was living among robots or Stepford people. I now moved to #2 house, neighbor of 25 years, ring, and ring. No answer. Maybe she has left for work. We talk in front of her house sometimes, two or three times a year—ring, ring. She's not home. She would answer. She has cats and I have a cat. We have bonded in this respect. On down the street I go, holding my robe tightly around me, house #3—ring, ring. No answer. Ring, ring—I know you're home. This woman has been house bound for years. She has round the clock help—ring, ring. No answer. Maybe she died and no one told me. Continuing on house #4, no I can't ring this bell. They just moved in last week. Maybe they are not home anyway. I don't want them to meet me in pajamas, a ratty robe with an unwashed face and disheveled hair.

On I go, house #5—ring, ring. No answer. Cars are passing, slowing down and giving me strange looks. I pull myself erect with great dignity and ring the bell again, but I don't hear the sound of a bell. Great, now even if someone is home, no one will hear me. I know this lady, met her years ago. I read in the paper her husband died about a month ago. I slipped a condolence card in her mailbox and she called to thank me. Did she leave town? Here I am just about out of options when I spotted a woman in the lobby. Waving madly, she saw me and opened the garage door. She said the front door is stuck and the doorbell doesn't work. When I informed her of my dilemma, she invited me in. I called up the steps and announced myself. My hostess was very hospitable. She gave me a cup of coffee while I looked through the yellow pages for a locksmith. Called one and proceeded to wait and chat.

Here were two women who in thirty years have only now and then said "Good morning." She said, "I always thought you were very quiet". This was no time to change her mind but if we became friends, she'll find out how verbose I am.

Ring, ring—the locksmith is at the door. I accompany him up to my house. Would you believe it, now my iron gate was closed. Obviously, the garbage men had returned and seen the can holding the gate open emptied it, returned it to the entrance closing the door securely. Behind the closed gate, I have now become double locked out! The locksmith took out his tools, as I stood underdressed in front of my house. After much poking and prodding and finally having to resort to drilling, the lock was demolished.

Home, sweet home—back in my house. He repaired the damage and I gave him a check that could have paid for a round trip to L.A. Did I want breakfast? I washed my face, brushed my teeth and sat down. It really wasn't too bad. It was a beautiful morning. The sky was as blue as the Aegean Sea. I had caused a minor disturbance; some cars driving past might mention seeing an eccentric woman walking around in pajamas. Not a bad morning. My locks have been changed. One key fits all; or mostly all. Today started with a bang but it didn't end with a whimper.

QUICK SAND

The river reflected the dying sun and there we were in the middle of the lake stranded on a sand bar. I had been at a picnic and with the bravado of a sixteen year old I had urged two young men newly arrived in America to man the oars of a canoe. Together with a younger boy we went for a sail. Two rivers merge together, the Brazos and the Bosque to form a large reservoir called Lake Waco including some sandy beaches. The evening was approaching with no shoreline visible and we were obviously stuck tightly. Being a tease, I had said "The sand bar is probably quicksand and we will all be swallowed into a pit of darkness". My two companions became terrified, literally frozen in fear. Finally in desperation, the boy and myself hopped out and after much shoving freed the vessel and off we sailed back to the shore just as darkness descended with an anxious crowd awaiting, we stepped on dry land.

I felt like a conquering hero, I really didn't know a thing about quicksand; it could truly have been somewhere in the vast lake. It seems my approach to life hasn't changed too much. I still would like an adventure.

P.S. One of the immigrants wrote to my father afterwards asking for permission to spend time with me, marriage as his objective. I don't think this would have been possible. He had showed cowardice and I wanted someone brave, at least as brave as I fancied myself.

THE EYES HAVE IT

I really did not want to write this story. In fact, I started writing this story several months ago and then disregarded what I wrote, tore it up and got on with my life. This has not been possible because the saga continues.

Way back in March, a good six months ago, I went to an ophthalmologist and he gave me a new prescription for glasses. Now to begin. First, I went to an optometrist I have known for years, a nice guy, a little flaky; he really wanted to be part of a barbershop quartet or a classic car collector. He ended up as an optometrist with a wife and three children with his dreams on hold. #1 glasses + my frame; glasses came back several weeks later and the optical centers were off. Whatever else was wrong I couldn't tell since I couldn't see out of them at all? The world through these glasses was arching and I, like Chicken Little thought the sky was falling down. #2 glasses came back in a brilliant pink tint. I was really seeing the world through rose-colored glasses but not very well. #3 glasses came back but they forgot to remove the tint and now I do see through a rosy glow. #4 glasses, ah hah, no tint, only non-reflective glass but what's the problem. Why do I see a shimmering across the room down the road and from my room with a view; even the skyline is glimmering. I really need to move on.

In between Glasses #2 and #3, I decided to go to another optometrist and supplied with the same prescription have a pair of glasses made. You can never have too many glasses when you are desperately seeking vision. The games began again. #1 glasses came back. First the lab called several times and told the new place of a variety of problems. At last, #1—well it had scratches. Vision, who knows? #2—Dark glasses—thought I would go all the way and get clear and dark. Dark glasses received. On my left side while looking through these glasses were perpendicular shadows. Back they went and waited for revised version. #3—Clear glasses alert! The office called me and hesitantly said hey they had been waiting and waiting for the glasses. After several calls were told this pair was lost in the mail. "Please to come in and pick out a frame and we will start over". I went in cheerily and started over. #4—Dark glasses came back. I was looking through a glass darkly and rather strangely, but was told you need to get use to them. Bulletin "Clear Glasses Due Any Day".

Went back to Dr. Ophthalmologist. He recommended a specialist—an optician he thought could analyze my lenses since he said, "Eyes are my specialty, and not glasses". Made appointment to see specialist and showed him my array of glasses. I said, "I'm not nuts but I'm coming close". He took glasses into his back room and came back with the good news. He said, "You're not nuts. These glasses are not ground to the prescription and they are optically distorted. Ask for your money back and if they refuse, take them to Small Claims Court where I will appear as an expert witness". I replied, "I don't know if I'm up to court but I will try to be reimbursed". I am really not a fighter, once a lover. He said "I will write letters to each supplier with complete details and you take it from there". Meanwhile, I sheepishly handed him a pair of old frames (which he said were fine) and said, "Would you make me a pair of glasses I can really use".

I left the frames and they will be my next step into the land of the sighted. Back to optometrist #2—It seems the lost glasses turned up but the lab which had been supplied with measurements for the new replacement frame put this info into the now found frames, placing reading portion in wrong position. They asked (the lab) if

I would come in and discuss this. I went in and showed them letters from optic specialist about my distorted lens in dark glasses. They took them from me and said they will send both back to CEO of lab. I am thinking of getting a Seeing Eye dog. At least I'll have a good companion. There really is no end to this story. Just picked up new dark glasses from specialist and I am still very much in the dark.

The saga continues. I waited a week after last encounter with an optician. Returned to Dr. Ophthalmologist to check new "Evening in Paris" glasses. He agreed they were too dark but he commented that my vision is becoming dimmer i.e. glasses should be clear to compensate from my "graying" eyes. Also I can't see to type so he prescribed typing glasses. Don't try to drive or try to cross the street with this pair.

Down again I went; downtown to see specialist. Returned "Evening in Paris" glasses to be transformed to "Morning in San Francisco". Also, old frame to be fitted with typing glasses. Off I went back to Lab #2—no glasses yet, it seems something keeps happening. Either lens doesn't meet requirements or maybe they are waiting till I become senile and forget all about glasses. At last, I am the proud owner and wearer of one pair of distorted lens. I'll settle for this, as I have no other choice. Wait, one more tidbit of news. Yesterday while dressing for an evening out, I put my glasses on and, yes, a lens fell out. Oh my God!

What do I do now? I can barely see with these—without, no can see—inspiration—with the use of a little scotch tape, inserted lens and went out for my evening of merriment. Took them to Lab #2 today—Guess what?—I had a loose screw. I could have told you that. Tightened screw and here I am waiting for the next call. Received calls, plural—today, drove over to Lab #2—clear glasses seem o.k. I'll keep them—"Tis better to see a little, than never to see at all". Still waiting for sunglasses.

Now to drive back downtown and pick up redo of glasses #4 from lab. I am really getting good at driving downtown. Entering the Sutter-Stockton garage, carefully taking the ticket from the machine; driving round and round and up and up. The first time, I parked on floor 9—the highest you can go and had to stop downstairs to find out the trick to exiting this hall of cars. Everything is technologized—no people, just machines and if you don't know the program, it's a no go. Second time, I parked on floor 7—a kind soul instructed me on how to insert ticket plus money in machine before leaving—I made it out at last. Today, floor 6—I'm becoming very proficient, or so I thought. On exit, I put money and ticket in machine. The machine kept telling me—*This does not compute.* Desperate, I finally realized, my dollar bill was facing left instead of right. That's the ticket. Once again I was given permission to leave. I'll be back soon, more later.

O.K. Picket up dark glasses from Lab #2. I guess they are all right. At this point I've become completely passive. I paid for them. I wore them. I don't see too well—but I see. Downtown, downtown—Sutter, Stockton Garage, floor 5—picked up typing glasses and tried on distance glasses. Would you believe it, I couldn't see. The optician #3 took them and said "I'll send them back"—(I remarked something about the base curve and he shook his head sadly). I paid for typing glasses and left. I don't know whether I'll ever type again but back to the garage. I am now very efficient. Insert dollar in machine—George Washington's face in correct position. Drive out of garage after inserting ticket correctly. One more trip to town and I can leave this story behind me, maybe, I guess so, perhaps or who knows.

GRUMPY OLD CATS

Finian just ran down the back stairs. Fuzz ball was lying on the deck. Finian walked over to him to say "Hello". Fuzz jumped up, looked around and gave a small hiss. Finian looked perplexed. "We've known each other for years, what's your problem?" Fuzz seemed nonplussed as the two exchanged greetings. Eskimo fashion and it seems, the Maoris in New Zealand do the same . . . . nose to nose.

Finian moved into the yard. He had forgotten Fuzz has been deaf this past year. Oh well, he thought at his age one couldn't be expected to remember everything.

Both he and Fuzz had been to the groomer within the month. They have a modified "Lion cut" shaggy around the face and shoulders. No one touches their tails. Uh, uh, Finian's tail is still quite handsome, full and fluffy. He doesn't hold it as high as he did a few years ago. This arthritis in his back hasn't gotten any better. Damn, this getting old. The spirit is willing, but the body does tend to break down.

Finian walked back up the stairs from the yard and started talking "Meow, meow, me-ow, me-ow." Oh for goodness sake, I forgot Fuzz couldn't hear. I have so much I want to tell him.

Firstly, my mistress got herself a fancy computer. It's in the den. I don't like to go in there. I am more comfortable in the living room. I've yelled at her when she stays in there too long. She yells back "Come on in."

I won't budge; I'm going to stay right here in front of the heater. I yell again, "Me—ow!" She comes in and says, "What do

you want? Are you hungry?" Occasionally, I'll follow her into the
kitchen and watch while she heats my food and carefully places it
in my plate. Sometimes I deign to take a few bites and walk out.
This infuriates her. So what, I've been the top cat in this house all
my life and I'm not going to change. She goes back into the den
but mostly, she settles down in the living room and that stupid
computer is forgotten at least temporarily.

People just have to respect age. It's taken me a long time to feel
secure in my skin, or should I say my coat. Who cares? I know I
don't look as good as I did, especially with this weird haircut.
Actually, I look like a peeled onion, with a little peel left on for
affect. I know my hair was a mess but what's the big deal. I've
always though I looked grand.

I like to go down on the deck, get a little fresh air and visit
with my friends. So what happens, Fuzz can't hear anymore, Molly
is still too shy (I think she's cute), but I can't get to first base with
her, never could.

The new residence next door is Inky. Did I mention they all
live together, must be cozy all running around bumping into each
other. Back to Inky, a dumb black cat that lived in the park. The
woman next door decided to adopt him and teach him to live in a
civilized society. He doesn't look too smart to me. He hangs out at
the end of the yard and never speaks. Maybe, he needs a bilingual
education course.

I think cat speak is the most eloquent language in the world. I,
myself, am very fluent. Sometimes I talk too much. Just blame it
on my genes. With a name like Finian McLonergan, you expect
me to be full of blarney. And a good meow to you, too.

WHAT ARE YOU DOING?

"What are you doing"? I asked. This was something I said often over the year to my husband who was sitting in the den. It would become very quiet and I knew he wasn't watching television. He had read only sporadically in his later years. I realize, especially now, that there is just so much you can absorb from books when your mind or body are otherwise occupied.

He has been dead almost three years and it seemed a rather frivolous and unrealistic question to ask. Today, as I am nearing the third anniversary of his death, I know I am not asking him what he is doing. I am questioning myself. I am doing many different things since he died. I have done the usual things—had the house painted, bought groceries, had the car serviced, took the cat to the vet. What I believe I've really been doing is starting a new life. I met people I would never have known. I've joined groups I'd never have joined. I've written pages and pages of my inner thoughts and remembrances of a life long past. I've moved out and on to a different plane. I am no longer anchored in a marriage where another's needs or wants are considered. I've become or am becoming my own self. I am discovering new needs and discarding unnecessary tasks.

In some strange way, I feel completely selfish. I do, go, feel only what and where is important or pleasurable to the new me. This does not bring me the contentment I would like. It is only a first step and I am very aware of the pitfalls of moving into uncharted waters. Each day, I awake and think what are my plans. I know for the short term. "What am I doing?" That's a good question. I guess at this point the closest answer is "The best I can".

MY SO SO LIFE

I sit here in front of the fire. My cat is curled warmly in my lap. His tail hangs languidly across my knee. This is a good time to reflect. How did I get here from there?

There, is a long time ago. George Crow no longer gave me crayolas or held the faucet on the water fountain. He left me for a girl with long curls. Begging my mother to make me long curls like Shirley Temple. She said, "I can't, your hair is too fine." I was six and in the first grade.

I used to ride the streetcar across the bridge over the Brazos River. My father had a store on the other side of the river. When it rained the river rose and covered the bridge. We sold the big house that had two porches. We moved into two rooms. We spent ten years in two rooms.

We always had outside. Summers were long so we sat outside on porches of grass. I had a dog-named Boy but a car hit him. I had a lot of cats. One was named Chesapeake and she had three kittens. She left our house after a year or so. She moved next door. They let her stay in the house at night.

I thought I was in love with Lawrence Dukas. He had a car with a rumble seat. He drove past everyday and I would stand in front of the house and wave. We drove to the park and ate watermelon. I didn't like him anymore. He seemed kind of dumb. I was fourteen. This was beginning of my so-so life.

STALAG IIB

For twenty-one months I wrote letters to a soldier taken prisoner in Europe during WWII. It wasn't until he was librated by the Russians that I learned his story. A Texas infantry division was sent to North Africa where after months in the desert they were transferred to a ship. The unit made land on the coast of Italy at Salerno. The enemy was waiting. He was wounded and taken prisoner but refused to ride on the truck into Germany hoping to be recaptured during their march. He finally could no longer walk and he was to ride the rest of the way to a prison camp, Stalag IIB forty miles south of Danzig, Poland. His leg became infected from the wound and German doctors examined him. He was told gangrene had set in and the leg must be amputated. He refused and told them according to the laws of the Geneva Convention; he should be given whatever drug was available. Sulfa powder was provided and for almost a year, he lay in a dirty bunk under the most primitive conditions unable to walk. Miraculously, his leg healed not without massive scarring but he could walk.

He felt surely God had provided this miracle. Every Friday night, he would open his small Hebrew prayer book in the presence of the German guards and recite the evening prayers. Over and over for almost two years, he tested God in this fashion and decided that he been chosen to live. Periodically, the SS would enter the camp and order all prisoners to stand at attention for hours in the bitter cold. Hunger was a constant companion and when the Russians liberated the camp, the men were sent to LeHavre, France for a month to regain their strength. He returned to California where we were married. His continuing relationship with God, his presence every Friday night in the synagogue was the mainstay of his life. He told me many times he was immortal and would never die. Only once did he tell me he was the reincarnation of Jesus. When I laughed, he became enraged and said loudly "Jesus was a Jew, why can't you believe me?" There was always this "other world" quality about him which in retrospect I did not notice early on. Years later, almost ten to be exact, he calmly told me it was time for him to die. It is very easy to become an accomplice in an illusion when you are emotionally connected.

I had never thought of leaving him but I could no longer fight his shadows and I became afraid. Since he said God had given him immortality, He had the right to take it away. I think of him often; a tall clear-eyed man who always seemed to see past the horizon. He did die but mostly I grieve for the young soldier who entered Stalag IIB and never really returned. Only in death was he truly free.

WAITING FOR THE BUS
AND OTHER STORIES

It's been a long time since I took a bus but I do remember waiting for a bus. I had recently returned to San Francisco, had just moved into my own apartment and gotten a job in the financial district. Mornings, standing in the fog was lonely and cold. Every morning, a group would gather, stand silently, board the bus and disappear among the other passengers. After a few days, I decided to break the ice and speak to my fellow travelers. I opened my remarks by saying something about the weather. They all turned and looked at me. No one responded. After the initial glances, they turned away and resumed their robotic stance. I had heard San Franciscans were a cold lot, but this seemed an extreme position. In time, I learned to accept my mute companions.

Months passed, and one morning completely unsolicited, I heard a man's voice and turned to face him. Brightly, he said, "It is a cold morning". I was completely taken aback. I thought to myself "It's too late for you fellow, you had your opportunity months ago". Each morning thereafter, he greeted me with a weather report. I was much too bored to start a dialogue. I moved soon after.

I wonder if he ever talked to anyone after I left. Over the last years, I travel about in my car. Buses are crowded and I am sure there is still no vocal interaction. The lonely crowd still exists. In the safety of my car, I have a radio, which talks or sings to me. Inanimate as these sounds are, it beats standing on a corner surrounded by faceless, voiceless people. I still have an irresistible need to communicate and I still talk to strangers. However, my expectations of a meaningful conversation are limited. I take what I get and move on, like I did long ago.

GUESS WHAT

We had a small grocery store in Texas. It was very poorly stocked. Outside of a dozen loaves of Jones Fine Bread and maybe six bottles of milk, the shelves were almost bare. I think we probably had four cans of Campbell Tomato Soup, two or three cans of peas maybe two cans of tomatoes. On most of the bottom shelves I carefully stacked my comic books. The big seller was Brown Mule Chewing Tobacco, light or dark; a small tin mule was imbedded in each piece. We had Bull Durham tobacco in a small sack and Garrett Snuff. My attention was always drawn to the candy counter. Inside were boxes of Baby Ruths, Milky Ways, Snickers, Butter Fingers and Guess Whats. Almost every day, I would casually slide open the back of the counter and take out a Guess What. Two or three caramels were carefully placed in a small rolled paper cone, twisted at each end; inside was a surprise. I didn't much like candy when I was a child, but the surprises intrigued me. I would carefully twist the end and reach in for the surprise. It could be a whistle, a small ceramic dog or cat, a teakettle, other small animals—you just never knew. I would remove the toy and play with it for a week or so, then exchange it with another toy. My fingers were not nimble enough to do the twist necessary to keep the original shape. Eventually every Guess What looked rumpled and disturbed. I was compelled to open every one and no Guess What was left untouched. I ended up with a small ceramic dog that disappeared years ago.

Guess what, I don't go for surprises much anymore but I do like candy!

EAST MEETS WEST

The sun was shining when our plane landed in Italy. As we flew through several time zones, during the last hours I spent looking into the black sky. As if someone opened a window, we flew into the bright sunshine that welcomed us to Rome. Rome, we stayed in a pie wedge of a room with a green door. The tub was large enough for two people. We did all the tourist things and learned the Romans are rather formal. When the stores closed for their siesta—noon until four—you leave the store, no dallying about, business or no business, everything closes.

On to Florence and Michael Angelo's David, a huge sculpture; no cameras were allowed but we all cheated. The last evening in Florence, we were treated to the Gala Dinner Dance. We climbed aboard the bus and were deposited at a large restaurant on a hill overlooking the city. We were seated at long tables. The music, the small band started playing. The musicians were seated on a small stage overlooking the dance floor. We all looked around at each other. Nobody got up. We all just sat, like beached whales. The dance floor was empty.

Across from us at another long table were men, a lot of men. Several moved across the floor and then we noticed they were Japanese. Very politely, they gestured at a few women at our table to dance. One woman arose and joined her partner, then another, and another. As we watched, the dancing began producing more couples. We all felt quite tired from a day of walking through museums, shops and more museums.

The music was lively and as my husband rose (presumably to

go to the men's room), a small Japanese man approached him, held his hands out. They both looked at me and I nodded by head vigorously "Yes, yes!" And off they danced—wow, did they dance; two middle-aged men, laughing, totally oblivious of the other dancers. Not one word was spoken. They were both laughing hilariously as was everyone else. They twirled, they dipped, and they jitterbugged. This Gala Evening became one of the most delightful times of my life. We all became one. At the end, my husband's partner bowed and my husband bowed. It seemed most differences could be settled by laughter. We don't need words to communicate. We need actions. As my husband returned to our table flushed and smiling, the rest of the group gave him a standing ovation. He asked me "Did I look foolish?" "No, you looked happy." He said "I was, I have never done anything like that in my life."

Sometimes, when I hear music for dancing, I start smiling . . . remembering the joy of two men from different worlds totally delighted with each other. Maybe I ought to check out a tour . . . . maybe someone will ask me to dance.

MONKEY ON MY BACK

A friend and I were talking about unresolved issues in our lives. I used the term "monkey on my back". I said I've never felt guilt. It has not been one of my demons. The use of the word "monkey" brought to mind a time in my life when I was about twelve.

I attended Hebrew School during the summer for several days a week. I would meet my father for lunch. We were each other's best friends for a whole summer. This was my first opportunity to spend time with my father alone. After lunch, we always visited a pet store around the corner. We took crusts of bread and fed the monkey. Day after day, into the pet store while my father patiently watched and smiled as I fed my new pet. I wanted this monkey and asked my father if he would buy him for me. He agreed but said you must get your mother's permission first. Bursting with happiness, I told my mother of my good fortune. She looked at me sharply and said, "It's impossible to keep a monkey in our small house, and there is no room. Absolutely not!"

I was very disappointed but as children do, forgot about the episode and life moved on. My father and I were never to resume the closeness we shared that summer. I mostly remember him as a quiet solemn man. We had very few dialogues; mostly he seemed distant and remote. I spent my teen years dancing, laughing with everybody and anybody I met. My father came from a world of order; there was a proper way to conduct oneself and I am sure he found his daughter had total disregard for the rules he had lived by. We barely spoke. My mother became the mediator between us. After I married and moved away, he wrote me several times. I still have the letters; that are filled with words of love and affection. He died when I was in my twenties so I had little time to become acquainted with him as an adult.

Why didn't I long ago tell my father I loved him? Why didn't we talk about the monkey he wanted to buy me and laugh together? Many years after he died, I met his sister, my aunt. She said, "Your father wrote about you all the time". He said, "You were his sunshine". Yes I do have "a monkey on my back" and it is guilt. Today November 30th is exactly 45 years since he died. I lit a candle for him and I would like to repeat the last line of the silent devotion in memory of my father "May He grant thee eternal peace. Amen."

HOT TAMALES

Bob loved tamale pie. I decided to surprise him and make his favorite dish. It takes several hours to assemble the ingredients but I did make the tamale pie.

It was a warm winter night. January in Texas can be many things but this night was really hot. I was sitting in sandals and a cotton dress reading. I smelled smoke and opened my door looking down the stairs. I was living in a small apartment house.

My downstairs neighbor came out screaming "Fire, fire." I saw wisps of smoke trailing behind her as she ran out the door. I retreated into my apartment. The smell of smoke was becoming stronger. I walked into my bedroom and calmly called the Fire Department. It was only two blocks away; I was sure they would be there in no time. As I was talking to them, the man asked me "How did the fire start?" I said "I really don't know but I am calling from the building; I think I'd better go." With that, I hung up.

I walked over to the closets and carefully looked around. In one was my newest purchase, a black and white check raincoat. I didn't think it was going to rain but I quickly yanked it out and took it with me, closing the door behind me securely.

I took nothing else. I saw no reason to worry. I had made a general survey of my apartment and then decided to go out the front door. As I approached the door, flames were rapidly coming up the narrow stairs. I turned quickly and went through the hall into the bedroom where a door led down the back steps.

As I reached the ground, I walked to the apartment house next door to warn them of the fire. I wandered back and forth in front waiting for the Fire Department. No sign of them, only a lot of swirling, hungry flames leaping out of the windows destroying everything in the apartments.

One of the neighbors ran up the back stairs of my building trying to get an older couple to leave. He came down the stairs and said, "I don't know what to do, they won't come with me." Without thinking, I said, "They know me, I'm going up." I ran up the back stairs and told them "You are coming with me." They protested saying "All we own is here in the apartment." I didn't argue, just grabbed their hands and pulled them out the back door, down the steps. The windows in the downstairs apartment exploded just as we reached the backyard.

I don't know how long it took; it seemed forever, but finally the firemen did show up with their hoses turning the street into small lakes. As I watched, I thought of all those dam cockroaches being burned to cinders. I was looking up at blazing building and all I could think about was the cockroaches. I had bought every product available. These were monster roaches, big shiny brown creatures. I was glad they were dead, burnt to a crisp.

Walking through the twisted hoses lying chaotically across the street stepping carefully over the puddles, my husband appeared. The first thing he said was "I thought you were going to make tamale pie". This was my introduction to "Grace under fire". In this case, literally fire.

The fire was brought under control and I looked up at a blackened wall. My husband walked casually over to the firemen and said he wanted to go upstairs to our apartment. They said it would be too dangerous. The stairs might collapse. He talked to them and quite persuasively said "I think I know where I have a bottle of bourbon, come on up and I'll give you guys a drink". They led the way carefully, testing each step gingerly and we entered a litter of burned furniture but . . . . But, the tamale pie in its fireproof casserole dish was on top of the stove, nice and warm. The top of the dish was black with a crack running through it, but the contents were intact.

He reached under the sink and sure enough, a bottle was found and he opened the charred doors of the cabinets and found some smoky cups, pouring out generous helpings of bourbon. There was a party like atmosphere, everyone was talking and laughing. Bob found a smoky fork, took the top off the casserole and stood casually eating tamale pie.

We removed some of the wet clothes from the closets. Since I had so carefully closed the doors there were remnants of our belongings, which would prove, unwearable and unusable. We drove over to his aunt's house where we spent the night. In the early morning hours, a fierce norther blew into town. The car wouldn't start the next day; the engine block had cracked. The temperature had dropped below freezing overnight.

I took a cab and went downtown to begin assembling a new wardrobe. I remember a beautiful wool skirt from France and a lot of inner and outer clothing. Life took on a new meaning. I started going house hunting. This turned into an adventure unlike the previous one.

I never wore the black and white check raincoat again. In fact, I have detested checks ever since. There were still a few cockroaches that showed up from time to time, but they never got the upper hand. I still make tamale pie occasionally and it always reminds me of this turning point in my life. I came out with new clothes, new furniture and a new house.

UNSHARED MEMORIES

"Remember when we bought our first house, remember?" I don't think he ever remembered. It was a brand new house in a new development, mostly purchased by families whose men had served during WWII. I was excited at the prospect of buying my first house; this would belong to me. No one else had ever lived in it. We argued about the color to paint the house. He said "You can pick the inside colors and I pick the outside". He chose yellow paint for the wood frame house and blue for the trim. I said, "It will look awful, the roof is already installed with red shingles". I lost the fight.

About a week later, we returned to view our home. The builder was standing in front and cars were slowly driving down the street. Our house, my beautiful new home looked like a badly painted clown. People were staring and laughing. I didn't say, "I told you so" but the builder said, "You'll have to change the color, sales on my other houses has stopped. No one wants to buy because of your house. Others who have already purchased want their money back". I looked aghast at the egg yolk yellow house with the royal blue trim plus the red roof looking down in dismay. I walked around the house peering in the windows. My kitchen walls were green but the ceiling was navy blue. My bedroom was a very, very shocking pink. I told the builder the colors inside were wrong, not my choice. He agreed and said his painters were probably drinking and after doing the outside figured why not give the inside a dramatic look. He said the inside would be repainted but we would have to pay for the outside—which we did, my choice—white with a touch of red trim to match the roof.

After we moved in our next-door neighbors hesitated talking to us for some time. Eventually, I convinced them we were quite normal. This was to be debated later. We bought another house a few years later. After the last debacle, I was given carte blanche. I spent days at the housing site (another new development), watching the foundation being poured, walls going up. It was interesting and exciting. After walking through the framework of my new house, I found a folded blueprint. Opening it up I began to examine the plan. It was all there, the rooms, the closets, the windows. I decided to do a little creative redesigning. Nothing major, only minor changes. Using a blue pencil (which was the color on the blueprint), I changed the closets designating large sliding doors, eliminating the small ordinary style. I found the small circles for electrical outlets. No home ever has enough electrical outlets. I cleverly drew the identical circles giving each room an outlet on all four walls, increasing the number by eight or nine. In the kitchen where the stove was to be placed, I drew the outline to indicate 220 wiring. We did not have an electric stove, but who knew when I would want one. In the garage, I again drew outlets for my washer and dryer; a good day's work, even if I say so myself. The house was completed to my specifications.

Bob, my then husband, died years ago and is not here to talk about the house that was the house that Helen rebuilt, but I remember.

TERROR IN THE NIGHT

I grew up, got married and bought a house. Went to the movies, out to dinner, many weekends at the beach in Galveston. Moved, bought another house, new furniture, a lot of new things. My biggest concern was to find the right drapes for the living room. At last, soft white cotton print with dramatic sprays of red and green; a perfect complement to the dark green walls and white ceiling. Very smart, very "House Beautiful".

Life was a known routine, not too many surprises. Time moved slowly and I continued to exist in a dreamlike state; days adding up to weeks and then years. Went shopping, did lunches, and I knew that my marriage was disintegrating. Maybe things will get better, change. No, the patient had gone from a chronic condition into a downward spiral and the end was in sight.

I returned to the workforce; I began to regain a sense of independence slowly, haltingly.

The words in the marriage vows read "Till death do us part" but there are no last rites for the death of a marriage, no final words of condolence or sympathy. When my uncle heard of my divorce he said, looking at me with distaste "I hope you know what you are doing". My so-called friends shrugged their shoulders and said, "Now, you know we're not going to take sides." I gained a rapid reputation going from a "wife" to a "swinger." The impending divorce made me an untouchable. It was frightening and unnerving. Several of my friend's husbands made suggestive remarks and one called me for a date. I was being condemned, but for what.

Insomnia and me have a long-term relationship. Alone at night, sleeplessness took on a new dimension. It became a full time companion. Went to a doctor for sleeping pills—no relief in sight. One night in desperation took all the pills left in the bottle. Didn't even sleep. Suicide attempt or not; I wasn't successful. The next day at work, I was pretty groggy. I decided then and there, I obviously couldn't kill myself. Death comes soon enough. I planned to live long and well. No more pills.

My life was busy, work and play. There were a lot of playmates. Not too much time spent anguishing over the past or worrying about the future. Sleep began to welcome me now and then. Coming out of the haze of uncertainty and confusion seemed on the horizon until that night, that night of terror.

That night of terror, I brushed my teeth, put on my pajamas, got into bed and turned off the light; something awakened me, I blinked and heard nothing. I'll get up and get a glass of water. I said, "I'LL GET UP—why can't I move? I can't feel my legs; I reach down, there they are. I could feel the warm flesh. I inhaled deeply and tried to pull up my leg—nothing happened. I CANNOT MOVE! I'm paralyzed. Oh my god, what am I going to do?

I looked around; I had exchanged a house for one small room. I had taken nothing with me but the two twin beds from the den; a corner table between the beds and a coffee table. The kitchen was not a kitchen, a counter and a small built in refrigerator. The air conditioner in the window was humming loudly. Panic set it— no one will hear me scream. I looked across the room at the television; at least I had taken the television. I wish I could turn it on but how to get across the room. Someone at work might call in the morning, maybe. How long had it been? I looked at the clock; it read 2:30 AM. Again, I try to move—nothing. I lay very quietly and waited; tried to move my legs gently; still rigid. I look at the clock on the table next to my bed—3:00 AM. Should I call someone? What would I say? The room began to seem smaller; the walls seem to be closer. And, I am frozen like a block of ice on a narrow bed. Maybe I could try to roll over on the floor. I try lifting my shoulders, yes that's good, now roll over—you can do it, no sensation at all below my waist. Relax for a little while. Think, do something. Oh well, why not. It's almost 4:00AM.

Call him—call your husband—you're still friends. Go—ahead call—I guess he's home. I reached for the phone on the table and dialed his number. A sleepy voice answered. "Bob, I'm paralyzed, I can't move." The voice said, "Oh, how are you doing honey?" "Bob, didn't you hear me, I can't move my legs." "Oh, that's too bad" he said. "Hey Bob, maybe you should call a doctor or something." By this time, I probably sounded hysterical. "Just try to go back to sleep, I'll call you tomorrow" and he hung up.

What did you expect? That's what you married. He was never there for you. Don't you remember when you went to the hospital? He dropped you off at the door and said to call him when you were coming home. He didn't like hospitals. He didn't like a lot of things. Remember why you are getting a divorce.

I began to breathe deeply, anger draining away to a trickle. I moved my toes. I did it again. I moved my legs—one at a time. I'm not paralyzed. I slowly got up and sat on the side of my bed. I'm o.k. What happened? It was as if someone or something had said "You did the right thing." Part of me had felt I was "a rat leaving a sinking ship." He was an American soldier, who had been badly wounded and spent the last two years of the war in a prisoner of war camp. I had made endless excuses about his erratic behavior to myself.

An inner tranquility flowed over me. I wasn't angry with him. Why should I be? The marriage is over. Neither of us is guilty. But, the night lives on in my memory—a night of terror, helpless and alone. Thinking about it, I was the one on the sinking ship; I had been clinging desperately to a phantom marriage. The man that returned from Stalag IIB was a ghost, not the young happy soldier I had met a few years earlier. He was to die five years later. The rats he left behind in Germany.

GOOD, GOOD, GOOD

The smell was tantalizing. The café was overheated and everyone looked tired. It was cold outside and the sound of sizzle from the large griddle made its own music. The cook moved quickly from side to side, dancing as he flipped the burgers over and then placed them gracefully on the open buns. Watching the hamburgers cooking, cooked to the right doneness by a proud craftsman gave it a special taste. The crisp edges of the meat joined with the crunchiness of the onions and the tartness of the pickle. I took the warm roll in my hand and savored the melody of flavors. Still feeling the juicy taste on my lips, I returned home filled with contentment. The streetlights reflected sullen shadows which gave the night a mellow, haunting aura. Pushing the door open my heart was filled with anticipation.

Nighttime is the best time for love. Warmth surround me, enveloped me. As my body was caressed, the covers taunted me as they moved away. Slowly, quietly almost purring catlike, I surrendered to the intimacy above me. Sleepily, exhausted I sighed, relinquishing myself as my down comforter embraced me in its soft arms.

OH LITTLE TOWN

I read about a comedy act in the paper. One of the issues discussed was about what Jews do on Christmas day. This has been a constant dilemma all of my life. Most years passed easily as the festive lights, the crowded stores, and especially the music surrounded me. It has become a cacophony of sounds, ergo "On the first night, I am dreaming of a white Christmas and a partridge in a pear tree. Here comes Santa Claus and the little drummer boys, hum, hum, hum."

Over the years I have felt alienated, rejected, out of the loop. Living in a Christian world has become the norm, but still, but still, as I get older, I don't think I have become more Jewish— maybe more aware of not being a Christian.

This year circumstances permitted me to do what some comic said Jews do on Christmas day, i.e. go to a movie and eat Chinese food. I drove to the movie, parking was easy, theater relaxing, and movie was superb. Continued to step #2, Chinese restaurant. Ordered prawns, won ton soup, mushu pork and sat happily among mostly Asians and assorted Caucasians. I questioned the people sitting across from us, and yes, they were Jewish. I don't know whether the Asians were Buddhists or Muslims or perhaps more were Jews. Here I was on Christmas day, no longer an outsider. There were a lot of us that didn't go to family dinners and hang out around a Christmas tree. "Jingle bells, jingle bells."

A FUNNY THING HAPPENED

We started out enroute to Santa Fe, New Mexico; a destination I had thought about for years. Across the endless flat expanse of the American west, we finally reached Albuquerque and settled in for a few days of sightseeing, sopapillas and a general look about of this sprawling city.

Around Old Town sat dozens of Navajo women selling their wares. No smiles were forthcoming from their grim faces reflecting the defeat of an Indian nation, now represented by trinkets. The sopapillas were superb—deep fried puffy bread.

On to Santa Fe, high in the mountains; the air was so pure, my chest ached deliciously as I breathed. The first night after settling comfortably in our bed, the sounds began. The roaring of engines and as we looked out the window of the room, cars were speeding around and around the square. Around and around they drove; the squealing of tires, the screeching of brakes was to be our undoing. Wearily, dressing and going to the desk clerk, we asked for another room. He said, "No more rooms." We asked about the racetrack in full throttle around the hotel. He said, "There's not much for the young people to do here, so they drive around at night." This ended our sojourn to Santa Fe.

We packed hurriedly in the early morning hours and drove down the mountains through Albuquerque and arrived in Gallup, New Mexico. The town was a convention of pickup trucks. Everybody drove a pickup truck. Young sullen Indian men drove each truck. Here were the sons of the women who sold their trinkets in the square in Albuquerque; here were the descendents of the

Navajo people reduced to driving back and forth in a dusty town. No goals, no ambitions; just dead end streets with dead end lives.

Heading west, we stopped at Flagstaff, Arizona. At my suggestion we turned south into Oak Creek Canyon and down into the town of Sedona. Around us in stillness, something magical permeated the atmosphere. As we looked around, the hills were covered with green rocks, boulders. Perhaps, a leprechaun had transported pieces of the Emerald Isle to this place nestled in the bleak hills of the high desert. I knew this was my special place and I wanted to keep it with me. We picked assorted green rocks, carefully placed them in the trunk of the car.

We soon continued west up and over a mountain, into Jerome, Arizona (a ghost town). No ghosts could be found but hundreds of tourists were walking in and out of the shops; souvenir shops, art galleries (paintings of Jerome by local ghosts). We continued on through Prescott, Arizona a mid-sized city on a high plain, inhabited by super patriots flying the American flag and gun shops supplying the good citizens with their constitutional right to bear arms.

Into the Mojave Desert we drove in a car with no air-conditioning. The blistering heat enveloped me and as I turned from pink cheeked to fire engine red, this place called Salome beckoned to me. Gasping as I walked into the large café inhaling the coolness provided by the swamp cooler on the roof. I protested venturing out again into the furnace that was eyeing me through the windows. Again driving well over the speed limit, the queen of the desert, Blythe, California greeted us and we checked into the gleaming white stucco hotel. Nighttime descended and braving the heat that hovered gently around 100 degrees, we went for dinner. On our return while passing through a pathway alongside the hotel, we came upon a large cage. I looked inside and saw a beautiful golden mountain lion looking at me with beseeching eyes. I saw a large ball on the floor of the cage. I called to the lion and said, "Bring me your ball." He picked it up and brought it to me. I took the ball from his mouth and we began a game. This large cat began to purr, a purr that could be heard across the yard. I scratched his head and rubbed his nose. Why would anybody put an innocent victim in a cage? The owners told me the next day that he had been raised by them since he was a cub. They no longer kept him in the lobby on a chain. They were fearful someone might tease him.

The next day, we drove to Los Angeles; one more stop before home to San Francisco. We were tired and the heat of the desert had left us numb. It was then I remembered the green rocks, my wonderful green rocks. These had been my trophies. These had been the award nature had bestowed one me. In Los Angeles, we opened the trunk of the car to examine our carefully wrapped treasures. I unwrapped the first one; it was a basic brown rock; then another one—an ordinary rock; this continued until all were exposed. All the rocks had changed back into common garden-variety rocks. What happened? They had been green, brilliant green. Sadly, we took them out and deposited them along a road with others of their kind. Did the bright sun in Arizona keep them green? Did the heat of the desert cause them to loose their brilliance? What happened? I have thought about this from time to time. Sometimes years pass and I still wonder what happened? My friend, the mountain lion should never have become a part time pet to spend his life away from his habitat. I suppose nothing in nature should be removed from their origins.

BLUE BIRD OF HAPPINESS

It was almost five o'clock on the afternoon of October 17, 1989. The World Series was about to start in San Francisco. An unearthly sound startled me and my house began rocking, swaying madly. The cabinet doors in the kitchen swung open and glasses began falling. Was this the Big One?

There was a moaning of inanimate pain from all around me. Pictures standing on the library table fell over, chairs moved, bookends were dancing. Pillows on the couch fell on their face. Suddenly the house came to a screeching halt, as if giant brakes were engaged. As I looked around, outside of a few broken glasses, everything seemed pretty much in order. There would be no World Series today, the very important Bridge Series (San Francisco Giants/ Oakland A's). All electric power was out. As night fell, I looked out at a city in total darkness except for huge fires lighting up the sky in the distance.

I felt insignificant and powerless. You can go to higher ground from a flood, hurricanes are anticipated and tracked; satellites show storms approaching but earthquakes are the most unpredictable. Even now at every sign of movement, my heart starts pounding. I sat at the table that evening surrounded by candles and was mesmerized by the surreal panorama of flames burning in the Marina district of the city.

By morning, power had been restored and I looked out on my deck. Sitting on the railing was a small multi-colored parrot. I opened the door and he flew in and followed me into the kitchen, sitting on a bar of soap while I washed a dish. I called the SPCA to see if anyone had reported a missing bird of this description. They gave me a number. I gave him raisins and dry cereal. I even named him Henry. This bright curious creature accompanied me as I moved from room to room. The woman (with a lost bird) whose number I had been given came to my house carrying the most beautiful birdcage I've ever seen. It was a replica of the conservatory in Golden Gate Park. She said, he wasn't her bird but I encouraged her to adopt him. When he saw his new home, he moved in quickly and settled down. My few hours with Henry helped me forget my terror of the previous day.

When they drove away, I missed his cheerful presence. I would have liked him to stay but my cat, Finian, would have welcomed him with open claws. I was grateful that Henry had found a new home and doubly grateful that I hadn't lost mine.

MOVING ON

It was the hottest day of my life. We had stopped at an Indian Trading Post near Gallup, New Mexico. My head was pounding, my face was flushed and the blinding sun reduced me to something inhuman. I climbed out of the car and stumbled into the shade. The pounding not only continued, it intensified. I followed the sounds I heard in the distance. In a yard in back of the Post, Indians in their native garb were dancing in circles to the beat of the tom toms. Tourists stood around carelessly watching these remnants of a proud people performing like animals in a circus.

I had left my long time home in Texas a few days before, refusing to look back as the car moved north along the highway. I did not dare look back. Like Sodom and Gomorrah—I thought if I looked back I would turn to stone. Leaving one life for another is one of the most difficult transitions possible. I had made it this far. Each day further from my past became a day closer to my future.

The day in the intense heat in New Mexico seemed to be the boiling point of my life figuratively and literally. I thought I can go no further, I can't think, I can't see, I can't breathe.

Slowly, as I watched the disheveled warriors going through their repetitive dance, tomahawks glistening in the sun, reality began to emerge. I was not a defeated tribesman; I was an embryonic creature being primed for a new beginning. My headache began to subside, my vision cleared. As we proceeded west, an inner peace accompanied me to my destination. My new life was awaiting me and it would be good and it was.

HEADS UP

On one of our Arizona sojourns, my husband mentioned his old Army buddy who had moved to El Paso. They had been closer than brothers during the years they served together in the war but had lost touch. As we were leaving Tucson, I took the wheel and turned the car south saying, ""Let's go to El Paso and find Pete".

I loved to drive, especially to a new place anticipating new adventures and possibly a recovered friend. Across the New Mexico border and there was El Paso at the tip of Texas. Across the Rio Grande River was the Mexican city of Juarez. In the middle of June, it was hot but dry. El Paso is almost 4,000 feet high and the air was pure and clear. The mountains surrounding the city were covered in gravel with absolutely nothing green. I said something to the effect that I felt I was in a gravel pit. Continued on to Ft. Bliss, a large army base; very little in the way of trees or flowers—each yard was neatly covered with gravel. Yes, for sure I was in a gravel pit.

Opened the phone book to see if we could find Pete. Amazingly, his name was there—Biagi Petrello—we called him and he was surprised and delighted. Pete, who had married a Texan returned from the war and settled in El Paso. Originally from Pennsylvania, he had made the transition and was now a school administrator, fluent in Spanish. We drove to his home the next day and were warmly greeted by Pete and his wife. He led me grandly into his Texas size house and as I entered the huge living room I looked up in horror. Along the wall looking at me were heads; mostly deer with their antlers thrust boldly up. There were other assorted animals. I was speechless but not for long.

At least a dozen pair of eyes was looking at me. I turned to Pete and said, "Why did you kill all these animals? Why? How can you stand to have your victims watch you everyday?" He seemed embarrassed and mumbled something about being a hunter. My husband gave me a hard look, which I interpreted to mean, "Be quiet". He was right, of course, but somehow I was so disturbed I asked if we could sit in another room.

I still have visions of all those mounted heads looking at me with imploring eyes. When we left, my husband said he was also taken aback but I should have kept my own counsel. Pete seemed like such a nice gentle man but he was caught up in the blood sport like so many others. When we left El Paso, I knew we would never hear from him. Whether I touched his inner core in some way, I'll never know. The heads were his trophies. Sometimes I think I suffer from spontaneous combustion and I'm damned proud of it. At least I am a rebel with a cause.

A REQUIEM TO UNCLE FLUFFY

Uncle Fluffy died. I heard it from Bill who now lives in Austin, Texas. For many years, Bill was our friend and cat sitter. He was also our next-door neighbor's cat sitter and she had a lot of cats.

Finian, my cat and longtime companion is almost fifteen years old. When he was a very small tike, he ran down the outside stairs and the first cat he saw was Fluffy. Embree, my neighbor, had warned me about Fluff's bad temper. She said he never met a cat he didn't fight and had the scars to prove it. I watched in alarm as Finian ran madly across the yard to meet Fluffy. He jumped up eagerly hoping to land on Fluff's back and start a game. Fluffy was watching and as Finian made his move, Fluffy ducked. Finian flew through the air and landed on the ground. Over the years, Fluffy suffered Finian's childish antics and I began calling him, Uncle Fluffy. Fluffy had a lot of siblings none related but all lived together.

Embree had retrieved several cats from the park where she went every morning before work. I think of her as the "Mother Teresa" to all the feral cats in Golden Gate Park. Her work there is still in progress. In the evening, her family of cats would gather in front of her house awaiting her arrival. Cars would slow and brakes would squeal as they rounded the corner. Sitting patiently, from six to eight or nine cats, different colors and sizes blanketed the sidewalk. It truly was a worth a stop or at least a long look.

There was the original cat, Sam; several strays who showed up one day, Linus, Rusty and Peanuts; Whiskers, a black monster who departed this mortal coil—none too soon; then a batch of kittens—Danny, Julius, Dippy and Molly; Pretty Boy Floyd— part Siamese; O.C. (Other Cat) beautiful black ringed eyes; Fuzzball, a furry gray bully of a cat (who Finian had to fight a few times before he got the message)—he was no Mohammed Ali; a cat called Daisy who never joined the group—only ate and ran. Embree never found out whether it was a boy or girl. Last but not least, Uncle Fluffy—a small, mostly white part Persian, a little tough guy. He had a long and happy life.

He was about twenty years old. He had become deaf and had a little difficulty walking recently. Not long ago he had wandered away and was taken to the SPCA. When Embree discovered his whereabouts and picked him up, they told her he was about to be put up for adoption. They thought he was only about ten years old. How's that for a senior citizen?

They are all gone now except for Fuzzball, Molly and Pretty Boy. Uncle Fluffy was pretty special to Finian and me. All my uncles are gone and now Finian has lost his.

Rest in Peace, Uncle Fluffy!

THE GYPSY IN MY SOUL

"Where's the baby"? She asked looking at the swarthy woman who was standing in her store. The gypsy said "What baby, I haven't seen any baby." The woman moved from her place in back of the counter and approached the gypsy. "I don't believe you", and with that she pulled up the gypsy's long full skirt and there looking quite happy with big blue eyes sat the baby ensconced in a large pocket among the gypsy's many petticoats.

The baby was my mother and maybe she inhaled some mysterious scent during her brief moment in close quarters with the gypsy. She was not a psychic nor could she read tarot cards but she had the ability to carefully scrutinize people and events. She was always accurate in her observations. We used to tease her and call her a witch—a good witch.

Since I am a second-generation witch, my powers have been genetically diluted. I would wish to have the clear-eyed vision of my mother. However, I did inherit a restlessness, which I attribute to my mother's association with that gypsy.

My mother said in Hungary during her youth, gypsy's did steal babies, especially light skinned, light-eyed ones. She said their children were taught to beg and they found people more willing to give to the fair-haired beggars. I assume this was true. A cast system has existed in all countries re light skin over dark.

The story of the gypsy who almost stole my mother was my favorite bedtime story. When I was small, I refused to go to sleep unless she told me a story about the "old country".

MEMORIAL DAY

GOLDEN GATE NATIONAL CEMETERY
May 1996

Thousands, thousands of flags blowing
In unison over marble markers
Neatly placed row upon row
Placing flowers in green metal vase
Speared into the hard ground
Sparkling, brilliant blossoms
Dance in the wind above your grave
Where did you go?
You left too soon
I haven't finished knowing you
No one is left to know me
You were a soldier once
Your last battle was with death
And death won.

RUB A DUB DUB

As I began to rethink my travels, one activity seems to take precedent. "Washing". As we prepare to take a trip, we packed along with a myriad of other things—liquid soap, portable clothesline, clothespins. As life goes on—so does laundry.

I have done more hand washing on trips abroad than I have ever done at home. In Italy, for instance, most of the women on the tour used the bidet in the bathroom to soak small items. While I didn't resort to what I thought was uncouth use of the bidet, the basin in the bathroom was usually filled with assorted under garments, socks and other unmentionables. In Florence, we had a rather large accumulation of laundry. I filled the narrow tub and spent the better part of an afternoon bending over hand scrubbing, rinsing, wringing out and hanging anywhere and everywhere items of dripping clothing.

I have spent hours in Athens trying to keep up with soiled clothes. I saw the Parthenon and sailed the Aegean Sea. Still at the end of several days, I was once again reduced to scrubbing clothes and desperately seeking enough areas to hang up to dry. The same task was repeated over and over again.

At least when we took cruises; several ships were equipped with laundry rooms where we women would gather to do our repetitive laundry. One ship had several ironing boards that were busy around the clock. Another had very small laundry rooms, which were usually full. Since there was no one in charge and you couldn't take a number, I was reduced to racing up and down the hallway trying to time myself to be there when the machine was being emptied. Several small fights erupted when two people arrived at the same time. On this trip, I mostly used the machine around midnight. Being a night owl has its advantages. Sometimes I think my itinerary should have read like this:

Day 1—Tour city (1/2 day); Do laundry

Day 2—Museum, native marketplace; dinner under the stars

Day 3—All day trip to historical ruins

Day 4—Do laundry before afternoon trip to scenic village

Day 5—Walk through Old Town; Evening Gala Dinner

Day 6—Leave one city to drive to other city (4 hours)— Unpack; Do laundry

Day 7—Visit three churches; view from high place

Day 8—Prepare to leave for home; Do laundry

Day 9—Arrive home; do not unpack luggage; Use clean clothes you left at home

Day 10—Unpack luggage; do leftover dirty laundry found in luggage.

THE END

WHERE THERE'S A WILL

On the fourth of July while returning from a trip to Lake Tahoe, we took a scenic side road and ended up in Grass Valley, a small town north of Sacramento. As we drove closer to the center of town, the traffic became heavier; a parade had taken priority on the main street. Soon we became stuck in wall-to-wall cars. The heat became unbearable and nothing was moving, absolutely nothing.

Without thinking, I opened the car door and stood looking at the traffic jam, which surrounded me. I calmly walked into the middle of the street and began to simulate the gestures of policemen directing traffic. I was standing quite dignified in the sweltering heat—slowly a car would back up a little; another would inch ahead. Like an orchestra leader with a baton, each driver was watching me carefully and followed my command. Without hesitation, my efforts began releasing the trapped cars. Soon a few were moving, then more; a crescendo of engines enveloped me and my symphony came to an end.

Elated, I climbed back into my own car and as we drove back to San Francisco, I felt very self-satisfied about this feat. There is always satisfaction in a job well done and especially as a first time conductor to achieve the desired results was most pleasurable. Needless to say, my husband thought I was completely demented but praised me when he saw my success.

AMAZING GRACE

How good it is; I was lost and now I'm found—one of the most beautiful gospel songs ever written. I heard Leontyne Price sing it a few years ago and I can still hear her magnificent voice.

I've never felt lost but I sure as hell, don't think I've ever been found. I'm probably going off on another soul search journey. My whole life has been spent in trying to define "Who am I?" It doesn't consume me. I live each day in the most ordinary way but I feel that I am not ordinary at all. Much of my writing I have labeled as "cracker barrel" philosophy. I had no idea that I would ever have pages filled questioning my existence; analyzing my emotions.

What really moves me is when sometime I look in the bathroom mirror and I find myself looking back through my father's eyes. His eyes were brown. My eyes are green. Still, he is looking at me with a sad wistful expression. I feel this connection and so many years have passed since he died but still, I believe we both share the same inner quest to find meaning in our lives. I would like to see him and say, "You were a success, and I remember you. You didn't fail—I am here to give you praise".

My Father—Age 24

SHIPS I HAVE KNOWN
AND LOVED OR NOT

WESTWIND

On our maiden voyage, first time out on the big pond our destination was a Caribbean cruise. First we flew across the country to Miami, flew again to Aruba and boarded the SS Westwind. Moved into Cabin #305, Monte Carlo Deck which turned out to be a really nice little room, very little, actually Lilliputian. The bathroom was designed for total intimacy. The shower was so small that you had to step out of it to turn around. We were cozily installed in an inside cabin. I was told that it really didn't matter since one spent so little time in their cabin. I am here to tell you it does matter. I never knew if it was night or day; I depended on the adjoining outside cabin to let me know the approximate time. Our neighbors usually took showers in the morning and when I heard the sound of plumbing, I always assumed it was close to daylight. Oh, well I was at sea. Visited St. Thomas, Curacao plus other islands and then spent the better part of a day in Cartegena, Columbia at the emerald market. I had my picture taken holding a three toed sloth that looked ferocious with its long nails but true to its name it was slothful and never moved.

We were encouraged to join a table of eight. It is considered proper etiquette to socialize aboard ship. We had three meals a day with three of the most scintillating couples I have ever met. One couple regaled us with stories of their numerous operations. We heard all the gory details plus listening to them reorder from the menu. They were on a low salt, low fat, no red meat, no sugar and a few other caveats diet. The other couple obviously took the trip for the food. They ordered everything on the menu and except for a few grunts barely looked up from their plates. The last but least lovable couple dressed alike every day, never talking to any of us. Once they wore western garb with red kerchiefs around their neck. On formal nights they both wore ruffled blue shirts. They barely talked to each other, sitting and eating like robots.

The Panama Canal was the highlight of the trip. We stood wide eyed on the deck looking at this marvel of engineering while the rest of the passengers were inside eating, playing cards, watching a movie, whatever. Except for a few wanderers, we were alone on the deck for the many hours it takes to pass through the canal.

NORDIC PRINCE

We upgraded and booked a suite (translated to "large room") on the Promenade Deck for our next cruise on the Nordic Prince. The bathroom was big, big tub with very high sides. Since the shower was over the tub, it was necessary to climb up over the side and carefully step, down, way down and then reach up, way up to turn the water on.

We sat again at a table for eight. It takes times to learn—socialize at your own risk. Two couples joined us, plus two women. The middle-aged man told us he was from Kansas City and he talked and talked. His small plump wife was very quiet. She ate and ate. He finally reached his plateau of conversation and informed us that he was German. He praised the Germans and admired Adolph Hitler. Our dinner companions became unusually quiet, except for my husband who suggested we not talk politics or anything controversial. "After all we are all Americans", he said. Big mouth retorted, "I'm a German first!" My husband replied in a cold stern voice "You're a Son of a Bitch, first!" After the meal, he and his wife left the table. The rest of the people congratulated my husband on his remark. The S.O.B. did not move to another table and continued to talk but no one spoke to him.

The Nordic Prince, she did toss about. As the Norwegian Captain announced over the loud speakers "We're going to have a bumpy ride". There was some talk that the currents can become strong where the Atlantic ocean crosses into the Caribbean. All I know is that we found out that this ship had been literally cut in half to add to the length and then carefully reassembled. This was probably the reason for its instability.

SEA PRINCESS

Ah, the Sea Princess, one of the last of the wooden ships; paneled walls throughout the ship. We sailed from San Francisco under the Golden Gate Bridge, Alaska bound. As we approached the Canadian city of Vancouver, the temperature hovered in the 90's very unusual at this time of year. I went ashore and went shopping at the Hudson Bay, an old fashioned store with worn wooden plank floors. Transactions still were taking place with little baskets holding sales slips manipulated by pulleys between floors and departments. I envisioned the cashier in a small dark cubicle.

On up the coast of Alaska, sailed the inside passage and stopped at Sitka, Juneau and then the magnificent Glacier Bay. The ship sailed slowly for hours surrounded by sparkling blue sapphire glaciers. On the large ice flows small harbor seals were scampering about. The temperature had dropped to freezing but I stayed on the deck for hours basking in the beauty of nature. By now, we had smartened up and dinner was for two. No intrusions just good food, service deluxe and in our cabin a small refrigerator complete with two bottles of good wine compliments of our travel agent.

DAPHNE

The Daphne, a smallish Italian ship was our last cruise. The ship tilted to the right or should I say leaned starboard. We went on deck and could look down at the prow of the ship. Several crewmembers talking loudly in Italian were moving heavy objects from one side to another. This went on daily but they never seemed to figure out what was wrong.

We had a suite again—this time two rooms plus bath. The beds in the sleeping area were comfortable enough but as the night progressed, our bodies moved closer and closer to the wall—head first. Every now and then we would awaken, rearrange ourselves before slipping back to sleep and eventually starboard. We talked to the people on the other side of the ship. They said we were lucky—they were sliding too but feet first. They would awaken to find their legs protruding from the end of the bed.

Again, the wonderful trip through the Panama Canal; again amazement at the giant chasm through a jungle where monster ships sailed easily through locks that were lowered and raised in the appropriate order. The ship stopped on the west coast of Costa Rica. We debarked in the tenders to reach the shore. We boarded small red railroad cars on the narrow gage line where we were whisked up to the capital, San Jose. The little train's engineer obviously was in training for the Indy 500 as we sped up the winding tracks looking down steep canyon walls. We were bouncing up and down on our seats like rubber balls while being served fresh pineapple and other cold tropical fruits. As we bounced from side to side, fruit juice splattering my blouse and face, I was overcome by laughter, which wasn't shared by most of the other passengers.

We returned to the ship by bus, stopped at souvenir stands where I purchased three small painted carts now sitting on a shelf high in my kitchen. I found a couple of small donkeys to place in front of them to make them more realistic but the last cart has yet to receive an escort.

The dining room (again a table for two) was bright but the Italians obviously did not cook the food. The waiters and stewards were mostly Guatemalans. Cooking American type food was obviously foreign to them. We had some very strange pancakes for breakfast among other culinary mistakes. One of the waiters was from Indonesia. He told us he never ate the food; he had brought instant dinners from the United States.

Some pipes broke on our deck and all the cabins but the half dozen up front (one of ours) were flooded. We were the lucky one but people had to salvage their belongings and were moved here and there throughout the ship.

All in all, I love the sea. I love to see the flying fishes play (and they do). I love to watch the dolphins as they follow the ship. Once in the Caribbean, we saw a school of blue dolphins off the bow, gleaming royal blue like a jeweled pattern in the sun. "By the sea, by the sea, by the beautiful sea—you and me and you and me—oh, how happy we'll be, by the bea-u-ti-ful sea"

MIDNITE OIL

Sometimes, I wish they wouldn't bother me. I sit down to read a book or watch television and they won't leave me alone. All those words scratching at the windows of my mind. I close my eyes and try to pull the shade down. It does no good.

I can hear their relentless movements. I finally give up and let them in. They are so disorderly; all the nouns bunch together; the verbs are scattered about; adjectives and adverbs push each other from side to side and I want to scream out "Stop!" "If you want me to do something with all of you, give you a place in my stories, you must wait your turn".

The story begins—what will it be—shall I write about my mother, my father, my teachers, boys I've known, girls I've known, places I've been or perhaps cats I've owned. Yes, today I need to feel soft fur and look into the knowing eyes of my cat. He sits so quietly, contemplating his inner thoughts while I do the same. The gentle warmth that is lying on my lap soothes the savage beast that followed me home. A long day, a weary day and the silence of my small companion give me pause.

Today as I looked around, the world made no sense to me; cars rushing back and forth; people going in and out of stores. All the buildings, all the roads—everything that man made and uses surrounded me and I could make no sense of it. I have been part of the crowd, part of daily life but now I feel it was a role I played. I was both the actress and the playwright—but the show closed. I am now out of a job and out of a life. How do I resume or perhaps begin another act. I have a general outline of the characters, a little dialogue, a vague notion of the locale but there is no real sense of substance. How sad it is to come face to face with your future and find it missing.

THE FLAGS

As I drove through the Presidio today, I looked up and saw the flag at half-staff. Somebody died; this time there were a lot of some bodies. Those were the ones that were killed by a terrorist bomb in Saudi Arabia. I clench my lips as tears formed in my eyes. I don't want to cry. I never cry. Well, occasionally I do cry.

I remember only too vividly looking at the flag at half-staff looming large, moving gently in the breeze as I was being driven to my husband's funeral. In Golden Gate National Cemetery, among the thousands of other veterans, the man I had shared much of my life with was being honored. The young Honor Guards fired their rifles in the clear blue sky and the deed was done; one more marker among the rolling hills and plains of the cemetery.

Every flag at half-staff brings back the memory of that day and the flag seemed to be following me no matter where I stood out there among the gravesites. When we drove away, it was waving to me in a goodbye gesture. Today, I saw it again; another goodbye. It is so sad, so very, very sad to acknowledge death, every death.

FOREVER—NEVER

I don't think I want to live forever. The only thing I would want to change is to have those I love to live forever if I could live forever too. If that could not be an option, it is very difficult to think how I would change my life.

It has taken me so many years to arrive at my present stage. Trial and error has been part of this long trip but I wouldn't have missed the potholes along the road. They have kept me alert, jarred me into decision-making. I have always been pleased with my gender, my appearance but I would have wished for better vision. Glasses, at times have been the bane of my existence. I would never wear them at parties when I was younger. I only remember groups of blurred people but possibly by this time of my life, they would have become a blur any way.

I sometimes wish that we had had more money so I could have gone to college or could afford to shop at upscale stores. However, I never had a burning desire for higher education or fancy clothes, so there goes that wish.

O.K. If I could live forever, in what way would I change my life? I guess I'd better start being more frugal. I don't think my assets are unlimited. Since I will continue to live, starting now, I guess it would be nice to philanthropic but since as I mentioned above, my assets will diminish long before forever, I am at a stalemate as how to change my life.

I guess it all boils down to my first sentence. I don't think I want to live forever. I love the world I live in and I love life. Living forever, never—but I did give it some thought.

HONEYMOON

I've never had a honeymoon. I have been married but my honeymoons could be labeled as "Non-existent". One was spent on a long train trip with the stranger I married who became stranger each day. There were days of fun and happiness during the following years but I certainly didn't have a jump start into marriage with stars in my eyes.

The next honeymoon (second husband) was an abysmal overnight in a beautiful hotel in the dead of winter. We couldn't find the thermostat or possibly the furnace wasn't working. Needless to say, my sexy black gown remained unseen under a pile of blankets.

Today, I found several small amber glass objects; two tiny pitchers and a basket, which glistened in the sun after I washed the dust off. This was my mother's honeymoon. She told me that after her wedding in 1919, she and my father went to a resort with hot baths, a version of the European spas. They went to a dime store and bought these small glass articles, returning to the spa and dipping them into a bubbling fountain of hot mineral water. They then turned into this lovely amber shade and haven't faded in all these years.

There are no more honeymoons on the horizon but wouldn't it be nice if we could be immersed in a warm spring and remain the same as we once were.

THE WAKEUP KISS

The girls were all watching from the bus window as the tall, handsome soldier swept me into his arms and kissed me. I belonged to an organization and we young girls from Waco had been recruited as goodwill ambassadors to spend a day in a large army camp in February 1942. During the early days of World War II, men from other state were stationed far from home and we girls were invited to participate in the activities planned for the day.

I had not wanted to go. I was the youngest and the other girls treated me with indifference. They talked and laughed with each other while I sat meekly on the back seat of the bus on the way to Camp Bowie, an army base about a hundred miles away. Once we arrived, a group of girls would get off at different mess halls to be met by a group of soldiers. The bus stopped several times as others departed. Soon it was just I and another teenager left on the bus. After a long ride across the bleak, treeless encampment, the bus stopped and the driver announced, "Last stop". We got off and there was only soldier standing there. He introduced himself and was eventually joined by another soldier. It was obvious that he chose to be my escort. This charming, suave man with the beautiful smile overwhelmed me. He showed me around the mess hall, the gym and the tents in which the men slept. We then returned to the club where the other girls were gathered and the dancing began. We danced but soon my bus mates implored him to dance with them and besieged him. Off he went and I was desolate. I wandered into the ladies' room and sat on a couch. As far as I was concerned I was ready to return home. I reentered the room and my "soldier" hurried toward me saying "Where did you disappear to, I'm going to marry you". I said nothing. He took my name and address. It was soon time to leave the bus was waiting. Then, he kissed me he really kissed me. I felt very inadequate—I had never kissed a boy before. As I got on the bus, the other girls were watching me; I knew what they were thinking. The best dancer, the best looking had spent most of his time with me and had topped it off with a dazzling display of kissing me in front of God and everybody.

I knew I had to learn how to kiss. What if he really came to see me and I was found wanting. I soon met another soldier and decided to practice. I liked him well enough but it didn't matter if I came off amateurish. I found out how much lipstick smears; I found out how to kiss without bumping noses. I wanted to be a sophisticated and adept kisser.

I got a letter from my erstwhile fiancé. He said his unit was on alert and he was being shipped out. He asked me to join him in Florida before he left the states and we could be married. He said he would send me a bus ticket. I refused but I did say that I would wait for him. It seemed the only honorable thing to say when a man is going overseas, possibly to be killed. Three years passed. We exchanged letters during that time and I pursued the art of kissing.

The war came to an end and even though I had moved to another state, my hero returned with the sole objective of marrying me. He was still handsome with a smile that melted my heart. Ten days after he returned, we were married. As the Army Chaplain pronounced us man and wife, one thing I had no qualms about— I knew how to kiss.

MY FATHER

I was living in Houston in 1952 when I got the phone call. My mother told me that my father had been taken to the hospital. I hurriedly packed and took the next morning's flight to San Francisco. This was my first plane trip and I was filled with fear and anxiety. As I boarded the plane, I looked around and found familiar objects, the rows of seats, the small round windows, and the narrow aisles surrounded me. I had been here before or more to the point, I had seen so many movies of airplanes, the transition to real life seemed very simplistic.

My father was ill, very ill. The doctor said they needed to perform exploratory surgery. I waited anxiously for the verdict. The doctor came out and took me aside. He said, "Your father has cancer, it has spread and is inoperable." I asked, "How long will he live." The answer was "About six months." The doctor said, "Shall I tell him." I said, "No, no I will tell him, but I don't want him to know he has cancer." I talked to my mother and told her of my decision. She agreed with me.

The next day I went to the hospital. I needed to tell my father something. He was very intelligent and not easily fooled. As I walked into the room, he looked up at me with question mark eyes. I said, "The doctor removed a small tumor. It will take several months to regain your strength but you will be fine." As I talked, I could not look into my father's face. I focused on the floor near his bed. There sat my father's slippers. Two brown felt slippers neatly placed together. As I looked up, I knew—he knew but he was willing to play this game for both of us.

I visited every day. He instructed me to withdraw his money from the Postal Savings. He wanted to pay off the mortgage on the house. I remember going down to the main post office but they refused to give me the money. I needed to bring in his fingerprints. They showed me how to smear lipstick on a piece of paper and how to roll a thumbprint. Back and forth I went and it was accomplished. We never talked about the surgery.

He came home and I found each day in San Francisco more and more difficult. We were deceiving each other and the truth was cutting through me like a knife. I was sick every morning and soon I returned to Houston promising to be back in a few months. I did return and we talked and continued to avoid the truth. He died a month later and the funeral was held in Texas. He was buried next to his son, my brother, as he had requested. The men who talked at his funeral knew more about him than I did. He had been very active in the Workmen's Circle and had written many political articles for their New York paper in the 1930's. He had also written several plays and skits. His dream was to be a great writer, but when he arrived in America he accepted defeat and knew his writing career would never be realized. He spent time going to a college in New York to learn to read and write English. I have many short stories he wrote, some in German and some in English.

Even now, when I think of my father, the first image are those neatly placed brown slippers. In my mind's eye, I am standing in his room looking down. I did the right thing. He did the right thing. We protected each other as much as we could. Isn't that love?

FIRST LOVE

When I was seventeen, I fell in love. I really fell—when he picked me up for our first date and opened the car door; I bounced into the car but I bounced too high, hit my head on the metal strip of the door and landed in a mud puddle. My new skirt was covered with dirty water and also much of the rest of me. I quickly gathered my wits, hurried into the house, clean up, redressed and rejoined my escort.

We talked about everything in the world. We spent hours on park benches, just talking. We spent hours on the phone. Being with him totally consumed me. Nothing he said was mundane and when I talked he seemed to inhale my presence. We were of one breath; one pulse and we were destined to be together forever. We had known each other for two weeks. He asked me to marry him and I agreed. We decided to elope. I didn't tell my parents as I was sure objections would destroy our perfect love.

He picked me up for our elopement day and began our drive to another city to get married. The further we traveled, the less comfortable I felt. My mother trusted me; she had told me many times "I know that whatever happens, you will always do the right thing." I should have told her. I said, "Turn around, we have to go back, I can't do this." He angrily turned the car around and all the way home he muttered about my change of heart. As he left me at my house, I knew it was over. He called once and that was the end. What happened? What would have happened if I had married him? In retrospect, I did do the right thing, I think.

SOUTH JR. HIGH

Miss Azalete Pidcocke, Science Teacher, South Junior High School looked around the room; her cold eyes narrowed and she said, "I will only make exceptions for orphans and those that wear glasses, all the rest of you will be expected to finish each project and do a good job on your tests. I will not hear any excuses." We were seated around two large rectangular tables. One was for the boys, the other for girls. Immediately, I felt safe; at least being nearsighted would finally pay off.

Miss Pidcocke, pacing back and forth on her bony legs and screeching voice intimidated us. She slowly scrutinized our faces. Her favorite perch was sitting on the boys' table, talking loudly and swinging her legs up and down, up and down. We girl nervously looked away, afraid of being voyeurs. She would lean coquettishly close to the boys while emphasizing a point. The boys would look down or away embarrassed. We, girls, used to tease each other if our skirts pulled up or we bent over awkwardly. We called out "I'm going to take your picture." When Miss Pidcocke carelessly tossed her legs about, skirt swinging from side to side, no one wanted to look, least of all literally "to take her picture." Maybe that was her problem, nobody ever wanted her.

She found fault with all my science projects. There were no orphans in my class and I felt singled out as a potential target. I had a sinking feeling in the pit of my stomach every time I entered her room. I never received any benefit in being an exception. Quite the contrary, she seemed to delight in my discomfort.

At the end of the term, she asked us to raise our hands when she called out in her nasal squawk "How may of you got all A's" and down the line. Then she said "How many got all A's, except in my class?" I raised my lone hand. She glared at me, asked for my report cards and left the room. She returned and handed me back my cards. She had erased the B+ and changed it to A-. Due to her largesse, I could now be on the honor roll. I learned very little about science but I did learn not to be exceptional again, at least not from a position of weakness.

BEST PLACE TO LIVE

"What's so special about San Francisco?" my husband asked me many times over the years. He would look at me, shrug his shoulders, narrow his eyes and in a bemused voice say, "Are you having a love affair with this foggy city?" I usually made some trite reply but thinking back, he must have been jealous. Like all love affairs, this one has had its ups and downs.

I lived here for three years in my late teens. I found the city exciting. Word War II was in its prime and the streets, restaurants, theaters were wall-to-wall uniforms. I was surrounded by young men who took me dancing, wooed me and left for destinations overseas. I was almost engaged six or seven times. I walked through foggy streets at night, in total darkness—all the houses had blackout drapes, especially those facing west toward the Pacific Ocean where our enemy might invade at any time. I was chilled to the bone and eaten alive by sand fleas. We lived on the west side of the city, which was still covered with sand dunes. This was "my town" and I found an element of bohemianism among new friends that I had never encountered before. These people talked about everything and being a radical seemed very stylish. I would proudly say that I am not a communist but I'm slightly pink. Actually, I was wet behind the ears.

When I married my soldier at Ft. Mason and moved to Houston, I felt I had left myself behind. I settled down to the domestic life. I never joined the women for bridge or mahjong; I never had dinner parties, never became part of any social group. I mostly read.

Ten years later I returned to San Francisco. This time I was mature, ready to make a commitment. I found a job, an apartment and a boyfriend. He was an artist and he opened up the Beatnik scene for me. We spent evenings in North Beach. Ate in every restaurant along Grant Avenue, went to poetry readings, jazz clubs, cappuccino at Toscas and drank coffee in the basement of city Lights Book Store; parked on Powell Street around midnight and people watched; up and down every hill in the city. Oh my, I did fall in love. This affair was going to be forever.

I left the boyfriend and married someone else. I guess my husband had a right to be jealous. I loved him dearly yet the city and I have a special bond. I look out my windows that overlook the city and sigh, "You're mine, all mine."

DAYS GROW LONG

I remember when life was endless. I read the title of a book that I had read some twenty years ago. All of a sudden I was struck by the memory of a dark haired woman reading. Was I that dark haired woman so totally immersed in the pages of that book? Life moves slowly at times and all of a sudden a week has passed, than a month and a year is almost missed because of the acceleration of time. Why couldn't time have stopped those twenty years ago? She had so much more to read, so many more places to go, so much more emotion to feel. Why didn't time stop?

Did I complete my life too early? I feel as if I am now at a stalemate—no going back and not much going forward. Twenty years ago, life was endless. The future was a wide expanse with no boundaries. Life now is a circle. I go round and round and the circle becomes smaller. Each day leaves me more tightly enclosed. My mortality is staring me in the face.

I would like to stare back with unblinking eyes and force it to turn away. Oh, I want my endless life back. I want to wake up in the morning and feel the pleasure of a new day. I want someone to smile at me over breakfast. I want to feel a warm hand caressing my neck.

My days now are filled with wants. This wasn't always true. Today, I feel new truths. Life is endless and for the many I've loved, life has ended. Maybe it is the dark outside, the thick fog obscuring the streetlights. I sit here in the glow of my lamp as a small bright spot surrounded by the blackness out my windows. I feel safe, alone and waiting. I am just waiting—that is my new truth.

Sometimes, I feel as if my head will explode. I pick up a book and another book. So many people have written on so many subjects. I know I can't read all the books or write all the words. I am so frustrated at my inability to do all the writing I need to satisfy my tormented mind. The tight band around my temples taunts me.

Where have I been these past years? Why didn't I start writing earlier? There are many reasons but now here I am and still no matter how many pages I fill, it's not enough. My philosophy has always been one of forgiveness, especially of my shortcomings and myself. Why now am I filled with despair that I won't have the time or talent to satisfy this yearning to cry out on paper "I was here, I lived, I loved, I was here"!

SOMEONE IS SITTING
IN MY CHAIR

PART I

Minnie Cloe lived down the street. She was a little older than me and I played with her occasionally. She didn't have the joie de vivre of my other companions. Her father drove us to school now and then. The car was a large black elegant marvel with canvas windows and a wide running board. I think my love affair with cars started at that time.

One day, Minnie Cloe ventured down the street and sheepishly said, "Do you want to play?" I probably said "Alright." She then proceeded to a large lawn chair on our lawn, climbed up and looked smugly about. I had long ago designated that chair as mine. I, too, would climb up, put my arms regally on the arms and survey my kingdom. I told her quite firmly to get off my chair. She replied prissily "Company is given the best chair." I politely asked her again "Please get down." Her reply again was no. I had no choice; she had overstepped her bounds. I walked over and punched her in the face. Her nose started to bleed and she ran crying from the yard yelling, "I'm going to tell my mother." I slowly pulled myself up into "my chair" and sighed with relief. Sometimes it does take drastic action to accomplish one's goals.

Soon, Minnie Cloe and her mother came down the street and up the sidewalk up the steps to our front door. My mother answered the door and was told of my bad behavior. Back down the sidewalk they went, Minnie Cloe looking at me timidly. My mother called out some mild reprimand and went back in the house. Within a few minutes, Minnie Cloe returned. I said, "You can sit on the bench." She followed my directions. Sometimes, one has to be harsh when people take advantage of your good nature. I think Minnie Cloe learned her lesson.

PART II

Many, many years later, I joined a writing class with other members of my age group. I had attended once a week for almost two years. I liked writing and I liked listening to other stories. I always sat on the left side of the table with my back to the window. Glare from the outside blinded me. This chair, this space had served me well. I had become familiar with my fellow writers and their different styles of writing. I had found a comfortable niche among all these aspiring authors. The room at times was cold, was hot, was noisy from the hallway filled with chattering people but there was a feeling of camaraderie.

One day the spell was broken. A new person emerged upon the scene. She quickly moved to my "chair." She literally took possession of my space. I was allowed to squeeze into a smaller space or more to the point removed to another side of the table. I tried to accommodate this interruption in my routine. It didn't work. I flashed back to Minnie Cloe who appropriated my chair and the steps I was forced to take at that time to regain my self-esteem.

This new person writes long, long sad stories and looks tragically around the room. The room now has a presence of gloom and doom. The rest of us have faded into the background.

I don't think I want to get attached to a chair or a space again. This reminds me of the children's story of the Three Bears "Someone's been sitting in my chair." I forget how it ended. Did any of the bears get punched in the face?

NO PICNIC

Sidney had a car with a rumble seat. I didn't really go out with boys much at fourteen but when he asked me to go to the weenie roast with him, I said yes. He was the tallest boy in the group, which gave him an edge over the others. The day of the outing arrived along with Sidney and his car. He was ever so polite. He got out and opened the car door for me. As I got in the car and thanked him, he laughed nervously. I was startled. Sidney didn't laugh—he brayed and snorted. Egad, here I was in this wonderful car with a boy who sounded like a horse.

I quietly told myself not to be amusing; I didn't want to start up this barnyard sound. We joined the others at Lovers Leap in Cameron Park. The smell of hot dogs roasting over the coals was fine but I did not want Sidney to laugh. I knew if he did, sooner or later the other girls would tease me about my escort. I moved around and away from the others. I spent long moments looking down at the Brazos River from Lovers Leap. The legend had passed down about two young Indian lovers whose families refused to give them permission to marry. The lovers jumped to their death from this high cliff so they would be together in the next world.

I wasn't about to do anything drastic but I couldn't wait until Sidney took me home. I was in a state of terror that he would start laughing and braying and snorting. This picnic couldn't end soon enough for me. I quickly ate a charred hot dog and said I would like to go home. When I reached my house, Sidney opened the door for me. I quickly thanked him and hurried into a safe haven.

I never went out with him again. Growing up is precarious enough but one needs to protect their fragile psyche until old enough to not let small matters become magnified. Sidney was a nice enough boy but my day with him was certainly no picnic.

SHOOTOUT AT THE HANG CHOW CORRAL

Saturday night—Once upon a time Saturday night was special. Went out for dinner, went to a show, went dancing. All dressed up for Saturday night.

Now Saturday nights are mostly stay at home, watch television or maybe visit with friends. Last Saturday night was different. I had an invitation to go out for dinner at a nice restaurant. My date picked me up; he even had on a white shirt sans tie but it was a start. I wasn't too gussied up but I felt special in a red jacket that said, "I'm cool".

The first restaurant was overloaded, crowded and as we pushed through the bustling throng, a decision was made to leave and look for greener pastures, i.e. a place to graze graciously. Back in the car to the next possible spot—a French restaurant that supplies very edible eats. Around and round the block we drove; no parking space. We began to make larger circles around and round two block areas, then three, and then four and that was enough. I suggested returning me to the original start of this futile foray into the madcap world of Saturday night.

My date suggested a small but good Chinese restaurant near his home. I acquiesced out of ennui and in desperation to end this fun filled evening. We only had to walk two blocks up a hill and down to reach this charmer. Sluggishly, I walked into a corner restaurant, typical small time Chinese with the usual Formica tables, bottles of soy sauce, hard chairs and the option of dining alone.

There was no one else in the restaurant. The waiter was talking on the phone, and talking on the phone. I made small noises and large gestures and he brought us the menu.

He returned to the phone. He stayed on the phone. I suggested leaving but my taciturn date was reluctant. I suppose he was hungry. Eventually, the inscrutable took our order. He knew not one word of English. I didn't think it mattered. I knew whatever I ordered could be assorted from the several pots. I have never been in a kitchen in a Chinese restaurant, but in my mind's eye I see the whole array of foods; large pots of bits of beef, bits of pork, bits of chicken; large pots of rice plus thin noodles plus thick noodles; large pots of mixed vegetables. All they have to do is to take plate, combine ingredients to complete order. Viola! Instant gourmet dish.

Waiting patiently, the front door was flung open. In came two large policemen; then two more followed. The sound of their heavy shoes as they moved across the floor brought me up short. At last I was going to see some action. One policeman spoke into his walky-talky "Suspect believed to be armed". This was getting better all the time. I am a fan of "NYPD" and "Homicide." I know how these guys operate. Meanwhile, my date was turning pale and repeating his mantra "I don't like guns—I don't like guns." I tried to calm him. I said, "If the shooting starts, we duck under the table. Haven't you watched any TV? It's done all the time."

This didn't seem to help. He just kept saying, "I don't like guns, I don't like guns." What a bore—here we were in a real life drama and he's missing the excitement, the rush of adrenaline. The cops moved into a small room at the side of the restaurant and then began pounding on an inside door (which turned out to be the bathroom). Bang, bang, bang—this was getting good. Two plain-clothes policemen came in dressed in plaid shirts both large with beefy faces looking around and sizing up the situation.

I didn't even look at my date, who by this time was muttering to himself over and over "I don't like guns." Soon a small Asian man was led out, hands cuffed behind him. With long stringy hair, he looked harmless enough but I wondered if they had found the gun. The police asked the waiter/owner if he knew the man. He said something like "Chow mien, crispy noodles" to be interpreted—he knew nothing.

I couldn't wait to go to the restroom. Maybe I could find the gun if they had not recovered it. I entered and looked in the wastebasket. I took the top off the water tank of the commode— no gun. I looked up and saw a high window with glass louvers. Perhaps, he had tossed the gun out the window. As I prepared to stand on the toilet seat and try to look out the window, two thoughts entered my mind. One, I might fall down and break something or two; the police had probably searched the rear area. I returned to the table and tried to eat the greasy noodles and drink the hot water called tea.

Later than night I paid for the meal with a case of heartburn and pledged never to eat Chinese again. However, the thrill of the evening lives on. I think of it as the "No Shootout at Hang Chow." Being surrounded by the boys in blue, I became for a few minutes the adventurous woman I used to be. I was part of a happening that fortunately never happened. I really have to get a life. Living vicariously has it's kicks, but dam it, I'm not dead yet!

PILE OF MONEY

The telephone rang and I answered: Hello.

H.A. Helen, this is Harold Adams from Richardson, Texas. Do you know William Gross?

H. Yes, you are talking about my uncle.

H.A. Yes, I am, do you know where he is buried?

H. If you are talking about my Uncle Willie—he died in the 60's. He is buried in the East Bay, Oakland or Alameda.

H.A. How old was Mr. Gross when he died?

H. I'm not sure—I think he was in his early 80's. How do you know him?

H.A. Well, I walked into his store when I was about twenty years old. His store was Standard Hat Works in Waco.

H. Yes, that's right.

H.A. He was a very smart man. I think he was an intellectual.

H. Yes, you are right.

H.A. I was in the air force for eighteen years.

H. Where did you get my phone number?

H.A. I asked your cousin in Dallas for your number. Richardson is just out of Dallas.

H. What are you doing in Richardson?

H.A. Well, I'm 78 years old. I have a house with appliances and a pile of money.

H. You're doing o.k.

H.A. I'd like to meet you. Maybe we could get together.
  H. Texas is a long way from San Francisco.
H.A. I am in San Francisco.
  H. You are—where are you staying?
H.A. I'm at Haight and Ashbury Street. Is that far from your house?
  H. It's too late tonight. Where are you staying?
H.A. I'm going to sleep in my car.
  H. Are you crazy? Get a motel room or something.
H.A. I'm not going to spend $40 for a room.
  H. Don't sleep in your car. Outside of being uncomfortable, you're in a big city.
H.A. No, I'm going to sleep in my car. I'll spend my money on something better.
  H. All right, it's your choice.
H.A. I'll call you in the morning and maybe we can get together.

I hang up the phone and called my cousin in Dallas. She said, "Yes, I gave him your address but that was a number of years ago. I think he's related to the Adams family in Waco but I'm not sure.

Next morning, Monday—phone rings—answering machine took this message.

H.A. Helen, this is Harold Adams speaking and your machine is talking to me. It's roughly around 8:45 now and this will be the last time I'll call you. I'm sorry I cannot come out and see you but this is the way the ball rolls. It's been a pleasure to talk to you so next time I come to San Francisco maybe we can get together. It's been good to know you and thanks for your information. Goodbye.

Next morning, Tuesday, 11:34 AM—answering machine took message. Helen, it's 20 minutes to 12 and I'm going out to the Legion of Honor Museum today and then I'm heading for home. I phoned you earlier and I'm sorry you're not there so maybe someday in the future I'll call you. Thank you.

I DON'T KNOW HER

My new Aunt Bette introduced me to my new sister-in-law, Ethel. My new husband had a sister with Down's syndrome, which at that time was called mongolism. I had entered a new world and Bette announced to Ethel "This is your brother's wife'. Ethel answered, "I don't know her". Later, someone would say, "Helen's your sister-in-law". Again the reply "I don't know her." Ethel could play the piano with both hands on the keys; not an expert but if someone sang a song, she would sit down and play the melody. She lived with Aunt Bette. My husband's mother had died many years before; she had four other children and she put Ethel into a mental institution when she about six or seven. Bette had no children and could not tolerate the idea of this child shut away. She brought her into her home and Bette used to call her "my daughter". Ethel never acknowledged this status either. When Bette said, you are my daughter; Ethel would reply, "No, I'm not!"

Ethel spoke with a heavy Latvian accent, as did Bette and her husband, Abe. She walked clumsily but did as she pleased. Bette and Abe would occasionally come to visit us on Sunday. Ethel sitting in the back seat of their car, refused to come in our house. Bette would try to cajole her out of the car saying "Don't you want to see your brother?" Ethel would shake her head angrily. Abe would throw up his hands in disgust and walk up the sidewalk. Bette persisted and sometimes she won, by dragging Ethel up the walk. Ethel would pull away and Bette would catch her but eventually Ethel's wishes prevailed and she stayed in the car.

My neighbors would watch this contest—Bette holding Ethel

by the hand and Ethel jerking away from her. No one said anything to us nor were we overwhelmed by southern hospitality. We lived there only a couple of years, which was just as well. We had become the folks with the crazy relatives.

I taught Ethel to play a simple card game. She learned quickly and won most of the time. She would laugh gleefully and say, "I beat you, I beat you". While having dinner at Bette's, Ethel would speak out at the most opportune times. My brother-in-law was always complaining about his lack of money. Ethel piped up "Who do you think you are, Rockefeller?" My Uncle Abe would tease her and call her Goofy Head. She called each of us Goofy Head if we displeased her in some way. Aunt Bette had a great heart and a wonderful sense of humor. I remember her generosity to me in many ways. She gave a full life to one of natures mistakes and loved every minute of it.

GOTTA DANCE

"What do you want to be when you grow up?" I always had a pat answer. "I want to be a dancing girl". My first debut was at age seven. My parent had moved during the Depression from our big house to a large compound consisting of a store, a church and six tourist cabins. I would knock each day at the three occupied cabins and ask, "Would you like me to dance for a penny?" I was always warmly received. I would start singing my song "Shoe shine boy, you work hard each day, shoe shine boy got no time to play, every penny helps a lot, so shine, shine shoe shine boy". This was followed by my tap dance and I closed with a flawless bow. My father ended my early attempt in show business. He said I was a nuisance and was bothering people.

A few years late, I moved my act indoors. The church had a large stage quite suitable for my performance. I tapped across the stage with large flourishes while singing "Anchors away m'boy, anchors away". Sitting on the benches watching me intently were the triplets, Mary, Martha and Joseph who lived next door. They weren't a very enthusiastic audience but they always came and stayed until the end.

At age 12, I went to dancing school. I was ready for a partner. Ballroom dancing—one, two, three, four. I mastered the foxtrot immediately and the rumba was a piece of cake. Halloween came and since funds were short, my mother made me a costume out of a white sheet plus a black witch's hat I bought at the dime store. My last dance turned out to be a huge success. I waved my magic wand and all the boys danced with me. I was truly queen of the Austin Street Ballroom.

By fifteen or sixteen, I went big time. My girl friends and I started honky-tonking. Honky-tonks were situated on the outskirts of town. The band played country western music. The only song I remember was one called "Ida Red, Ida Red, I'm a plumb fool 'bout Ida Red." It was good foot-stomping music. I lived in a dry county (no booze sold) but all the fellows had brown paper bags (with a bottle of bourbon resting easy inside it). They would buy setups—ice and water. You could drink to your heart's content. I didn't like the taste of liquor but lordy me, I loved to dance. The most popular honky-tonk was called The Bloody Bucket. I have no idea why, but Texans have a unique sense of humor. "Never judge a cowboy by his boots".

I danced my way all through World War II and continued for another ten years. I married a dancing man. Since all things must come to an end, I left the dancing man and ended up my career, married to a great guy who could only do what I called the Los Angeles dip and not very well. I continued dancing by myself at home. My husband always said I should have been on the stage. He recognized my talent.

I am now reduced to snapping my fingers and moving my shoulders when the music starts. Still deep within my heart lies a dancing girl. She's still gotta dance!

AMOST A GHOST

Driving back from San Francisco, we took the southern route; down the coast of California through Arizona into the tip of Texas. We spent the second night in El Paso. Houston was at least 700 miles away. We took off down the scenic highway; miles of scrub brush, treeless plains, and dirty service stations. There wasn't even a decent place to eat. We survived on soft drinks and candy bars.

Civilization as I remembered it ceased to exist. The bleak landscape and the heat were my constant companions as the miles rolled by. It was one of the longest days of my life. We arrived home in Houston about two or three in the morning. I went into the bedroom to undress and wandered into the kitchen for something to drink.

As I started to walk through the dining area, I saw a blue object moving about the kitchen. It seemed to float here and there. I saw no form, only a blue blob moving silently. I began screaming. I couldn't stop. Where was my husband? I looked in the other rooms. No one was there. I kept screaming. My husband came running into the room. I couldn't talk; I couldn't say a word. I had completely lost my voice.

Slowly regaining a semblance of sanity, I noticed my husband was wearing blue shorts. That must have been him moving soundlessly barefoot in the dark kitchen. The long tortuous drive had reduced my brain to a quivering mass of jelly. It took me almost two days to regain my voice. On our trip home I had been reading a mystery/science fiction by Frederic Brown, the Night of the Jabberwocky. I really thought it was a jabberwocky in my kitchen. That's about as close to a ghost I've ever been. If the real thing would have come along, I don't think I'd be here writing this story.

NIGHTMARE
ON PALM AVENUE

We had just moved to a four-plex in Houston; two apartments upstairs and two down. Married only a few months and starting life in a new city was bewildering. I introduced myself to the woman across the hall. She didn't seem overly friendly but I had no idea how unfriendly she was to become. The games began soon enough. Every time I left the apartment, she would open her door and scream "You have to keep the stairs clean". I didn't think I looked like a janitor but to appease her I suggested we take turns sweeping the steps. She slammed the door. I think I swept the steps once and decided I wouldn't let her intimidate me. She continued to open her door whenever I left, screaming at me.

I started sneaking out, hoping she wouldn't hear me. Sometimes it worked but not always. I told my new husband about this ongoing harassment. Ever the peacemaker, he knocked on her door and suggested we be friends. He even had the gall to suggest we kiss and makeup.

I would hear her door open when my husband was coming up the stairs. She would invite him in or ask him to fix something. Fortunately, he didn't oblige. I had married a man who didn't know a hammer from a screwdriver. I looked out once upon hearing their conversation. She was wearing the lowest cut blouse and the tightest shorts; I knew she did want to kiss and makeup but not with me.

I spent the better part of a year nervously entering and leaving my apartment. Mostly she would stand at the top of the stairs glaring at me. I have spent my whole life trying to avoid confrontation. This early episode reinforced my belief that when push comes to shove, I am a coward. I used to blame my father's genes for my dismal failure when dealing with a bully. I saw him silently take verbal abuse from his boss when I was in my teens. Looking back and realizing how hard it was during the Depression, my father was not a coward but a victim.

Two positive things emerged from this unpleasant experience.

    a.   I learned how to use a hammer and screwdriver.

    b.   I still dislike confrontation but I don't run from a fight.

        I do believe I've inherited my mother's genes as well.

GROWING UP

Mrs. Grass lived next door. I don't remember seeing her but I probably did. She never came out of the house. I heard she was crazy or something. Later on, much later someone said she was going through the change. I wondered what she was going to change into—a frog or a prince.

Oh well, I had more important things on my mind. A mean, old man occupied the house on the other side of us. I really hated him. One day when we returned from the movies, stretched across our front steps was my beautiful orange cat lying dead. I sobbed and sobbed. I overheard my parents talking. They said Mr. Karns; the mean old man had threatened to get rid of my cat. He said it was killing his chickens. My father said he probably poisoned my cat. I was sad for a very long time.

Margaret Ann and Doll McNally were my very best friends. They went to Catholic School and learned catechism. I had no idea what that was but it sounded very important. Mr. McNally was always taking his razor strap and whipping Billy. Billy McNally was only a few years older than his sisters. I never saw Billy do anything wrong. Mr. McNally worked in a factory that made coffins. I went there once and tried to climb in a coffin lined with shiny pink material. Mr. McNally got mad but he didn't whip me. My father had a razor strap hanging in our bathroom; he never whipped me. I always felt sorry for Billy.

My home was my castle. I was the princess who held court at the dinner table. My parents were very reserved and my brother ignored me. He thought I was a bother with my constant talking.

He did take me with him now and then when he went exploring. He was my big brother and knew exactly what to do and where to go. Once I followed him into an empty house and we found some silver candlesticks and a songbook. We buried them under our house. Later I went to dig them up but they were gone.

We had a big garden in our backyard. There were some vegetables, string beans, corn and carrots. We had a row of six peach trees. Once I ate a green peach and did I get sick. I learned a lot growing up and I'm still learning. Life is full of surprises and you need to be prepared.

AIR WALKING

If there was ever a time in my life when I felt *I was walking on air* it was when I fell in love. I was in love several times, so I did a lot of air walking.

At age fourteen, my heart raced when Lawrence Dukas drove past our house in his car with the rumble seat. He noticed me and took me for a ride. We went to Cameron Park and ate ice-cold watermelon. He didn't say much. All he did was laugh and spit watermelon seeds at me. That ended my first walk.

Next it was Ray McCracken. I was seventeen. We talked and talked. I was sure this was the real thing. We were so much in love we decided to elope. As Ray was driving us to be married, I changed my mind. Ray got mad and turned the car around. We drifted apart after that and the walk was over.

Later there was Douglas, Bill and finally a Bob showed up. This was really love. This lasted for ten years. Sometimes the air literally went out of my walk. Eventually, symbolically nothing was left but a flat tire.

I wasn't through loving though. Monroe was very nice but he had a short run, then Jack and Milton. I was working up to the grand finale. I met Len and my life was filled with joy. I spent two years in playful wonder. Reality reared its ugly head and I was again available for love.

This time I wanted it all. It was delivered to me in a very handsome package. For the better part of thirty years I was walking on air. My life at last was complete. I had reached the ultimate goal. It ended four years ago. No one lives forever but even after his death I am surrounded by the years of love. I still feel his embrace and hear his words. I am still walking on air.

RAINDROPS

First a drop, then gentle tapping on the roof; an overture to a storm. I hear the wind slowly warm up the string instruments then the crash of symbols, the rumbling of drums; the symphony has begun. I have always loved the sound of rain beating against the windows, thunder rushing across the sky just before the crackling blades of lighting join forces in a grand crescendo. I feel swept away by the percussion of sounds.

From my beginning, I would run to the windows to watch the rain dancing across the lawn. When the rain stopped, I would hurry into the sandy road and pick up handfuls of moist earth inhaling the sweet odor. My big brother died when I was ten years old. Each night I would plead with him to tell me a story. The one I remember most vividly was the story of the rain. He said when it rained, encased within each raindrop were tiny people. When the rain fell to earth, they were released and started new lives among the flowers, the trees and bushes.

After each rainstorm, I have a feeling of renewal and a sense of freedom. Do you think in another life I was one of the rain people my brother told me about?

I CAN SEE

Three days ago I had eye surgery; only three days—a new eye, the old one had a long life and needed to be retired. I don't want to talk about all the steps preparatory to surgery. The operating arena seemed large, user friendly with four adoring fans hovering around me—two doctors and two nurses.

As I lay there listening to a language totally foreign to me, approximately an hour passed. I saw a green bug moving about in a rosy halo, which changed to violet arcs and silvery threads sliding mysteriously along an unknown path. Outside of a headache that provided me with more laying of hands, infusions of sedatives into my veins, I emerged upon the scene a born again visionary.

Yesterday I was told to leave the eye uncovered and a miracle occurred. I looked out and saw Tiburon across the bay, little tiny white dots of homes along the hillside; the peaks of Mt. Tamalpias. Out, way out I saw the skyline of the city; perfect miniature buildings elegantly etched against the sky and the mountain range of the Oakland Hills. I looked across and saw the forest on Mt. Sutro. The trees were fat bushy greenery that covered the slope. I saw a car coming up the street and a very small person at the wheel (of course I was looking down from almost a block away).

For years I've become accustomed to seeing the world through a pleasant haze. I am really born again; a whole new world has opened to me. It has been very disconcerting to look around my living room at the number of stuffed animals that are perching here and there. Snoopy, Goofy and the Waco lion are watching me. The big lion king I got a couple of years ago at Macy's is laughing—his eyes are peering at me unblinking. The pair of furry white cat slippers on the floor are both staring at me intensely. I called them Heidi and Ho and Ho looks dumber than I remembered.

The most amazing thing of all is my cat, Finian. When he came upstairs yesterday, I thought wow, look how big he is; he couldn't have grown overnight. He has lived here for fifteen years and has always been a middleweight or so I thought. He is still a beauty but he's big. I can't wait to explore the rest of my universe. As Humphrey Bogart said to Ingrid Berman in Casablanca "Here's looking at you kid".

TO: DR. JOHN STANLEY

My Ophthalmologist

To be song to the tune of *A Partridge in a Pear Tree*

On the first day of Christmas, I looked around and said
I can see, I can see, I can see
On the 2nd, 3rd, etcetera, Dr. Stanley gave to me
A new eye, that can see, that can see
Before the Easter bunny starts coloring his eggs
I will get another eye that can see
That can see, that can see
Thank you Dr. Stanley for the gift you gave to me
That can see, that can see, that can see
From a grateful patient, Helen Lewison
Who can see, who can see, who can see
And a Merry Xmas to all, even Tiny Tim.

A NO HOST PARTY

My husband came home and said, "How would you like to give a dinner party?" I am sure I turned pale and said, "I don't do dinner parties. I fall to pieces when I have to decide what to fix, whom to invite, it's just not one of my skills'. He laughingly said, "You won't have to do anything". "I won't have to do anything, what is the gimmick?"

He said, "A friend of mine stopped by the store. He and his wife are selling some kind of waterless pots. They will provide the food, cook it, serve it and clean up. They just need a home to demonstrate their wares. Be a good sport—I already told them its o.k." It didn't sound too bad, so I agreed.

The Wilsons, the chefs for the evening called up and asked if I had any preference in regard to the main entrée. I suggested pot roast. I invited two couples I knew. The big day arrived. Mary and John Wilson enter my house with an assortment of pots, pans and sacks of groceries. I gave them carte blanche and set the dining room table. My guests arrived promptly at 6:00 PM. I served them drinks; I can do beverages quite well.

I was called into the kitchen and told dinner was ready. They asked when the meal should be served. I said, "I'm still waiting for my husband, it shouldn't be long". Time passed, an hour—another hour, it now past 8:00 PM. I reluctantly told the Wilsons to serve the food. My guests were getting restless and I was getting mad. We ate in silence while my cooks and bottle washers moved rapidly in and out of the kitchen. A sense of foreboding hung over the evening.

As I remembered, the food was good. My guests were patient and I had a strong desire to make a scene when and if my husband came home. Sure enough, with the clock approaching ten, he came into the house smiling. No apologies, just said, "I bet you folks had a good dinner. Would you like an after dinner drink?"

The Wilsons hurriedly cleaned up, packed their pots and pans and left. No sale was made. There is a saying "No good deed goes unpunished." I was embarrassed, my friends left with no comment. I had literally participated in a "No Host Dinner."

TEENAGERS

Finian is going to be sixteen this summer. He's smart enough but very dependent. I've catered to his taste buds, his sleeping habits, his hobbies and it seems I've never done enough.

Every since I've become a one-parent household, I can really empathize with those thousands of people who have to handle all the problems, emergencies and decisions alone. It really is very beneficial to have another adult to share the ever-present burden of daily life. I don't mind doing all the driving, all the shopping; sometimes though I feel the world is too much with me, i.e. my world.

For instance, Finian hasn't been well lately. He hardly touches his food; he's very moody and sleeps a lot. When I try to touch him or stroke him a little, he yells at me. I made an appointment with his doctor today. Getting him into the car wasn't too difficult but he bitched all the way to his office. While we waited, I talked to him gently and he turned his face away from me. Eventually, we were ushered in and as the doctor started to examine him, he really got mean. I said, "He's usually a good patient." The doctor said, "No problem, he just isn't in the mood to be handled today." He was taken into another room where they took samples of his blood and urine. When he was brought back in, the doctor said, "He's really a very good boy. He is running a little fever so I gave him an injection of antibiotics. We will call you in a few days and let you know the results of the test." I asked "What should I feed him if he decides to start eating." The answer was "Anything he wants."

I came home and cooked chicken soup. Isn't that what you give sick people? He didn't improve over the next few days and I really got worried. I called the doctor's office. They said the tests were positive; all was fine. I informed the doctor that my kid is in a lot of pain. Back we went to the doctor's office. Finian wouldn't talk at all; he was completely dejected. After another examination, a very bad lesion was discovered and it had become infected. The doctor said, "He must have been in a fight—we have to keep him overnight and do minor surgery."

Finian, Finian you're the only man in my life now. You're going to be fine but just forget that macho stuff—no more fighting. I'm going to keep you under house arrest for your own good. Every dog or in your case, cat has its day; you have to hang up your gloves and become a stay-at-home like me.

YOU'RE THE TOPS

I had just returned to San Francisco after a ten-year absence. I was once again single, gainfully employed and starting a new life. After a company dinner, one of my co-workers suggested we go to the Top of the Mark for an after dinner drink. Walking up Powell Street on high heels was an experience. I mastered the technique by walking pigeon toed to keep from slipping backwards.

Into the hotel we strolled, entered the elevator to the top. I had forgotten what a sumptuous view of the city as I glanced around the room looking through the large windows. We sat down at a small table and ordered a drink. It wasn't very long before two men approached us and offered to buy the second drink. We acquiesced—we were young—we were single and the night had just begun. Before the drinks arrived, a man in a black suit came over to our table. He said quite curtly "The Top of the Mark is not a pickup bar" and suggested we leave. Not one to be intimidated, I told our two new companions to meet us over at the Fairmont Hotel across the street in front of the Tonga Room. They were both agreeable and we met, entering together.

One of the men was tall and handsome. The other was short and unassuming. Since I was the most enterprising, I chose the good-looking one for my date. We each danced and changed partners now and then. Milton, the short one was funny, bright and interesting. Before the evening was over, I decided I wanted to know Milton better. He later told me that he had only just met George that evening at the bar. They decided to team up when approaching us and the rest is history.

Milton was from Tucson, Arizona and was attending a conference in San Francisco. We spent a few days together. I drove him around the Bay Area and we talked and laughed like old friends. He said he was planning to return to San Francisco in a few months. He did come back as he had told me and I saw him briefly. By this time I had become involved with another funny, interesting man. Milton asked me to marry him; he said we'd live in an adobe house and drive to Nogales on weekends. It sounded exciting but my heart was now in North Beach.

Since I have acted impulsively all my life, I thought if Milton had asked me to marry him during our first meeting, I might have agreed. Foolishly, he went back to think it over to return when I was spoken for (so to speak). I do believe he would have made a great husband but I did O.K. I married a tall, handsome, funny and interesting man, plus he bought me a wonderful house on a hill overlooking San Francisco. You can't do better than that!

MY BROTHER'S BIRTHDAY

I don't know where I got the rabbit. I don't remember what happened to the rabbit. I think it got out of its cage and ran away. I just remember its white fur and pink nose. This was the year my brother died. I needed someone else to love and I guess I must of loved petting this furry creature. I've had a series of pets, mostly cats that like petting and one dog.

My brother way lying on a daybed in the big kitchen; I guess he was too sick to be left alone in the bedroom. My mother spent most of the time around the kitchen; she was always cooking or doing something near the sink. When my brother was in the hospital, I was taken to see him. At the doorway of his room, I became very scared; there lay my brother frothing at the mouth like a rabid dog. I must have been at his funeral but for the life of me, I can't remember. It seems I do remember most things he did, especially when he looked at me with his large gray eyes. He was never a little boy; he was born a grown up.

Once I followed him all he way to town. He was always on an expedition. My mother said she didn't worry about Morton because she said he would be home for dinner. One day he could not shake me off his tail. I was always trying to follow him but he very cleverly eluded me. This day I succeeded in keeping up with him and we traveled a long way from our house. We ended up downtown and walked into a dime store. He gave me a dime to buy something. It took me a very long time to make my selection. I finally bought a very small doll; her arms moved but that's all. She was certainly easy to dress; all I did was tie different color ribbons around her and call them dresses. I certainly had no sense of style but I really didn't like dolls much anyway.

My mother got worried that day because I was missing. She called Uncle Willie who had a hat store downtown. He sent his delivery boy to hunt for us. He found us all right. He rode a motorcycle with a big box on the side to deliver the hats. He put my brother up front on the seat with him and I rode in the box.

I just remembered today is my brother's birthday. I wonder what his life would have been·like. I'm sure he would have been the best at any job. It has been an awful lot of years that have passed since he died. I was only ten and he had his fourteenth birthday two months before he died. I still see his unruly sandy color hair, his olive skin and those intense, knowing eyes. I get goose bumps thinking about him even now. There is a saying when a chill passes over you that someone is walking on your grave or is it just any grave. I still see the stone above my brother's grave, name, date of birth, date of death and a small stone that reads "Beloved Son".

THE VCR IS GOOD—NYET

I took my VCR to the repair shop. I program more shows than I'll ever watch. In this technological age of wonderful machines, the joy is in the doing. My VCR had revolted and was now showing silver streaks across the screen. The magic word is "tracking" but the machine did not respond to the control marked "tracking". Obviously, it had derailed.

I brought the confused VCR to be repaired. The man behind the counter plugged in electrical socket, inserted tape, pressed button. "See", he said "Good picture, nothing wrong". I said, "Give it time—in a few minutes, you will see something is wrong". I was right, of course—the screen began streaking. "O.K". He said, "Leave VCR—we fix".

A week later, I picked up machine, paid bill and took it home. Connected it to TV, plugged in, programmed movie. Next day, rewound tape—played movie—egad! It's still streaking. Took machine back to shop. Man plugged it in, inserted tape and said, "Look, good picture". Again, I said, "Wait a few minutes, problem will return". I was right, second time.

Week passed, two weeks. I called the shop. Man said "It's on the work bench, waiting for parts". One more week, again I picked up my VCR. I waited a few days before using machine. It must have been fixed. In three weeks, you can build a house. Last night, I hooked it up, programmed and waited for results. Rewound tape, alas, alack, the streakers back.

One more time back to the shop. Man plugged it in, inserted tape and said "Look, good picture". Again, I said, "Wait a few minutes, there is a problem". I was right, third time. Man said "Use tracking button". I said, "I've tried that many times". Man pushed button—waved his hand to the left of machine, to the right of machine—aiming remote control at all angles. Took out tape—inserted another tape—streaking continued, accelerated—took over screen—one wild streaking machine.

Man's face became livid—took fist and slammed top of machine, pounded it again and again. I said quite calmly "Is this how you fix machines in Russia?" Man took top off machine, blew on circuit board, placed fingers here and there and gave up. Tried to put top back on machine. Couldn't replace it, screws fell on floor—pushed machine among others on shelf and looked at me. No words just looked. I said, "I guess that machine has seen its last streak, how about a refund?"

Man said, "Must call manager". He called somebody; spoke in Russian. "Well" I said, "Do I get a refund?" "Manager will call you". All the way home, I was laughing—my machine had been destroyed—I didn't get a refund—maybe some day I will, who knows. Somehow watching Igor or whatever his name is punching my machine out seemed so ludicrous, I felt I had been watching a Charlie Chaplin movie.

My VCR has good picture—Nyet

P.S. I did get a refund.

TO DR. STANLEY

Dr. Stanley—you did it again. Merlin the magician has nothing on you. You waved your magic wand i.e. scalpel, whatever and now I am composing a duo for two eyes. First, though I want to describe the new colors that emerged while lying underneath a canopy of lights for the second time. The rosy halo that enveloped my eye was reduced to a half circle. The bright green previously perched in the center, appeared and faded to white with a tinge of green. The most interesting sight were the small warriors throwing silver spears down among sparkling crystals. For the finale, again a bright green spot (a picture of an emerald) framed by a narrow band of white. Sadly, the spectacle ended and the operation was over.

Again I was presented with a headache. Happily, the headache disappeared to be replaced by another eye onto the world—

My new song goes something like this:

Two for tea
And two that see
My life is like a melody
And I'm as happy as can be
For sure—lah—dedah—dah!
Thanks again for being there
I—now have—a matched pair
I can see anywhere that's there
My voice is really not sublime
But what the heck, I'm feeling fine
De—dah de—dah dah—de dah . . .

ALMOST ST. PATRICK'S DAY

My Irish cat, Finian, is sprawled across my lap; the end of his bushy tail gently moving. Tonight I think it is time to address the ghosts in my life—the most important, the most loved, and the most remembered. I look over at the couch and my mother is looking at me with a twinkle in her eye. "Mom. I miss you; there is so much I want to tell you. You always said to me "You can do anything you want to do". I followed no grand plan but I find no fault with the life I've lived. I have been lucky but my belief in myself you encouraged and nurtured. You were a success. How glad I was to be your daughter, how proud".

"Daddy, don't look so sad. I've never forgotten you. You bequeathed to me your love for words. I never knew you well and I am sorry. You were caught between two worlds—the one of your youth and the new world that treated you harshly. Your love of poetry and plays had to take second fiddle in a life that left little time for art. The every day was filled with basic needs. I wish I could put my arms around you and say how proud I am to have had you for a father".

"Morton, don't leave. You left my world when you were barely fourteen and I was ten. You were my big brother, my silent brother, who moved through his short life with a single purpose. You knew exactly who you were and what you wanted. You never engaged in small talk but when I begged you at night to tell me a fairytale, you would finally let me crawl in your bed and cuddle up. The stories would begin; wondrous tales came flowing out of your imagination. You were the magician; you gave me magic. You always held yourself apart from the world; you had a grand purpose. Was the world not ready for someone like you? I was left wanting—after you left, the magic in my life ended. I lived with fear of the dark for years, the dark inside the house not outside.

The last ghost I will talk to this evening is a husband of many years. It was like living with an encyclopedia, unabridged dictionaries, and a hundred reference books. You knew everything and were willing to share your knowledge. You loved me unashamedly and your heart was filled with compassion not only for those you loved but the whole world. I still see you looking at Finian, our cat and saying "Finian, you're a caution". You knew I would laugh and say that's a very old fashioned phrase. As we looked at each other I can still feel the pleasure we felt in being together. How can I encompass a lifetime in a paragraph about my ghost husband?

Some people say they wish they could have said more to those they've lost. I think we talked long and well. I have no regrets on that score. I would like, I would wish, I would hope that I could reach out once more and touch you, just touch you. Sometimes I think I've lived a dream and when I wake up I'll be someone else. I have lived a dream and someday I will sleep the eternal sleep. Oh, if I only believed in ghosts, I could look forward to dying.

EULOGY TO ALLEN GINSBERG

I was, I was North Beach
Grant Avenue
Blabbermouth night
The coffee houses
We stood outside
Grayline buses, watching
From windows
The denizens of
Beatnik nights
Vesuvios's "Come and
Romp with our Dancing Girls"
I was love love
Among glass bubbles,
Nets at luas
Instant parties, hoping
Crowding, looking
For love
New Pisa, olive oil
Garlic, jugs of
Dago Red
Across tables, we
Gazed

Ah, love
Paul Klee, tansu chests
Lost artists, The Black Cat
Indifference
Tinged with anger
Shredded love
Defying death
I was North Beach

THE CAT'S MEOW

I don't think I'll ever forget the day Charlotte and Pete put Ti in the oven. Ti was an elegant Siamese cat, a little shop worn from living with two heavy drinkers.

In the late '50's, the North Beach area was a conglomeration of semi-artistic people . . . . some with talent, some hopelessly enamored of the excitement emanating from the cafes, the art galleries, the bookstore and the Italian delis. Craftsmen, who designed jewelry, color etchings, silk screens, leather sandals, etc, surrounded us.

Charlotte came from Eastern Brahmin roots, slim, haughty, and very chic. If she wasn't always tilting, she could have posed for the cover of Vogue. Pete, handsome, fine features, premature gray hair held his liquor quite well. When he became deep in his cups, he had a tendency to get violent. Charlotte had a black eye more than once. To put it in rather foolish terms, I don't think she ever knew what hit her.

They lived up on Telegraph Hill—a very arty house—delightful backyard, rather unkempt. The cramped rooms were filled with expensive furniture littered with papers, magazines and the coffee table was strewn with remnants of many evening imbibing the elixir of the Gods . . . martinis, martinis, martinis!

I don't think I ever saw Charlotte empty handed. Always a glass in her hand—always very gracious, very polite until she passed out and landed still attractive on the chair, on the couch and occasionally on the floor leaning against the wall.

My friendship with them was short lived. As I remember Pete

locked Charlotte out one night. She wandered into a bar and bed with the bartender, a handsome Italian named Dante; and forgot to come home for a week or so. Pete left town or at least, he left North Beach.

One particular evening spent with them, I heard a howling from the kitchen. I wandered in and located the source. Opened the oven door and a bedraggled Ti, blinking his beautiful blue eyes looked up at me. I gingerly, pulled him out, gave him some water and proceeded to tell my hosts exactly what I thought of them. I said something to the effect "I think you are the dumbest animals I've every known". Life moved on and God knows what happened to Ti. They both apologized profusely and picked up the cat and stroked him. He looked up at his owners and if looks can kill, they should both certainly be dead by now. They probably are.

WHOSE LIFE IS IT ANYWAY?

Surrounded by gurus
Articulate, non-stop
Talkers
Giving us enlightenment
Into our spiritual selves
Huge audiences sit
In wide eyed
Wonder
At the feet of these "holy men"
My reality, my life
Belongs to me!
I am my own guru
Others' metaphysical
Utterances are only
Sound bites
Designed to mesmerize
Confuse and cloud
Our troubling issues
My life, I live on
A "need to know" "need to do" basis
One magnificent life
I do not intend
To waste
Searching for ephemeral
Answers to questions
I haven't yet asked
Whose life is it anyway?

PRIME SUSPECTS

The woman was dead as hell. She lay on the floor in her pajamas with her brains scattered all over the rugs and my gun was in her hands . . . . I closed the book I was reading and thought about this scene. I had thought about doing away with her for many years. She had been a source of unbelievable misery.

Shortly after we were married, I met my new stepdaughters; two small girls who gave me the once over and then proceeded to ignore me. I never expected much, but I got less. I never met their mother; I had suggested we meet. I felt the girls would be more comfortable knowing they had their mother's approval. She refused to meet me. The children made their two-week visits throughout the years. As they grew older, they became more demanding and more insolent. I knew they were following their mother's directions. They made long phone calls back and forth to her while in my home. I had two phones in the house and each would monopolize the line when talking to their mother.

I did try to placate them. I drove them around the city, to Chinatown, the zoo, the park, out to eat, anything they liked; all to no avail. As the oldest girl told me quite openly "You're living in my father's house". In between their visits their mother periodically sued for more child support, pleading lack of funds. Back and forth we went to court, overwhelmed by lawyer's fees. She never won a case but it didn't deter her determination to destroy us financially and emotionally.

My husband became ill and the child support check was sent out a month late. She sued him for Contempt of Court; the penalty could be jail time. Again, we went to L.A.; again the case was dismissed. We were beside ourselves. The girls were now teenagers by this time and had become totally insufferable. I never knew how to handle this situation. Their father loved them dearly so I tried desperately to survive their visits knowing they would leave and life could then return to normal.

During their last visit the two girls were moving about my home oblivious of me. They were doing something in the kitchen; they always said they would fix their own breakfast and didn't need my interference. I gladly relinquished the job and mostly stayed out of the way. As I came into the room, I saw that the water from the faucet was turned on high, hitting the edge of a cup or some dish. The water was spurting upward hitting the ceiling and splattering over everything. At long last, I gained my voice and yelled, "Turn the water off and stop it". A cold voice came from the kitchen. "I'll stop it alright". I heard the sound of a drawer opening; the older girl came out flashing a large butcher knife back and forth. Smiling, she walked slowly toward me and said, "I'll stop you". As I backed away toward the stairs, I stared back, moving very deliberately. Suddenly, the younger girl called out, fear in her voice, "Put the knife down, put the knife down". This seemed to puzzle my attacker. She slowly lowered the knife and said very coolly "Maybe I'll stop you next time".

When my husband came home, I told him of the incident. That was their last visit and we decided to leave the country. We applied to become residents of Canada. Neither of us could continue to live under the constant bombardment of lawsuits, threatening phone calls. I saw a man taking pictures of our house once; went out in front smiled and posed. I had no idea she would bring this picture to court to show our home, which she had told her lawyer was a mansion in San Francisco. Needless to say, the picture proved it was just an ordinary house.

We received papers from the Canadian government telling us

to come forward and we put our house on the market. I really
didn't want to leave and as the real estate people started showing
our home, I started becoming ill. We soon found out Canada had
a reciprocal agreement with the United States and we could still
be pursued over the border. We took the house off the market.

All these years later I have pictured her dead as hell, laying on
the floor with her brains scattered all over the rugs and my gun in
her hands. I talked about this occasionally with my husband. I
even suggested finding a hit man. He said "Don't you know we
would be the prime suspects if she was murdered and she sure as
hell isn't worth going to prison for." I don't know what happened
to her. As far as I know she's still alive. As least in my imagination,
I've killed her over and over again and enjoyed every minute of it.

ALL OF A SUDDEN

All of a sudden
I am truly a widow
All of a sudden
The only sound I hear
Is the sound of silence?
All of a sudden
I know I will surely die
All of a sudden
I am afraid
Not afraid to die,
Afraid to live
All of a sudden
I will wake in the morning
Another long lost day
Spinning lazily into night
All of a sudden?

MY HUSBAND

He had the strongest face I've ever seen. I think it had more to do with his eyes . . . eyes that seemed able to penetrate steel walls. Even when smiling, his eyes refused to be taken in by the laughter in the room. They were eyes that never slept . . . always wide, open and scrutinizing. The nose was elegant, straight and perfect. It seemed that it should have been larger, more prominent in keeping with the face. A chin thrust out at the world, daring it to do battle but the gentle softness of the cheeks tamed the warrior scowl that could explode when provoked.

This was a face that should and would have graced old Roman coins; a lion's face that any sculptor would have welcomed in marble. I lived with this face; I loved this face. I will never forget the look of amusement at my insolent remarks. He knew me well enough to realize my defense mechanisms took the form of careless gaiety and cynicism.

Even at the end of his life, no weakness or lack of character dimmed this remarkable countenance. As he slipped into eternal sleep, only the heaviness of eyelids closing suggested his inability to maintain his usual regal bearing.

SISTERS OF THE HOOD

Widowhood. The word "widow" conjures up many images. Widow's weeds, black widow; yet the reality is beyond words. It is just a fact of life.

One day a few months after my husband died, I opened the Resource Magazine, a guide to Jewish life in the Bay Area. As I turned the pages, staring me in the face were the words "Widow/ Widower Outreach Group." I hesitated to call. I didn't want to talk to strangers about my husband's death but I wanted to talk. I called and left my number. Within thirty minutes at the latest, my call was returned. We exchanged names and small talk. She called every morning. I looked forward to her calls; a friendly voice, no questions. She urged me to come to a meeting. I was hesitant. My grief was too raw and I cringed inwardly at meeting strangers. I never cry in public—I wanted no pity but I was left wanting.

Soon I did attend a meeting. Everyone greeted me warmly and especially Carolyn Lustig, who had become my phone mate. We talked and laughed and . . . . we became friends. No longer was I a widow; I was a woman, now living alone in the world of women. Each time I went to a meeting I gained more self-assurance. We all had traveled through the long tunnel of sadness and there was a light at the end of the tunnel.

There are still times the light become dim but it never goes out. By sharing our common need, we have strengthened our inner resources. The flow of friendship between each of us gives me great pleasure. How glad I am Carolyn didn't give up on me when I became so reluctant to come out.

I still feel great sadness when I think about my husband, but I feel great happiness in finding I was not alone. We *women of the hood* are very special, we really are.

FOOTSTEPS

I've only just begun to realize how may imprints are on my body. There are heel marks, kick marks, numerous bruises that are not visible.

When Mrs. Brock who lived across the street called me "Jew baby", I cringed but said nothing. I was about ten or eleven when she started calling me "Jew baby" and she continued to off and on until I moved away. I did not know how to fight back or even if I wanted to since Mrs. Brock was just a stupid woman who lived across the street. I actually kind of liked her. When she smiled, most of her teeth were missing. She spent hours watering her flowers and the rest of the time dipping snuff out of a small tin; then spitting into the empty coffee cans that were scattered throughout her house.

I was only seven when stones bombarded our house and our windows were broken. I remember the sound of the rocks falling on our roof. The police were called and said it was probably some kids. They drove away. I knew something bad had happened but I wasn't sure exactly what it was. We were the only Jewish family on the block. In fact, there were only two other Jewish families on the south side of town, which covered a lot of blocks.

When I graduated from high school I applied for a job at the Amicable Life Insurance Company. I had won the typing and shorthand award. I was a member of the National Honor Society. They didn't hire me though other girls in my class did get jobs there. On the application there was a space that read "Religion". I filled it out correctly but it never occurred to me how carefully

I Forgot to Get Old 293

they scrutinized these applications to weed out undesirables; of which I was obviously one. I found out later that they didn't hire Jews. The footsteps were beginning to make their mark.

When I went to work for the government, religion wasn't an issue. I worked in the personnel department and read the files. This was during WWII. I found out one of my bosses was suspected of being sympathetic to the Germans, our enemies, but nothing was done about it. In fact, it was reported he was a member of the German Bund in the United States.

I changed jobs, another government job and really got in trouble. I was working at the switchboard and Mr. Steel walked into the room. "Those dam Jews in Washington started this war". I said "I'm a Jew and I don't want to talk to you about this". He said, "Oh, you're Jewish, well . . . you're a "white Jew". I responded quickly "Do you believe in Jesus?" He self-righteously said, "Yes, man!" I said, "Jesus was a Jew". He came across the room as if to hit me. I grabbed a long pole that was used to open the transom and was waving it precariously in his direction. The fight was stopped and I was fired. I was not given an opportunity to give my version of the confrontation.

I got married and traveled to a city 2,000 miles away. At a party given by my new family, I was approached by my new husband who said "My family don't think you're Jewish. Can you read Hebrew and prove you are". I could and I did; I felt trapped. Would I ever be accepted just for me? I have spent my life trying to be fair, not judging people by their color, race or religion.

However, when there are incidents in Israel, I find myself taking out my Star of David pendant and placing it around my neck. I need to identify with my people. I am not religious but I have innate pride in my heritage.

THE WAITING GAME

Lily's husband had died three years ago. Her home was an array of color, oil paintings on the wall, ornate drapes behind the sofa; a silken background to an inviting environment. The living room was bright; crimson velvet covered the armchairs. The long sofa against the window was charmingly arranged with pillows of every shape and size, but, but . . . . it was the dining area that caught your eye. A long mahogany table waiting for a dinner party; a pink damask tablecloth set with crystal glasses, silver forks, knives and spoons at each side of an elegant china service. In the center, candles expecting to be lighted as they sat in their silver candlesticks; a table set for six. As I moved closer, I saw a covering of dust on the dishes, the silver turning dark here and there. The party had been delayed or was there to be one?

I hesitated to inquire about the table. However, my curiosity got the better of me so I asked Lily when she was having guests. She smiled cheerily and said, "I set the table shortly after my husband died". I didn't ask any more questions. Obviously, the table was set for her family. I knew she had two sons, plus their wives and of course, she and her husband. She said quite oblivious and with certainty "I am sure they will all be here soon".

I talked to her briefly on the phone a few times but lost touch. I don't know what happened to her but I visualize the dishes sitting elegantly on the table having gathered more dust and the silver is no longer gleaming. If she is still alive, I am sure she is still waiting for her guests to arrive.

BORN TOO LATE

May 12, 1997
I was born too late
Too soon
My emergence is long
Into my life
I would wish to be
Reborn
To begin anew and yet
Be what I am
I look back forever
Miles of living
Cannot be repeated
Except on paper
Years of inhaling
The scent of life
My entire senses tremble
Life's candle's flickering
In the wind of
Time running out.

HORSES MAKE ME CRY

I saw a movie not long ago. In the beginning a beautiful white horse is running across the beach. The ocean is tumultuous; the waves are churning and thrusting their white caps across the water covering the shore with frothy bubbles. Sadness overwhelmed me; a new sadness I have never felt.

On television, a graceful brown horse is running through the grass, going nowhere in particular. Again, the sadness rises up in my throat; I breathe with great difficulty. Why do horses make me cry? What symbolic vision do they trigger in my subconscious? I've never been near a horse in my life. I don't think it's the horse itself that engenders my emotion. Is it the running, the trip to anywhere? Is it the pure grace of movement against the landscape? Is it the isolation I feel watching a rider less horse? Is it their natural beauty, so sleek and shiny? Is it their strength that I feel lacking in me? Is it their eyes, soulful and large?

Mostly, I feel the wind blowing against my face as they run gracefully. I watch and feel such a sadness of being left behind as they disappear from view. I still don't know why horses make me cry.

MAGGIE SUGARBUM

Faye got a divorce. Actually, her husband left her for another woman. She joined AA—I didn't know she had a drinking problem but anyway, she met Larry there, and he moved into her house.

When we went to Los Angeles to visit Faye, we met Larry and Pepe. Pepe was an apricot colored toy poodle. He was the smartest dog in the world or so he led us to believe.

On our return to San Francisco, Mel said, "We have to get a dog like Pepe". My reply was "We don't have a yard; its not a good idea." Anyone who knew Mel, would know when he wanted something, there was no stopping him. The search began. Calling ads in the paper. We embarked on scouting trips to kennels. At last, we found a kennel in the East Bay with several toy poodles and one apricot. I wasn't impressed with Mr. Apricot. He just didn't have that certain something. I wandered through the kennel and stopped to look at a black puppy. Now that dog was special. We made eye contact and I knew we were meant for each other.

We bought her—did I mention, she was a female—not an apricot boy dog—a black girl dog. My husband said he remembered his folks talking about a blowsy black haired streetwalker in New York named Maggie Sugarbum . . . . Perfect, I thought. This puppy's coat was sure a mess, so the name stuck.

Maggie came home with us. Our house is not puppy friendly but we put cardboard boxes at the entrance to the kitchen and covered the floor with paper. Every morning before my husband went to work, he would walk gingerly into the kitchen and began to complain loudly about the mess.

"She's just a puppy," I said. I bought a pink leash and walked her everyday. Across the street were empty lots high with weeds. People driving by would look curiously at me. They couldn't see Maggie, just a woman holding a long pink strap walking near the curb. Maggie was smarter than Pepe; in no time I taught her to retrieve.

The kitchen disaster continued. Within the first week, my husband said, "She's going back. I can't handle the mess in the morning". I protested loudly. He called the kennel—they said, "Sure, bring her back". I continued to protest all the way across the bridge and back.

Later that evening, my husband said, "I'm nuts! I shouldn't have taken her back". He called the kennel and said he had made a mistake; we would be back the next day; back across the bridge, back to pick up Maggie. This time, he said, "We'll give her the downstairs room". We had a large round hooked rug in the room. Maggie got hold of one end and pulled and pulled. The rug ended up the size of a place mat. It didn't matter. I had placed papers here and there and everywhere.

I took her to the vet for puppy shots. I asked his advice about house breaking. He said when she looks like she's about to squat, put her on the paper. I stayed downstairs with Maggie for hours. This dog wasn't about to let me know her bathroom habits. If I left the room for a minute, she must have sighed with relief and quickly did what she had to do. I called the vet. He said puppies go often, so just be patient—you'll catch her in the act. Day after day, I spent hours with her—dashing up and down the stairs—no luck. My husband became jealous and said, "You spend all your time with the dog". Actually, I did. In fact, I lost seven pounds in a week and was still counting . . . . Up and down the stairs.

Without my knowledge, my husband placed an ad in the paper "Pets for Sale". A woman called and said, "I'd like to come and see the puppy". I took her name and number. I called my husband at work. "What are you doing, you took her back once and now you want to sell her". He said, "You look terrible, you haven't been well. I shouldn't have started this dog business. Please let the woman come out. Maybe, she won't even want to buy her".

I had been sick and I thought maybe he's right, so I returned her call. She came out and fell in love with Maggie. True to her name, Maggie liked everybody. I told the woman I really didn't want to sell her. She pleaded with me. She loved Maggie. She had never loved any dog this much. She had a long history of owning black toy poodles.

I was confused and called my husband told him of my dilemma. He said, "Please let her have her. She'll have a good home, you've been sick. Really, please let her have Maggie". I relented and she took Maggie away. The new owner called me a few weeks later. She said Maggie was the smartest, best dog in her whole life. She was taking her to England on the Queen Mary. She had bought her rubber boots and a raincoat. Would I like to see her before they left?

I refused. How many times, can you have a broken heart? I'm glad Maggie got a good home and went to London. Sometimes, I think about her and her trip abroad. I guess I'm a little jealous too; I would have liked to have a little bit of a dog's life.

LOST WORDS

I'm afraid to read a book. Every time I open one, I hurriedly put it aside. What happened to the eager creature I used to be? I started reading early; every fairy tale in the public library; all the current best sellers, the classics; to read was as big a part of my life as breathing.

I stopped years ago. A book here and there, but I finally slowed to scanning the newspaper and magazines. Yes, my life was busy with a lot of illness, a lot of doctor visits, a lot of everything that detracted from my ability to settle down with a book.

And then, then my vision began playing dirty tricks on me. Cataracts reduced my vision to the point that my casual perusing of the papers ceased. And then, wonderment happened, an operation on my eyes gave me back vision, wonderful vision. I can see. I can see to read, I can see to drive—I can see!

Now I come down to my moment of truth. I keep opening a book. I read one sentence and close it. I'll read it tomorrow—but I don't. For months, I've been looking at all the wonderful books that surround me and I became fearful. What's the matter?

Have I forgotten how to read? No. Have I lost the ability to concentrate? Probably. When I open pages and see hundreds of words looking at me, I become intimidated. Are they out to get me? Don't be silly. What has happened to the avid reader "me"? Do I not want to be engrossed in anything except the now I am living? Do I not want to take the time to become involved in characters I've never known? I'm really not sure of the answer. Is it because I've missed so many years of reading and I can't make up for the past?

Once upon a time, a world without books would be a dead world. Somewhere along the line, part of me quit living. I've overcome many obstacles in my life. My challenge now is to gentle myself, as one does a wild horse—to tame my restlessness, to calm my impatience, to again recapture the pleasure I felt at the sight of a book. I must try I must try.

GOLDEN GATE NATIONAL CEMETERY

MEMORIAL DAY 1997

Flags blowing in
The wind
Thousands of Americans
Under the red, white
And blue
Thousands of stones
Marble names
Engraved on
Our hearts.
Flowers, red, white
And blue
Remembering,
Remembering
So many wars, so
Many lives
Under every flag
A hero, my hero
Among the stones

GOD KNOWS

I said, "I'm an atheist". Anne said, "Do you know what an atheist is?" "Sure" I said, "An atheist doesn't believe in God or a supreme being". Anne said, "How can you not believe in something you don't think exists".

Yes, she's right I thought. I began to really think about God. Maybe I'm an agnostic. I reached another puzzling conclusion. An agnostic is a fence straddler, a play-it-safe believer. In the end when you fall off the fence, you would land on one side or the other. This didn't appeal to me. I wanted something more to believe or disbelieve in.

Take God for instance; whose God I thought. Is it the man, Jesus, hanging on the cross in Christian churches? Not for me. I don't care for martyrs much. Is it the unseen God with the long white robe and beard? Uh-uh, he doesn't seem to satisfy my image of a holy deity. Buddha, he's totally foreign to me. All I know about him is a big fat statue and Confucius writes books with very wise sayings. I'm really not trying to be disrespectful.

The God of my people is categorized by the SHMA:

SHMA YISRAEL ADONOI ELOHANU ADONOI EHUD "Hear oh Israel, The Lord our God, The Lord is One".

I will simply sum up this essay very simply with these words. I am still an atheist, but if perchance there is a God that I don't believe in, it will be the one that commands us to say the *Shma*.

ROOTS

My father was forty when I was born. There is much of him in me but we never knew each other. He was an intellectual, given to reading poetry and writing plays and stories (unfortunately most of them were written in German.) I recently had his plays translated from German into English. I was amazed, impressed and overwhelmed with the intricate details and stage directions of his plays. How sad that his talent could not have been acknowledged. Coming to America shortly after the turn of the century did not afford him the opportunity to pursue his art. The objective was to work, earn enough money to live and perhaps, just perhaps at some late date, he would be able to become the writer and share his creations with the world. As Thoreau wrote "Most men lead lives of quiet desperation and go to the grave with the song still in them." I am the only one left to sing my father's song.

My mother was never cherished for her quite wisdom. Her easy going exterior was viewed as being ordinary. Her family took for granted her lack of apparent emotion as weakness. I knew my mother best. Her stillness allowed her to conveniently keep her strength private and her intellect she secreted way. My mother was one of the strongest women I've known but since it was always in deeds not words, it was barely noticed except by a select few.

Through the twists and turns I've traveled, I look back at my parentage. I am my father and my mother. More importantly, I am myself. By a very narrow margin, I might have ended my life as another housewife in another house. Somehow I escaped that fate. A driving force like a strong wind was always blowing at my back.

I let it carry me without question. At times, I felt airborne with no destination. Yet, I always landed and lived a life of order for long periods of time. In my life of order, there were unconventional decisions, flat unthinking days and moments of delight.

My father's genes say *think*. My mother's genes say *feel*. My father's genes say life is only a trip to death. My mother's genes say death is the end for everybody, but life is just for you.

Why am I debating with my parents' genes? I am myself. Soul searching is pointless for the most part, yet I search. I am looking for my core. The essence that lives inside me, long languishing undisturbed always evades my scrutiny.

I wanted to write a story but again I ended up churning restlessly with no answers, only questions.

MENORAH PARK

Today is Memorial Day, May 26, 1997. I was invited to a festive lunch at a senior housing facility, called Menorah Park. I entered the room crowded with about a hundred people. At long tables seating eighteen, were wall to wall—canes and walkers. Many spoke no English, communicating their wants mostly in frowns. Since all these people were my "parents" for the day, I smiled and clapped my hands to the music. The band played "America the Beautiful" and segued into songs representing all the services— Army, Navy, Air Force and Marines; music from WWI—"Over there, over there, over there".

I watched the faces; slowly a small smile, embarrassed glances in my direction. A woman handed me her key ring. Inside a small plastic object was hanging from the key ring; a Spanish dancer in a bejeweled dress. As I handed it back, I made the gesture of a flamenco dancer. Her face brightened as she looked at me. I thought so many years of living on all the faces around me, and so little attention is paid.

I presume I am viewed the same as those around me, but I didn't presume. I was still young, wasn't I? I badly wanted to have a camera that would take pictures of all the faces around me; not an ordinary camera but one that would peel away the age lines, the dulling eyes. I wanted to see beyond the obvious. Even though I own no such camera, these worn and happy faces surrounding me gave me innate pleasure. Age is in the eye of the beholder, the same as beauty and I did see beauty in each and every face.

INTO THE FRYING PAN

Joe said, "You married the wrong brother. Bob is dumb and can't appreciate you like me". Trying to breathe in the hot humid air of Houston, I didn't know whether I had chosen the right brother or not; actually I didn't know what I was doing there most of the time.

Aunt Bette lived in a big two-story house—it was a total bedlam of chairs, tables and pictures. Nothing matched. It had the feel of being furnished from odds and ends picked up at garage sales. Their small grocery store jammed with merchandise. The shelves reached to the ceiling. The meat market on one side held a small selection of meat . . . . headcheese, pork sausage (the type of meat their customers could afford). The store was in the colored part of town and a hall attached the house to the store.

What was I going to say to Joe? He lived at Aunt Bette's and I visited often. "Joe, I'm glad you like me but stop kidding". "I'm not kidding. Do I look like I'm kidding"? We were in the dining room and Ethel was sitting at the table. She said, "Who's kidding"? I looked up. I had only recently met Ethel. I hadn't even known she existed. Ethel was Aunt Bette's niece and my sister-in-law. She was a mongoloid whose mother (who had died ten years before) had placed her in a mental institution when she was about eight years old. Bette couldn't stand to think of her being cooped up in what she called a crazy house.

She had taken her out and had been her guardian for almost thirty years. Ethel spoke with a Latvian accent just like Bette and her husband, Abe. When she looked at me, she was usually frowning. Later I found out that she could play the piano, which I thought was pretty amazing. I taught her some simple card games; she usually beat me.

Bette came in and said, "What would you like to eat"? I said, "No, thanks, I'll be eating dinner later". "No" she said, "I'll send Russell to the kosher meat market". She left the room to talk to Russell. Russell was the butcher, a tall, lanky man who had that— *I know something you don't know look on his face.* Bette and Abe couldn't read or write English. Russell would open the newspaper every morning; spread it dramatically on top of the meat counter and in a loud, clear voice begin to read. He only covered the more spectacular events . . . a *war was going on somewhere in the world or possibly some grisly murder.* Uncle Abe would stand quietly listening, shaking his head from side to side.

Bette came back and said, "Russell is going to get some veal chops, it won't be long". She hurried back into the store to join Abe who was usually standing behind the cash register.

"Joe, are you going to stay and eat with me. You know when Bette decides to do something, there's no stopping her". He said, "No, I don't eat here". "But you live here". He replied, "Only temporarily".

I said, "I'm going to go upstairs and talk to Nancy".

Joe gave me a cold look and walked out of the room. I said "I'll see you later." Ethel said, "I'll see you later goofy head". Uncle Abe called a lot of people "goofy head". He liked to tease; Ethel had picked up this phrase and used it generously.

I walked upstairs to talk to Nancy. She had worked for the family since she was fifteen. She had married, divorced and had three grown children. She always wore a white dress and went to church on Sunday. She was keeping company with the preacher. She was a whole lot more than a maid. She was like a top sergeant running the household. She knew as much about keeping a kosher kitchen as Bette. I remember hearing her more than once telling Bette "You're mixing up the (milcha) milk with the (fleishik) meat dishes". And, Nancy was always right.

Nancy had become my confident since arriving in Houston. "Nancy, Joe says I should have married him instead of Bob. Isn't that silly"? "Oh, Mr. Joe, he thinks he's a big shot. You know he went to Julliard".

"Does he ever play the violin? I know he's supposed to be very good".

"Mr. Joe plays by himself sometimes downstairs; he plays in front of his mama's picture".

' "Nancy, what should I say to him"?

"Don't say nothing. He liked to start trouble in the family".

I heard Bette's voice calling me. I went down the stairs. I smelled the chops cooking on the stove. I had married into a pretty strange group of people. However, Bette was a great cook I thought as I pulled out a chair and started to eat.

UNCIVIL RIGHTS

"Walter, sit down" I said. He looked at me startled and stood stiffly in his army uniform. "Come on Walter, sit down". He moved slowly over to the window seat across from the dining room table where I was seated. He cautiously sat on the edge; his face solemn and unsmiling. Walter was black. He was one of Nancy's sons. Nancy had worked for the family since she was fifteen.

I had newly arrived in Houston, just married, returning to the Texas I had left only three years before. When I arrived in San Francisco at age 18, I began a job and an education in civil rights. I listened eagerly to these new and exciting people who talked about things completely out of my frame of reference. I was eager to change and try to relate to what I heard. For the first time in my life, I had deliberately sat down next to a black man on the bus. I nervously took the seat and nothing happened. He didn't smell or try to attack me; things I had heard growing up. He looked out the window, his face worn and tired.

I became part of a bohemian group in San Francisco. Most of the men were in the Army and wrote for Stars and Stripes Magazine; all the people talked about books, politics, civil rights and equality. I was more or less the mascot, the youngest and was teased about my Texas accent but I was allowed to sit at the feet of these wise and knowing people. I bloomed in this rarified atmosphere of intellect and drama. I was becoming one of them or so I thought.

Returning to Texas, I was going to practice what had now become my beliefs. Walter sat across from me waiting to be dismissed. I asked him what he was going to do when he was discharged from the Army. He replied it would be soon and told me he had been stationed in England for two years as a radioman. I said "Walter, get out of Texas. Go west or east. You'll get a good job. If you stay here, I don't think anything has changed. You'll end up as a ditch digger and you're better than that".

Looking back, I wonder what gave me the right to lecture him. Was I condescending and patronizing? At the time, I truly believed I could save someone from a life with no opportunity and no future. Walter listened quietly, got up, nodded and left.

Within a few months I saw Walter in work clothes. I asked his mother where he was working. She said "On some project, they're digging the sewer lines". A few years later, Nancy told me "I'm worried about Walter. He gets his paycheck on Friday and then goes out and gets drunk".

I don't know what I expected to accomplish by my inspirational speech. Walter, who had left this country and spent time in England, slipped right back to the role that he had been assigned since birth.

When Nancy and her daughter came over to help me clean my new apartment, I still thought I'd show them we're all equals. I worked along with them and when time came for lunch, I set the table for three. I heated up some chili and sat out three bowls calling them in to eat. They came into the kitchen and sat down carefully, not picking up a spoon. I joined them and said "Come on, let's eat . . . there's more in the pot and we can have ice cream for desert". I started to eat and when I looked up, they were just sitting, not moving. I realized they were too uncomfortable to eat with a white woman so I quickly ate my food and said something to the effect that I needed to do something in the other room. When I left, I heard them talking and the sounds of dishes coming from the kitchen. I had failed twice but I had other methods or so I thought.

I would go into the department stores downtown in Houston where the water fountains were marked White or Colored. When I had an audience, I would point to the fountain designated Colored and ask quite loudly "Could any of you people tell me what is the color of this water?" I never got a round of applause or even an answer but I did get cold looks.

Once some of my husband's army buddies came over and after dinner they were sitting on the porch talking about the "coons". They were laughing; this was all very amusing to them. I became enraged, walked out on the porch and told them to leave. My husband said that they didn't really mean anything, it was just talk. I said they were not welcome in my house and if he ever talked like that he could leave too.

I became known as the girl from California. California was viewed as a place where people were obviously different and not well bred. I reveled in my difference. I had learned from people who were to be admired, not these narrow minded Texans that surrounded me.

There were other incidents but it wasn't until I joined the League of Women Voters in the early '50's and found these women were really going to make a difference. They had money and power. They drove their cars with large signs calling for the end of segregation. Many of their cars were bombarded with eggs and other things but they continued. In the middle '50's, the civil rights movement had come center stage, Brown vs. Board of Education in 1954 and the Montgomery Bus Boycott in 1955 with Rosa Parks.

Shortly before I left Texas in the mid 50's, I was driving through the black district in Houston. I stopped at a stop sign and before I started to move, a large group of black men surrounded my car. They were laughing, and yelling; then they began rocking my car back and forth. I sat frozen at the wheel; I was sure they would turn the car over. Just as suddenly as they had started, they stopped, walking away laughing. I heard one of them say, "We sure scared that white woman". I wanted to yell out "I'm on your side, I'm on your side".

CALIFORNIA,
HERE I COME AGAIN
AND AGAIN AND AGAIN

My first trip to California occurred when I was nine years old. We stayed with my aunt and uncle. My cousin, Joe was two years younger than me and we soon became friends. Every evening during dinner, his parents were constantly urging him to eat. He always dawdled with his food. I became very impatient with their nagging and I said, "I know how to make Joe eat". I tuned to Joe and said, "I bet I can finish my food faster than you". His eyes lit up and the race began. He finished his dinner.

He was very fond of artichokes. I had never seen one in my life. He would carefully peel the leaves, dip them in mayonnaise; the heart of the artichoke was the prize, which he finished with obvious delight. I came to appreciate this funny vegetable. When I returned to Texas the second time as an adult, I searched the markets for artichokes. I talked them up to the produce department of many stores. Eventually, they began appearing and people would ask me what I was buying. More and more appeared; I shared my love of artichokes with my fellow Texans.

The second time, I came back to California—I noticed salads on many tables in the restaurants. I began to think of California as being green, cool and rather detached. How can you fall in love with a bunch of cold leaves? I have come to appreciate their appearance, but I like my food with more substance.

The third time and last time, I crossed the state line, I fell in love with North Beach and Italian food. I had never heard of veal scaloppini, saltimbocca and of course, sour dough French bread. Italian food has character, warmth and flavor. In San Francisco now, we have restaurants serving food from every country in the world. Somehow, we have lost our unique California cuisine, which was probably an illusion anyway. I'll drink to that preferably with a Picon punch with a brandy float plus a lemon twist; the drug of choice during my beatnik days.

FATHER'S DAY

Bouncing Baby Girl

The most vivid memory of my father goes back many, many years when I was about four or five. My mother would sit on the front porch on warm evenings waiting for my father's return from work. I, as usual, was playing. "Play" was the most important word in my vocabulary. Every answer to "Where are you going? What do you want to do? Come in for dinner. It's time to go to sleep," elicited this response "I'm playing!"

This particular evening we were sitting on the porch, I asked my mother to go in the house and get my ball. I needed it "to play." She said, "Go in and get it yourself." I went into the room that held my assortment of toys. The room was too dark; I searched and searched. I couldn't find my ball. I went back out and said, "I can't find the ball, it's too dark". My mother said, "Your father will be home soon, just sit down with me and wait."

I wanted my ball. I went back into the house. The light was in the center of the room high on the ceiling. There was no light switch to turn it on; only a dangling string that I couldn't reach. I pulled my old high chair to the center of the room. I climbed unsteadily up to reach the string. The chair fell over and it was "lights out for me."

I awoke lying in my father's arms on the front porch. A damp washcloth pressed to my forehead. As I looked up at his worried face, I was overcome with pleasure. How good it was to have a father to love you, how wonderful to be held in his embrace. I wanted to stay there forever, loved and safe. I had never felt this way before.

This was the last time my father held me. I was getting bigger and still playing. The memory of that evening stands out—a warm breeze, the dark skies and my father's face watching carefully over me. I did have a very special daddy. My life passed from playing to living. The last time I saw my father, his face showed the concern and affection he felt for me. I didn't know how to impart my love of him. I followed his directions as he got his house in order. We never talked about his imminent death; it would have embarrassed both of us. We both played the game of life, talking about tomorrow and tomorrows. He had given me the gift of life and he didn't want to diminish this in any way.

ELLIS ISLAND—1907

She was so young. Leaving home to go to the United States was overwhelming. She knew she had to go; there was no future in Hungary. Leaving her mother was the most painful, but she climbed up on the wagon that would take her to the train station.

Arriving at the station, she saw the policeman examining the papers to see if you were leaving the country legally. She wasn't old enough; you had to be eighteen or escorted by your parents and she was only fifteen. She had been sent back the year before. She looked around and saw a woman surrounded by many children. She hurried over and told the woman of her dilemma. The woman told her to stay with her and that she would take care of everything. As the policeman approached, the woman said "Look at all these children; do I look old enough to have so many?" The policeman laughed and moved on. So began my mother's sojourn to America.

Her father had upgraded the ticket her older sister had sent from New York. "No daughter of mine travels steerage, like an animal. You go second class," he said. Clutching the ticket, she boarded the train and joined other young people en route to the "land where the streets were paved with gold." Surrounded by all the happy, excited faced, the journey was pleasant until they reached Hamburg where the ship was waiting. "All aboard" came the cry. They hurried up the gangplank. All her train mates were escorted down the stairs to the dreaded steerage. She said, "I'll go with them." "No" the purser said, "You go upstairs." "Can I see them later?" "No" he said, "No visiting in or out of steerage." Again she was alone on the beautiful ship "Kaiserin Augusta Victoria" on its maiden voyage to America. She went into the dining room and was served the most elegant meal she had ever eaten. It was the last meal of the trip. Seasickness accompanied her the entire trip.

At last, Ellis Island, this was America—a big drafty building, being prodded and examined by men in white jackets; lined up to receive food from a long counter. The people moved slowly, still dazed by the long sea journey of eight days. She was putting food on her plate and looked up. She saw a big black woman. Was this what Americans looked like? She reached out; the woman pulled back. She reached out again; maybe she was painted black. The black woman yelled something at her. Why wouldn't she let me touch her? She wished she were back in Hungary. She was very homesick. It would be a long time before she felt at home in this new country.

FAMILY TREE

"This is Luann Gelber and I'm trying reach Helen Lewison. I'll call back later." I had checked my answering machine and a voice or I should say, an accent from the past brought back memories.

I was born a Gelber but my father's family all lived in New York. Gelber, where else were there Gelbers? Yes, I remember— my father had a distant cousin who lived in College Station, Texas, the home of A. & M. College. Every boy who was going to amount to anything went to A. & M. My father left New York and went to College Station, presumably to work in his cousin's store. I never knew what happened but his stay didn't last long.

Thinking back, I remember a day when a car pulled in front of our store in Waco and a large smiling woman came in. My mother greeted her and the woman said, "I'm Morris Gelber's wife from College Station." The women talked and finally she said, "Why don't you let me take Helen home with me for a few days. She can meet my son and daughter; they are about the same age." My mother looked at me and before she said anything, I said, "Let me go, I want to go, it will be fun." She agreed; she usually did. I was always chomping at the bit and here was an opportunity to go somewhere new. I packed a few things, got in the car and off we went. About three hours later, she pulled up in front of a big two-story frame house. It was very imposing but rather gloomy.

We walked in and she called her daughter, Cecil. We looked at each other. I said, "Do we look alike?" Cecil said, "I think so." We looked for a mirror and there was a big one over the buffet in the dining room. We did look alike or we thought we did except for our noses, hers turned up and mine was straight. As the evening skies darkened, we were called in to dinner. A long table covered with a white tablecloth stretched before me. There were a lot of people already sitting there. We joined them and dinner was served. A colored woman brought in the food. She seemed friendly enough but who were those other people. I talked to Cecil and her brother. Her mother went in and out of the kitchen. Who were those other people?

Two middle aged women and two middle-aged men eating silently. They weren't talking. I hadn't been introduced so I said nothing. I began to feel very uneasy; they seemed like robots; very mechanical, using their forks and knives very properly, showing no emotion. I heard a voice coming from one of the men. "How's your father?" I was startled and jumped for a second. "He's fine." One of them could talk and knew my father. Who were these people?

Later that evening when we went to bed, I passed one of the bedrooms. The two women were just sitting quietly in their chairs unmoving. I felt I was in a haunted house. When I returned home, it was many years before I even had a clue to this mystery.

I pieced together bits and pieces of the puzzle. The elder Gelber, Cecil's grandfather contacted syphilis passing it on to his wife and unborn children who outside of Morris, developed different degrees of mental retardation. What a terrible crime to pass on to your children. The culprit was long dead but his cruel legacy lived on. I never knew what happened to this family of sorrow.

Here was Luann Gelber calling me almost fifty years later. She was married to the grandson of the one son who was unscathed by his father's disease. Luann called back. She had twin boys—two years old—a new batch of Gelbers. She sounded bright, intelligent and curious. She asked questions about her husband's family. What should I tell her—the truth, as I know it? I don't think so. Let the dead past bury their dead or something like that. All truths don't set you free, that I do believe.

I WAS KISSED AT SAFEWAY

I had a few odd and end places to stop—the vet's office for special food for Finian, my cat; the police station to report a series of sinister phone calls.

On my return home, I decided to stop at Safeway. On the radio, I heard the announcement—two cantaloupes for $1.00 why not stop, I like cantaloupe. After parking the car, I headed into the produce department and deposited two cantaloupes into a bag. On the way out, I passed the bakery—the sweet smell of pastries; I stopped, I looked—I started to move away. I stopped—I looked in the large glass case with its array of pastries, doughnuts, sweet rolls, and éclairs. I moved over and gave the pastries further scrutiny. Weakened by the sight of the Danish pastries, I picked up a bag and carefully placed two bear claws inside. Guiltily, I turned to the man standing next to me and said "Oh well, I'm never going to lose weight anyway/"

He turned to me and said, "You are a very beautiful woman, you are a very beautiful woman." I said, "Thank you, it's always nice to hear compliments." Again, he said, "You are a very beautiful woman, do you liked to be kissed?" I smiled demurely, being taken aback by these charming words. Again he said, "Do you liked to be kissed?" I just stared at him and with that, he reached over, took me in his arms and kissed me on the mouth. I looked over and there were about six or seven customers watching us. One of the women asked "Were you embarrassed?"

I felt my face flushed, looked at the man—a tall well-dressed man wearing a hat and now also, a very pleased look on his face. I said, "I blush easily, but I've never been kissed in Safeway." That said, I walked into the line at the checkout counter. Two of the people in my audience followed me. We talked about men and kissing. I told the man at the checkout "I've just been kissed in Safeway." He said, "Too bad, Herb Caen is dead. He could put it in his column." I said "Forget Herb Caen. I need to find another columnist." The checker said, "I agree with you." All the way home, I was driving and laughing. How many people get kissed at Safeway? I kept laughing, eventually just smiling. How about that! Not everybody is a beautiful woman who gets kissed at Safeway.

THE OLD LADIES

Today, I was brought up short. Someone referred to a friend and me as two old ladies. This term passed over my head until later in the day when it entered my mind—"old lady". How dare anyone call me an "old lady?" I know I've gotten older but old, never.

The two of us "the old ladies" were at a Senior Center. A young man in his 20's was discussing writing and literature with us. We had been involved in a small creative writing class and in his role as "teacher" we had listened, sometimes impressed with his broad knowledge of writers and his articulate views.

For reasons unknown to me, they moved us from room to room (in a barely used Center) and finally deposited us to a corner in a large room behind a blackboard. Seated at a long table on hard folding chairs; this was to be our permanent home. I protested—there were other places, more private, more comfortable. I found the director of the Center or assistant director and questioned this move. I was told that the City Park and Recreation Supervisors were now installed in our former room. "Sorry about that" she said but this was the best that could be done to accommodate our class.

Our teacher, our "wet behind the ears" teacher was told of my displeasure and he reprimanded me. He said, "You're giving me a bad time. You're making trouble." My retort was "Why don't you protest too, possibly they'll give us a more comfortable room." He said, "I can't do that. You'll have to petition and send it to City Hall for any changes to be made."

City Hall—my god, an empty Senior Center with a handful of people going to such lengths to get a room for two hours a week. When he asked if we were coming back the next week, my friend said, "I don't know, I travel by bus from Marin County and it has become a hardship." I said nothing. He said, "I really have to push myself to come over here. I am working several jobs" and then he used the words "old ladies." He was giving his precious time to us "old ladies."

I gave him what I think of as my Cheshire cat look; like the cat in Alice in Wonderland who vanished slowly and all that remained was its grin. I was planning on vanishing myself.

To quote from Alice in Wonderland: *"You are old, Father William, the young man said,*

And your hair has become very white; And yet you incessantly stand on your head—Do you think, at your age, is it right? Father William, obviously, I too, am standing on my head!

TO BE OR NOT TO BE

I knew what my father wanted to be. I knew what my mother wanted to be. My father wanted to be a writer. He arrived in this country at the age of 22 with a portfolio of two plays and a book of poems. My mother arrived in this country at the age of 15. She worked briefly as a cook and housekeeper before her sister told her to get a job in a sewing factory. Her sister told her that she was nothing but a servant. My mother listened to her sister and learned to sew joining hundreds of new immigrants in the sweatshops of New York. She confided to me many years later that she really wanted to be a cook. I would watch her in our kitchen. She lovingly basted the roasts; she hovered caringly over the stews; she stirred the soups ever so gently. She used a large blue porcelain bowl to mix and knead the dough for marvelous coffee cakes of assorted shapes and sizes. Neither parent achieved their dream.

My father studied the English language and wrote a few plays in English. The need to get a job was of primary importance. His dreams remained a dream. My mother left the sweatshops and married. She partly achieved her dream. She did cook for her small family with the same grace she would have offered to a larger audience. I was the recipient of delicate pastries and well-seasoned food.

My dream—what was my dream? For years, I told everybody who asked that I wanted to be a dancing girl. We owned a tourist court consisting of five separate cabins. Early on, I would knock on the occupied cabins and would ask "Would you like me to dance for a penny?" The answer was always "Yes"—and I would go into

my routine; singing and dancing. Door to door I went for a few
weeks until my father caught my act. He brought the curtain down
on my early career. I did love to dance but I no longer considered
dancing as anything more than fun.

What did I want to do? I had no great ambition. The best
option open to me was marriage and so it turned out to be a full
time job. I seemed to be pretty good at it. Learned to be an interior
decorator, learned to drive, learned to shop, learned how to keep
house, learned how to cook but that was always my weak suit. It
didn't matter because I married a man who didn't care what he
ate.

Life moved on and I became an executive secretary. The job
was simple enough but the repetition bored me and I moved from
job to job—some a little more interesting but there was very little
need to be creative. Back to marriage and the home again. At least
I had years of experience in this field. I was still weak in the cooking
department but I was included as a minor partner in my husband's
job. I became an "independent contractor; the definition these
days of people who work as their own boss but have no benefits,
i.e. sick leave, vacation time, pension plan, etc. On the other hand,
I was lucky; I had sick leave, vacation time and a pension plan. I
had a very benevolent boss. I guess I really had the best job in the
world. I never thought of it as a job; it varied day-to-day; always
changing, never monotonous. If someone had asked me what I
wanted to be, I would never have said a wife and yet it turned out
to be the right choice.

LEARNING

My mother asked me "Do you want to go to kindergarten?" My answer was "No, I haven't finished playing." I had not had enough of playing—all day if I wanted—or anytime. As the year progressed, I tired of just playing. Other children were going to school and there was no one to play with.

At age six, I was ready for school; more than ready. First, my mother gave me instructions 1. Never take any candy or ride with a stranger; 2. Look both way before you cross the street; 3. Wash your hand before you eat. These conditions were not too difficult to tackle and off I walked to the first grade. I learned that little boys liked little girls and I liked them back. George Crow gave me crayolas and turned the faucet on the water fountain for me. Just like big boys, George Crow became enamored of another girl with long curls. Oh well, given a few days, I forgot all about George Crow.

By the second grade, we had moved to another part of town. I missed a lot of school. I got sick, really sick—my appendix burst. I got a very big get well card from my classmates. There is nothing like being in a hospital to impress the other kids and I reveled in this attention for a while.

By the third grade—reading was the highlight of my life. The teacher would spend part of the day reading us stories. I would go home and ask my mother to read me a story. She read very slowly—she had been born in the old country; she could read and write English but she wasn't up to my standards. I snatched the book away from her and said, "I'll read to you." Very patiently, she said, "Fine." She sat quietly while I read her stories from the Wizard of Oz.

We left Texas and moved to San Francisco. The fourth grade found me in California, a cowgirl who had never seen a horse but spent the better part of the year trying to live up to my reputation as a girl portrayed in western movies. The teacher asked the class if anyone could play an instrument. Myself, among others held up our hands. She asked me what instrument I played. With a straight face, I said, "I play the comb." She said, "Those that can, bring in their instruments and play for the class." I brought a comb, carefully wrapped in cellophane and played. No one laughed; maybe they were impressed or confused. I never knew. I was completely serious.

Back to Texas by the fifth grade—this year is a total blank. Maybe I didn't learn much.

The sixth grade was special. My teacher was Willie Mae Scruggs, a tall, thin unsmiling woman. I was constantly chattering with my classmates. The classroom was divided; boys on one side; girls on the other. She moved me to the boys' side to try to silence me—to no avail. She separated the room with all the girls over to one side and the boys another. I was seated in the middle seat, the middle row; each row to the right of me and the left of me was unoccupied. With total disregard of my embarrassing position; I passed notes on the floor to the left of me; the right of me. Miss Scruggs caught me in the act and kept me after school. She said, "I give up, tomorrow sit wherever you want. You are a very good student and I sure would like to know what is going to happen to you when you grow up. Come back and tell me." I was the only one in the class who refused to say "yes, mam". Miss Scruggs had tried. She would say looking at me; her face stern and say "Yes, mam". I would answer, "Yes"

I moved on to Junior High. I was no longer as rebellious. I was growing up and starting to become a woman. Of course, this was not the end of my impulsive nature. In fact, I really haven't changed that much, internally that is.

WAY, WAY BACK

I climbed the steps
Back in time
Twenty-five years ago
His hair still black
His eyes, shining
Warm tears tumbled
I couldn't go back
Years away from him
Black hair, burning eyes
Words, more words
Fell upon the floor, the
Table and all was
Quiet
I wanted yesterday
Or maybe not
White wine, scotch
Never knew what
Happened, yesterday
Did I leave, no the
Wind blew and I
Became a leaf
Tossed about, someone
Picked it up
Years ago.

OLD COUNTRY

Old County, what
Is old country?
Mother, father once
Upon a time
Lived in old country
"Mama, tell me about
The old country"

Bedtime stories
Only old country
Walnut trees, dirt
Floors
Bread baked in brick
Oven
Wooden spoons, two
Dresses
Cut colored buttons from
Shirts hanging on lines
To make pretty beads

Old country
Oil lamp flickering
Plucking down from geese
Children dying
Children born
Every night, closed
My eyes in the old country.

LET ME OUT

Words keep bumping into
Me, black, blue
Bruises, words, thoughts
Sentences clamoring
Let me out, let me
Out
All my life, waiting
To find their place
In stories, essays
Poems let me out
I've lived long with
You, the time is
Now
Time runs out
And we sit huddled
Put me on paper
Let me speak, I sing,
I dance I live
On paper
Let me out.

MRS. BROCK

Mrs. Brock was watering her garden; she was always watering her garden; a chaotic, careless colored tapestry of flowers. She never seemed to spend any time in her house. I crossed the street and walked up to watch her. She looked up from her watering and said "Hello, Jew baby." She always greeted me with the same words. Inwardly, I cringed but never said anything.

She was short, stocky with coal black hair. She always talked a lot about everything. She knew all the neighborhood gossip. She and her next-door neighbor, Mrs. Geezler had a running feud, which had been going on for years. Each had rose bushes climbing up on the fence separating the houses. Each would complain that the other's roses were crossing into their yard. It really had nothing to do with the roses.

Mrs. Geezler lived alone. Her husband had divorced her long and ago and she had moved to Texas from Mississippi. She lived on a small stipend in a neat house. I was in there once. One room had old newspapers piled high in neat stacks. I never asked her why. She would come over to our store and quietly ask for a tin of Garrett's snuff. This was her secret vice. She was very fond of my father. Whenever she saw him, she would hurry over and say "Mista Gel'bah, isn't this a beautiful day? Do you think we're goin' to have a wet winter?' My father would nod politely and move away as quickly as possible.

Mrs. Brock bought tins of Garrett snuff too but she made no secret of it; she would put a portion in her mouth, swill it about and the spitting began. Every room in her house had an old coffee can used as a spittoon. She lived in the dirtiest house I ever saw. None of the beds were ever made; the white paint on the metal frames peeling covered with torn blankets and the stove in the kitchen was crusted with years of grease. The Brocks had a cow in their back yard and they made homemade ice cream on their back porch. I would join in turning the handle on the container. It seemed to take forever to get the ice cream thick enough to eat. I really didn't like the taste but I liked to be part of the family; they were always laughing and talking. I thought her daughter; Fleeta was the prettiest thing I ever saw with her long black wavy hair. She was a lot older than me and would let me brush it until it shone. Her brother Ollie was tall and skinny. He married and had two children. Frankie the youngest was always in trouble and the police were parked in front of their house often.

Even though I resented her calling me a "Jew baby", she brought over a beautiful gardenia for me to wear on one of my first dates; I sorta forgave her.

THE LITTLE CUCKOO

All my life, I longed to be a dancer, an actress—anything that would give me an audience. Growing up as an only child, my parents were a captive audience; my mother in particular.

In high school, I joined the drama club. I learned my lines quickly. The first play was titled "The Little Cuckoo". It was a play within a play. I got the part of the cuckoo. At one point in the play, I climb on a chair—stood up—faced the audience—and spoke the lines "cuckoo, cuckoo". My audience was mesmerized; actually "cuckoo, cuckoo" resounded through the auditorium as the boys in the front row mimicked me. I began to giggle and almost fell off my perch.

The second play was about a group of girls in a finishing school, very lah de dah. I was to come strolling in, ever so sophisticated holding this elegant doll dressed in silk pajamas. These types of dolls were placed against the pillows on a bed, like the throw pillows of today. I was to casually toss the doll on the couch and begin speaking. I, very so, indifferently walked in, my face totally devoid of expression; I was a woman of the world. I snapped my wrist and hurled the doll across the room. As it missed its mark, it hit the lamp on the end table, which came crashing down. Again, I brought my audience to their feet with exclamations of "Nice shot, you got a hit" and then a thunder of laughter.

My last role was a very serious part. I was to be the old woman who sat in a rocking chair and dispense words of wisdom to members of her family. Wearing a wig and a long apron, I walked slowly on stage and seated myself. One of my "granddaughters" came seeking my advice. As I placed my hands on her head, my chair rocked; and rocked. With each rock, the chair squeaked. Here I was a woman of serenity and insight sitting in a squeaking chair. Eeek-eek, eek—eek; again my audience burst into laughter and down the rows of students the sound went rolling—eek—eek, eek—eek! I could barely contain my embarrassment and laughter.

My mother who had been present at each play never said anything. Finally, I asked "Mom, did you like my acting?" She solemnly looked at me and said, "You're alright, but don't count on going to Hollywood."

MISTAKEN IDENTITY

The phone rang—"Hello"

"Do you know a Todd Andrew Lewison"

"No" I said, "Who is this Todd Andrew with my last name?"

She said, "I lived with him in Phoenix for several years; then I got pregnant and had a baby."

"And then, what happened?" I said.

She said, "He left me when my son was six months old and now he's five."

"Why do you want to find him?"

"My son wants to know his father. I have twenty two more Lewisons to call."

"You're very ambitious. Do you think you'll find him?"

"I don't know but all the people I've talked to so far are either Jewish or Norwegian."

"Well, I'm Jewish. Was Todd Jewish?"

"No, he was Norwegian."

"Do you have any idea where he is?"

"He went to San Diego to enter a rehab center."

"Oh, that's interesting. He was on drugs. Did he complete his stay there?"

"I don't know; they said he had been there but there was no follow up."

"Do you really want to find a druggy? You're probably better off not finding him."

"Oh, yes I want to for my son's sake. I think it's important."

"Well, good luck. Where are you staying her in San Francisco?"

"I'm not in San Francisco, I'm in Chicago—I just have to keep trying."

"More power to you girl, I hope you find what you want."

BROWN SLIPPERS

I close my eyes and
See the slippers
Worn brown slippers
Neatly placed side

By side
My father looked up
Cold hospital, white
Sheets
I looked away
"Everything is fine
Operation fine"
I say, staring down
Watching the
Brown slippers.
I looked up
My father's brown eyes
He knew, we both
Have a secret
The games began
"In time you'll be better"
Takes time, brown eyes
Watching, I look down, the doctor told
Me about six months
Shall I tell him?
No, no, he's my father
"Everything's fine Daddy,
You'll get stronger, takes time".

Time is running out
Brown slippers waiting to
Leave, go home
Reached over and touched

The soft brown felt
Still warm, still alive
Only six months, not
Enough time
I close my eyes and see
Brown slippers discarded
Thrown away like my father
Only I am left to remember.

FIVE YEARS

Everything stopped
The world became
A framed landscape
Silence, as I looked
around at art
lifeless beauty
No longer, did
I live
Yet ordinary needs
be satisfied
Everything stopped
My waiting days began
Sitting on the
Cusp
Everything stopped
Crippling minutes
A clock with
no hands
Sounds of traffic
Sunlight running
bumps its head
against the dark.

Been five years
since you died.
still feel the warm flesh
on your arm
as I stroked, pushed
Death away.
Fingers tingle at memory
Life reduced to
ashes, placed beneath
a stone
you in a metal
container, buried.
I glance secretively
across the room
your watchful eyes
scurry away as
you hide,
you're here, I know
you're here
Why can't you show
yourself.
I didn't see the flames.

I went out to
The stone and
dug a hole.
carefully placed
your watch so
You would know
what time had
done to us.
When I become
dust, will we be
together, turned
Into topsoil to
perhaps to grow a
wildflower or
a weed. Perhaps?

IS GOD THERE?

"Is God there?" I answered the phone and a woman's voice asked "Is God there?" I started to laugh nervously. She quickly said, "I must have the wrong number." I wanted to say something but was cut short when she hung up.

Today is Yom Kippur, the Day of Atonement, the holiest day in the Jewish calendar. I didn't attend services; I didn't even say a silent prayer. I wondered after the call "Is God here?"

I've questioned the idea of an omnipotent deity for most of my life. There are so many churches, so many beliefs with assorted Gods. Is there a special God for me? Can one glorious presence exist to be revered by millions?

I really don't know whether God is here, in my house, in my life. I wish it were true. I have a lot of books he could read; I have food and drink if he wants. I find the idea of a living God refreshing. I can relate to that image. I would want Him to know me and cherish me. We are all small miracles who live on this earth for a limited time.

I sit content in the remaining cycle of my days. The quiet around me is warm and comforting. My only regret is that I no longer have a husband to love. I would hope he is with You. I am still filled with love but it is diluted now and spread lightly among my friends and surroundings.

I do believe God is here. Sometimes, I even think I hear him breathing. I know something has guided me all my life. I am one of His creatures and I wish I knew what awaits me. Today God is here and I am here. That is enough.

SEVEN DAY JOURNAL

Day 1. October 14, 1997, Tuesday

Left class went to post office, mailed a bunch of stuff to newfound cousins in Texas. They have discovered a link between us. We are very, very distantly related. Maybe I will meet them one day. They have extended an invitation. Since my husband died I have had no desire to go beyond a few miles of my home. For someone who loved to travel, I've certainly done a turn around. On to bank—it's about time I use cash instead of MasterCard. Wow, what a beautiful day. Got home and would you believe my cat had thrown up on the rug exactly in front of my favorite chair. Using elbow grease and rug cleaner, I repaired the damage. He is usually a lot neater and goes out to do the dirty. Well, he is a cat and an old one at that. I guess a sixteen-year-old cat is equivalent to a 100-year-old person—so I forgive him. Had lunch with a friend at Joe's. For eating, it doesn't get much better than that. I've been eating at Joes since 1959. I have said that a plaque with my name should be on one of the booths. On to get my car washed at the "Brush less car wash". Back home, I put a movie into the VCR, which shall remain nameless, the movie that is. I guess I'm just bored watching naked people jump on top of each other after tearing off their clothes. I think lovemaking is passionate and loving, not a frenzied screeching roll across the floor. I think I'll write a screenplay—it would have to be better than this. I think I'll watch NYPD in a few minutes and settle down for the day.

Day 2—October 15, 1997—Wednesday

Boy, is it hot today. Attended a lecture at San Francisco State—the Humanities Club. It was about murals, which turned out to be more interesting than I expected. They pulled the blackout drapes in the room so we could see the slides; everything from caves drawings to graffiti. The retired physics professor who sat in front of me laughed from time to time, which I felt was a break through. He's usually so intense; I think he's about to crack. My friend, who writes so well, came back to my house where she read me some of her essays. It was still too hot to think straight. Took her to catch her bus to Marin. Off to grocery shop. I like the people in the Humanities Club—sooner or later if we all live long enough, I might get to know them better. One lecture a month leaves little time for socializing.

Day 3—October 16, 1997—Thursday

The memorial candle I lit last night is still burning. It has been five years today since my husband died. It still seems unreal. I keep thinking he'll show up. My cat was sick again this morning. My surrogate daughter was planning to come and walk around Stow Lake with me. I called her and she insisted I make an appointment with my vet. She said, "Tell them to x-ray him." (She has a cat too.) I did. She came; we walked a little around the lake. It was time to take Finian to the vet. She held him as I drove. It was an eventful trip. He used her as a litter box. I said "We'll wash your clothes when we come home, it was only urine." In we went, my damp friend, my befuddled cat and me. After examination, the vet said, "I feel a large mass. You are right; we will have to x-ray him. I don't want to alarm you but it might be cancer. Of course, wait till the x-rays are developed and come back in an hour". I took my friend back to her car. She said she would go home and shower and call me later. I returned and thought, actually I didn't want to think. I went back and the vet took me in, showed me the x-rays and said, "It is very puzzling, what I thought was a mass is Finian's kidney. It is large but we think still in the normal range—but he has only one kidney". I said, "Is that normal." She said, "No, did you ever have an x-ray before?" "No, never—what do you think happened to his other kidney?" She said, "Maybe, it deteriorated—I have no idea but outside of a little arthritis, he's fine." I took my cat with one kidney home, fed him and decided I had had enough excitement for one day.

Day 4—October 17, 1997—Friday

I taped "Seinfeld" last night and decided to watch it. I have been watching this sit-com for years. It has had the highest rating on TV. I don't get it, it's stupid—and then why do I watch it. I guess I'm trying to understand what makes a show popular or maybe I'm trying to define human nature. I think I'll quit trying. I sit in front of the TV watching this program and making faces at the screen. Minako came to clean my house. She was excited and told me she bought a house; actually her husband bought the house. He is a sushi chef and works in Oakland. They've been separated for years but no divorce. They have a very pretty daughter who has just entered U.C. Davis. She's planning to be a veterinarian. Minako's husband will now be moving back into the new house, as he will be paying the mortgage. Went to see my good friend, Carolyn, who is very disabled. She has a great sense of humor. Bought her a few things but mostly put batteries in her small radio, which she listens to, in the wee hours of the morning. Went back to the commissary again. Seems I spend a lot of time there. I know some of the people and I always hear part of a story—today it was about a chihauhau who intimidates his owner. Back to the homestead and tried to get my cat to eat his food with a little pepsic (the vet's suggestion). It didn't work—wouldn't touch the food. I gave up and cut up a slice of chicken untarnished by a medicinal flavor which he decided was more acceptable.

Day 5—October 18, 1997—Saturday

Turned out to be a big day, very big for me. Made plans to go see the play "Pentecost" at the Berkeley Repertory Theater. Planned to meet a friend at the Daly City Bart Station and take the 12:54 train to Berkeley. As I drove down 19th Avenue surrounded by wall-to-wall cars, I thought, "Let the devil take the hindmost." or whatever that means. By the time I got to the Bart Station, the entrance to the garage said "Exit only". As I drove up around and back, I saw the 12:54 moving away from the station. I parked on the lot and went down two flights of stairs to find friend. There she stood saying, "The train left and I forgot my Bart pass at home anyway. I gamely replied "Come along, I'll drive to Berkeley". She agreed and after getting directions—how to get on the freeway, off I drove down the road, over the Bay Bridge, all the way to Berkeley. You see, what really made it a "big day" is I haven't driven the bridge for several years or hardly anywhere that's there, there. Thank you, Gertrude Stein. I was a bit apprehensive, but my car was overjoyed to be out of the garage and on the road again. I said several times (to my car) "Aren't you glad we're up and running. We should get out more often."

Now to the play. Good seats. The play, the play—the plot is much too complicated to summarize. Most of the characters spoke their lines in Russian, Hungarian, Slovakian, a tad of German, some English and a lot of lines ending in "Okie Dokie, Tally ho, Hunky dory" and other bon mots. All good things must come to an end but to review the performance in brief—two priests, one American, two English (one Oxford—one cockney); one very phony Hungarian, a couple of Russians, a gypsy and his daughter plus baby, a Mozambican, a Pakistani and a woman either from Lithuania or Afghanistan who played the cello. The highlight of the play was the Palestinian (a woman) ordered a naked priest (to be sure he was not concealing any weapons) to deliver an agreement before killing the hostages (who spoke English). When there was a knock on the door, the naked priest entered—total frontal nudity.

I whispered to my friend "Well, at least he's circumcised". She chose not to respond to my observant remarks. Needless to say, the play ended with shooting, dead bodies, some philosophical remarks and downcast eyes. I drove back through Berkeley, again across the Bay Bridge, into Daly City to the Bart Station where my friend's car was parked. As I drove home, I told my car "You did real good, I'll have to take you out again." Made a fried egg sandwich, settled down and watched TV. It's Saturday night!

Day 6—October 19, 1997—Sunday

Let's see—Sunday—the big paper. Started to scan it, cut out a couple of coupons, which I'll probably never use. I am committed to looking through most of the paper. Starting with the comics; I am very selective—only Doonesbury, Peanuts and Cathy. Miss D. came over at noon. She is very excited—she has auditioned and been hired to sing Sister Sophia in the Sound of Music to be performed starting in late November. She usually brings stacks of C.D.'s over to use my stereo system to record songs on tape. Busy, busy—she runs back and forth to the machine. After a drink and cookies, she almost settled down. Then my other young friend came over and I listened while they verbally thrashed over the events in their lives. The energy they expended seemed very unimportant. Of course, I must bear in mind I have reached the age of reason. Actually, I was never perturbed about insignificant things. I have what I think of as my Scarlet O'Hara syndrome "I'll think about it tomorrow" or maybe never. Thank God for a mother with the genetic disposition to never "make a mountain out of a molehill." I have despaired in my life for short periods of time but most things have rolled off my back like water on the proverbial duck.

Think I'll go out for hamburgers later with my salt-of-the-earth friend and dine at the Pit Bull, commonly called the Bullshead. Couldn't find a parking place; drove over to New Chinatown—Clement Street—parked, goody, goody—Clement

Street Bar and Grill. Hamburger very good. Looked around and didn't see an Asian face in the restaurant. I think this is where old San Franciscans go to dine. At least this one did. Whoopee!

Day 7—October 20, 1997—Monday

Obviously, the hamburger wasn't as good as I thought. After a fitful night, I proceeded to do almost nothing today. My friend's birthday was yesterday but she offered to share her second cake with me. Talked with my European friend who disagrees with most of my views. I know she thinks I'm one of those "Liberals" as she disdainfully calls everybody that disagrees with her. I don't particularly like labels but I don't think "liberal" is a dirty word. Couldn't figure out what to have for dinner. Made a scrambled egg sandwich. This should clear up the age-old-question." What came first, the chicken or the egg?" It's obvious to me it must have been the egg.

CATALOGUES

I planed to write an essay on "catalogues", the class assignment. The word, the thought left me completely clueless. Catalogues come and go into my mailbox, upstairs on the table and eventually into the garbage.

I've looked through some of them. The catalogues from the many museums, Metropolitan, New York, Boston, Chicago and so forth hold more interest. They are filled with reproductions of pictures, artifacts, jewelry of a time long past. The jewelry holds my attention the most; glittering beads, flowing moonstones, shining gold and silver.

I have accumulated my own artifacts, beads, silver and gold over the years. For instance, on my mantle are two very small-carved wooden cats. I purchased them in Sacramento's Old Town. I have another small brass cat with red-jeweled eyes from Portugal. One of my friends gave me a small "worry wart" in bright orange from Oaxaca, Mexico. When you touch it, the head bobs. I have a carved wooden jewel chest I bough in Chinatown. Inside, every item has a story. A silver bracelet from Mexico, a necklace from Venice, turquoise colored beads from Athens, gold rings from two Caribbean islands, a harem ring (eight bands) from Istanbul, a jade ring given to me many years ago, pearls presented to me in an act of undying love; on and on it goes.

None of these are antiques. Their history started with me—I am the original owner. I live among my art; these include pictures, Eskimo art, an ironwood seal and turtle, tapestries, and needlepoint; assorted colorful items. I, indeed, live in my own museum.

I should have my own catalogue where nothing is for sale. It seems I have written an essay about catalogues anyway. Once I start "The moving finger writes; and having writ moves on."

IF

If I had to move somewhere else, where would I move? I don't have to move, because I have lived everywhere I've been.

There have been many places I could have called home. We used to drive through the 49er country, the foothills of the Sierra. There was gentleness in the green covered slopes and a quiet in the towns, Sutter Creek, Sonora, Nevada City. I used to picture myself living in a house near the Tuolumne River.

I've spent time in Tucson, Arizona. After being intimidated by the heat and the barren hills, I found beauty in the high desert, the adobe houses, and the midnight skies where the stars were like beacons. I wanted to live on a high terrace and hear the sound of the wind as it swept the sand across the roads.

In Jerusalem, I felt I had lived there before. As the sun was setting, I watched as the buildings caught the last glow and turned each slowly golden one by one. I walked through the cobblestone streets of the old city. I could feel my ancestry all around me. This was my home.

But Venice, ah Venice, the most magnificent; three hundred bridges connecting each island. A city built on water, a floating dream. As I looked across one evening and watched a family at the dinner table, I marveled that they could live so easily in this spectacular place. This should be my home. I would wake each morning and hear the water splashing against the back steps. My house with the ten-foot ceilings and stonewalls would make me a part of history. I would walk down to St. Mark's Square, look up at the Bridge of Sighs, knowing I had been here years ago.

Back to the present, San Francisco. I have deep roots here. There has always been a magic relationship between the two of us. It wasn't love at first sight. I was a new comer and the city stood scrutinizing me. As I opened my arms to embrace it I was accepted slowly and we became lovers; an inanimate partnership that has continued to grow and deepen. I cannot imagine leaving. We have watched each other mature. The intimacy of living together so many years is irreplaceable.

INTROSPECTION

I don't quite know how to write about this uneasy feeling; this fictitious fly buzzing about my head; this sense of total alienation between the me I was and the me I've become. The realization that all I've seen, touched, heard will disappear when I die has somehow settled in some crevice in my brain. I start to question my very existence. How come everything that was important to me once, suddenly seems frivolous. Does it matter, should it matter?

The stock market will go up and down. There is a war going on somewhere all the time. People are still starving in Africa. The price of homes is going through the roof. The excessive use of energy will be depleted and mankind will choke on his own pollution. To be well dressed, coordinate your accessories. Eating less fat and sugar should control high cholesterol. Natural fibers are better than synthetics. Crime should be controlled by better educational facilities in inner cities. Always wash your hand before you eat. Invest your money wisely. Eat a lot of whole grains and vegetables. And the bigees, *exercise, exercise*! If not you risk, a stroke, a heart attack, arthritis and god knows what else will get you.

The admonitions to living are endless. The problems the world faces are overwhelming. Man's inhumanity to man continues at an alarming rate. I feel totally helpless. What can I do improve the quality of life for my fellow earthlings? How do I quiet the unquiet that is invading every pore of my body? How do I desensitize myself yet maintain a sense of worth?

Come to think of it, what the hell am I thinking about? You see once I begin my journey of introspection I get lost along the way. I suppose I should bring this essay to some conclusion. What goes up comes down. Most questions have answers that are followed by another question. I am full to the top with questions and I know there is, and never will be any satisfactory answer. "Enjoy the moment, smell the flowers." Platitudes, platitudes, they name is man/woman. A rose by any other name—platitude, platitudes. Ah, I have the answer; the one I have been seeking all my life. After long use our lives become stereotyped and we are limited by our mortality. Life is a cliché within a cliché. Now that's an original thought, isn't it?

EAT TO LIVE

We were invited once to my Uncle Willie's house for Thanksgiving. I was seven or eight and was always very pleased and impressed on the rare occasions, we were invited. They lived in a brick veneer house and had a maid.

Uncle Willie had four children. Lily, the youngest was about five or six years older than me. I spent the night at their house once when I was about thirteen. I asked Lily if it was all right to kiss a boy. She looked at me with cool displeasure and haughtily replied, "It's up to you". Growing up an only child, I needed a lot of questions answered, but Lily wasn't about to give me any advice.

Thanksgiving—the table was quite elaborate, but mostly the turkey, the centerpiece of the table was brown and moist. My uncle carved the turkey and carefully placed a slice on my plate. I ate, quite aware of the royal presence of my aunt and uncle sitting at each end of the table. I asked if I could have another slice of turkey. My uncle looked at me and remarked, "We eat to live, we don't live to eat." I don't remember if I got any more turkey or not.

I have eaten a lot of Thanksgiving dinners since then and nowhere was I reprimanded if I requested a second helping. Still, every Thanksgiving, the prerequisite turkey brings back my uncle's stern warning. He obviously held to this credo, he was very small and thin. The pleasure in eating shouldn't be condemned and viewed as only a means of survival.

"Pass the turkey, please!"

"DON'T FENCE ME IN"

He was tall and blond. His sailor suit gave him the appearance of a little boy with a mature face dressed for a masquerade party. He was in the U.S. Navy and the war in the Pacific was raging. I don't remember exactly where we met but the first time we spent hours talking in my girlfriend's apartment; talking and talking until the skies began turning bright orange.

I was in love, really in love. He would call me from his duty station. He was temporarily assigned to the Shore Patrol; keeping other members of the Navy out of off limits bars or similar night spots. Once I met him at the beach in a dingy bar. The jukebox was playing the song "Don't Fence Me In". I thought of him as a lonely cowboy who was now serving his country wearing a silly suit, which was totally incongruous on his lanky body.

He began bring classical records to my home. I remember one in particular "Finlandia" by Sibelius. After listening to various records, he would question me. "What did I feel when I heard it?" He would quietly discuss music and I became his student. He told me I needed to widen my knowledge of music, literature and many other intellectual aspects of life. I, joyfully, acquiesced.

He suggested I spend a weekend with him at a hotel downtown. I agreed and proceeded to formulate a plan. First, tell my mother I was visiting a girlfriend across the bay. Since I wanted to appear worldly myself, I bought a wedding ring at the dime store. Next, I bought beautiful sheer black underwear. I was anticipating my entry into a romantic liaison.

We met for dinner before checking into the hotel. As I looked at him across he table, I felt more and more uneasy. Finally, I blurted out "I can't do this—I just can't do this." He looked at me coolly and said, "I've already made reservations at the hotel." I continued to protest. I was sorry, but I just couldn't go through with the plans.

He said, "All right, we'll go have a drink and talk about it." After dinner, we wandered into a bar and he ordered drinks. He went over to the jukebox and played "The Warsaw Concerto." It was the first time I had every heard it and found it magical. We didn't talk much.

Sounds from the front of the bar began moving down in our direction. An M.P. (Military Police) came up to me and asked for my health card. I looked up at him mystified. He asked again. I asked why and he said "All the other girls have cards, where is yours." He said he would come back after a few minutes while I found my card. I looked up dumfounded at my *prince charming* who seemed very amused by the episode. He had brought me to a bar inhabited by the local prostitutes. I, the innocent bystander was condemned to be included with them and provide the identification necessary otherwise be arrested and hauled away. I panicked and said "You can't do this to me." He said nothing just smirked. I pleaded "I am wearing a wedding ring, tell them I am your wife." As the M.P.s approached me, my escort said casually, "She's my wife, she's fine." I had been granted a reprieve but I became angry. I became very angry. I said, "I'm leaving and leaving alone." He smiled briefly and said, "Fine."

I do remember waiting for the streetcar around midnight in the cold foggy air. I was so mad I didn't feel cold. I did feel total relief that I had avoided the most disgraceful act of my still very young life. I was nineteen.

A few days later, he showed up where I worked. I really had no desire to see him. He said urgently "I want to talk to you." I said, "No, I don't think so." He said, "Please listen to me; just step outside for a few minutes." I sighed and said, "O.K. only a few minutes." We moved into the hall and he said, "You win, let's get married." "What did I win?" "Isn't that what you wanted?" "I would never marry you." "I called my parents in Florida and told them I met a wonderful girl and we're going to be married." "Well you'll have to call them back and tell them, she's not going to marry you." "What's the matter, you said you would spend the weekend with me and changed your mind. Isn't marriage what you wanted?" "After the humiliation I felt by taking me into that bar, I wouldn't marry you if you were the last man on earth." He looked surprised and said meekly "I'm sorry but I love you." I just looked at him and walked away.

Ah love, how easy it was to fall in love and oh, how easy it was to fall out. As my mother would remark often during my late teens "Who are you in love with this week?"

OH JOY

When I was six
I wanted to be a
Dancing girl
When I saw sixteen
I was dancing
When I was 26
I was romancing.
When I was 30-40-50
I did lots of stuff
Time moved on and
Them I had enough
Now that I'm . . . .
I don't really want a lot
I have a house, a car and a cat
Life doesn't get much, better
Than that
Oh joy!

A DAY IN THE LIFE

Finian hadn't had his shots. I've been ever so prompt in seeing to this every year. The doctor usually sends me a postcard when the time rolls around. This time, no card—I just all of a sudden happened to remember.

Our vet, Dr. H. Killed himself last spring. He took a gun and blew his brains out. He was the best veterinarian I had encountered in my many visits to pet hospitals. He could examine Finian, gently pressing here and there with both hands. I wish he were still around. Someone told me he was a manic-depressive. I never knew or would have guessed. Anyway, I called and made an appointment with a new vet in his office.

Finian is moving into old age. He's sixteen, which is pretty old for a cat. I have been told that cat's age is determined by five to one year as a human. This adds up to eighty but I think he looks very good for his age. The new doctor did a few things while Finian eyed him warily. I was informed they were taking him in back; he was dehydrated and need an injection of fluids. I waited thinking about my poor cat being subjected to needles. When the vet brought Finian back out he said, "Well, he's fine but he peed on me." I said, "So sorry" but I didn't mean it. At least my cat had initiated the new doctor by christening him, sort of like a ceremony of naming a child.

I took him out to the desk and sat him on the tall stool so he can look out the window while I paid the bill. The girls that work there recognize his elegant demeanor. They are always holding him, nuzzling him and telling him what beautiful eyes he has. He suffers their demonstrative advances and just looks out the window. I always say "Finian, you can drive home." When I get in the car, I place him in my lap. Sometimes, he stays there, paws on the wheel—sometimes not. I always sing, both on the way to the vet and on the way home. My voice would probably not tame the savage beast but he seems to be reassured by my out of key songs. He sits quietly so my musical ability must have some measure of serenity. Home at last—"Finian, we're home." He looks up at me— large green eyes assessing my voice. Sometimes when I talk to him, which I do often, I have wondered when I speak how I sound in his pussycat's head. It seems by the look on his face, my words reverberate "blah, blah, blah, blah." He talks to me often himself. A meow bordering on a howl "Meow, wow, meow." I will say "What do you want, what are you talking about?" I think, I just think he's mimicking me and in his language he's saying "Blah, blah, blah, blah.

PRESENTS

Looking back and trying to remember presents I received, all of them had worth, merit and from my standpoint "somebody liked me."

The woman, who cleans my house, always gives me a Christmas gift. The first year, she gave me two padded clothes hangers and two candles, shaped like red apples. The next year, she gave me a teddy bear that is sitting on my library table with a red ribbon around his neck. This year, she presented me with a doll sealed in cellophane with the words "This is not a toy." It is Mrs. Santa Claus complete with white hair and gold-rimmed spectacles holding three wrapped presents. I don't know what to do with Mrs. Claus. I'll probably put her in a drawer where she will reside the rest of her life.

When I was five or six my mother gave me a big doll. Her eyes would open when you picked her up and close when she lay down. Also a small wicker doll carriage accompanied this gift. I took the doll out of the carriage and proceed to roll it outside. I picked up my big orange cat, dressed him in the doll's clothes, put the doll's bonnet on him, put him in the carriage for a stroll down the street. This did not last long. Within a very short time, he jumped out, bonnet askew, dress dangling as he ran madly away.

My mother came to the door and said piteously "You don't like the doll; I'll make her new clothes." I said contemptuously, "I don't like dolls." I didn't get another present that I can remember until the radio.

By then I was eleven. This was the year I had my tonsils out. My mother took me on the streetcar to the doctor's office. He removed my tonsils—I can still remember the sweet smell of ether. After I regained consciousness, we took he streetcar home. There sitting on the table was a radio. I listened to Ma Perkins, First Nighter, One Man's Family, Vic and Sade—the Saturday morning show called "Let's Pretend." I can still hum the tune. The world of technology had entered my life—as I got older and married I bought a combination large radio and record player—then one of the first television sets; a black and white picture, blond cabinet, 16" Motorola. The television repairman spent a lot of time at our house. But, oh how, I loved Playhouse 90, Omnibus and even the silly comedians.

I, now at this point in my life have five television sets of assorted sizes, three VCR's, a small stereo with four speakers and a C.D. player. I, also have many, many electrical kitchen appliances, most of which I never use, except for the toaster and the microwave to heat up the cat's food.

I've come a long way but I am facing one very large obstacle. I don't have a computer. I have three typewriters—but no computer. I'm sorta planning to take a class later this month in the basics of a computer. It would be a shame not to test my skills and admit defeat if "I've never tried." However, if I go no further in mastering another machine, I would like to be judged by my record up to now. I don't think it's too shabby.

P.S. Several years later, 2000, 2001, actually starting in late 1999 . . . I got a computer, I learned how to use it and it sits regally in the corner of my den surrounded by its mates; a scanner, two printers; three speakers; a cordless mouse and of course, on the shelves above it is a series of manuals plus a clock, small stuffed animals—a Chihuahua, a rabbit, a puppy, a duck, a leopard, a penguin, an octopus . . . . I have moved into the 21st Century and I have learned the jargon—download, cut & paste, I know how to go online,

boot up and there are times my computer rears up and flashes
"CRASH". I have been thinking about getting a DVD player; I
understand the picture is far superior than on a VCR. I'm still
moving on . . . and on and on.

DIET DRINKS

The shelves in the supermarkets are filled with two kinds of soft drinks, Coke regular, diet Coke, Pepsi regular, diet Pepsi, Dr. Pepper and diet Dr. Pepper, etc. That is where I draw the line— diet Dr. Pepper. Does anyone else in the world know or care about Dr. Pepper's origins. I do or at least I'm a lot closer to the truth than most people.

Dr. Pepper was born in the same town in which I made my entry into the world. The story goes this way. A young man from South Carolina, Georgia or Alabama arrived in Waco, Texas in the early part of the Twentieth Century. He obtained employment at Pipkins drugstore on Austin Street, the main street of the town. He worked behind the long marble counter making sodas and sundaes. He began mixing different syrups and experimented making tall cool drinks. One of them became very popular. The demand increased and the customers asked him the name of the drink. He scratched his head and said, "Let me think about that." It seems wherever he came from; he had worked in a drugstore. The pharmacist that owned the drugstore was called "Dr. Pepper" using his last name. Our hero had a crush on the pharmacist's daughter. The good Dr. Pepper found out and fired him, thusly he ended up in Waco. "Hey, he said, "I'll call my drink Dr. Pepper, that ought to show the old coot what I think of him." I don't know if Dr. Pepper ever found out we were drinking in his honor or not. However, somebody else bought the formula and Dr. Pepper went big time.

Now to get to this "diet thing." I personally will not buy

anything that says "Low fat" "No sugar" "No fat" and certainly nothing with the word "Diet" emblazoned on its side. I do feel since I was privy to the beginnings of this drink I have a personal stake in its good name. Putting "Diet" on the side of a can of Dr. Pepper is not only offensive but also somehow sacrilegious. Anyone who grew up in Waco in those years will remember going into Pipkins Drugstore, ordering a Dr. Pepper and being handed a tall glass of dark liquid ambrosia surrounded by crushed ice. Later I would buy it in a bottle, put it in the icebox until it froze then slurp it joyously in the hot days of summer. My childhood is long behind me but Dr. Pepper and all it meant to me is still as vivid now as it was then. "Diet Dr. Pepper", think about it. Just about everything in this world has been reduced to reducing. Maybe I ought to get on the scale—is there something wrong with this picture?

EPIPHANY

The word of the month or probably the last year is "epiphany" which has now been broadened to "euphonious." Once this word was only associated with religious revelations. It has become the word of choice among people announcing to the world their truly divine internal emotions are culminating in ecstasy.

During the O. J. trial, I must have heard the word "disingenuous" at least twenty or thirty times a day. During the olden' days, I was confronted with the word "dissemble." My new husband used this often. With a critical look on his face, he would accuse me of dissembling. I went along with what I thought was a gag or just words. Eventually curiosity took over and I looked it up in the dictionary. The next time it was uttered, I became the caustic rebel that lies beneath my calm demeanor. Needles to say, "dissembled" never crossed my path again.

Since that time I have never let a word pass me by. I have to know, want to know what it means. I think perhaps that was my "epiphany." A wake up call to not neglect words foreign to me and be on guard to what is being said. I don't think I'm being disingenuous.

GHOSTS

I believe in ghosts. Actually, I don't think of them as ghosts; they are just people who have moved into another dimension.

My cat, Finian has been quite ill this at week. According to the vet, he has diminished renal function; liver disorder and something abut his electrolytes. To top off all this bad news, I was informed he is blind. This totally blew me away; my beautiful Finian with large green eyes. Of course, the first words out of my mouth to the vet were, "Well, I'll just get him a Seeing Eye dog."

I brought him home and set about doing everything possible to make him comfortable. I drove out in the pouring rain and bought chicken breasts. I came home and cooked them, no seasoning, as instructed.

Every evening this week I have been looking up at the ceiling and speaking to my late husband. "Don't take Finian away, he's my main man. I know you loved him, but you've got a lot of good company there."

My cat seems to be doing better today, so maybe he's been given a reprieve for a while. I don't really think my message is getting through. Sitting alone at night with Finian nestling on my lap, I really do think someone is listening.

I am caught up in
The unstoppable
Longer days, shorter
Nights.
Turning calendar pages
Month after month
Only time is immortal.

DESPERATELY SEEKING

The fire engines were racing down the street in front of our house. I ran out to see where they were going. I waved at the passing cars that were following the engines. One car stopped; I jumped in and off we drove. Several miles into the country, I saw the fire. All the cars were stopped; we got out and the firemen yelled at us "Get back, get back!" A large store was burning and we were told it carried a large supply of firearms and bullets among its inventory. The possibility of an explosion forced us to retreat. Sadly I returned home. Our adventure sabotaged by responsible firemen.

My search for adventure was still very much in tact. The rains came the rain did not stop. I stood in front of the house and watched the downpour. A car pulled up. It was Mr. Rubel, my friend's father. "Helen, I'm going across the bridge to East Waco to pick up my files from the plant. Do you want to go with me?" Wow, did I! I jumped in the car without hesitation. I was about thirteen or fourteen. We drove to the bridge. A policeman stopped us and said, "No one can cross, the river is above flood stage and water is already on the bridge. It's too dangerous."

Mr. Rubel convinced the policeman how important his records were. The policeman shook his head and said, "O.K. Proceed at your own risk." My heart was pounding as we moved onto the bridge. The churning brown water of the Brazos River was lapping over the roadway. Mr. Rubel drove carefully and I looked across at the high water. I loved the sense of danger. He pulled into his plant, quickly retrieved his files and crossed the bridge again. When he dropped me off at home he said, "You are awfully brave, none of my kids would go with me." I was pretty proud of myself; my need for adventure had been satisfied for the moment.

STORE CLOTHES

I wanted store-bought clothes. My mother had always made my clothes. The sewing machine was moved from the house to the store every year. In summer, the big widow in the store was the coolest place to work. I had to stand still a lot. She would carefully pin here and there as she turned around. I always complained, "I don't like to stand still. I want clothes from the stores downtown." My wailing went unanswered.

Later, much later, I realized my clothes were lovingly made and also, we really didn't have enough money to shop downtown. In high school after taking a semester of typing, my uncle gave me a summer job in his shop for two days a week. I was to type his business letters and he paid me the royal amount of fifty cents a day. He was a hard taskmaster. He owned and operated a hat store. He made hats, cleaned hats and sold hats. There was a large wooden tumbler in the back of the shop in which the hats were cleaned. I liked the sound of the machine and the smell of chemicals. It smelled to me like gasoline. There was a sense of power in the air "Thump, thump—thump, thump."

Back at my typewriter, life wasn't much fun. If I made even one error on a letter, I had to type it over. No erasures were acceptable. The letters were short but sometimes I had to redo them three or four times. My uncle would look at me coolly and say "You must get it right; when you go to work fulltime, you will appreciate how well you have been trained." At the end of the summer, I had saved the grand sum of $12.00.

Now, I was ready to go downtown and buy store clothes. I

bought two wool skirts, one a deep rose color, the other navy blue plus two white blouses. At last I would be going to school looking like my fellow classmates and not in a silly dress. Ah, success—I had it that fall. I looked the same as the well-dressed students.

Sadly, I must add a footnote. My typing skills continued to be imperfect even to this day. No matter how I tried or try, I make mistakes, many typing errors. I think back to that teenager working in the hot summer desperate to have the money to buy store bought clothes. My uncle's discipline had the reverse effect on me. My whole philosophy has been to view life in a more casual manner. I have always given myself room for error, fashion wise and especially in typing.

WILD FLOWERS

Yellow wild flowers
Running down the hill
Chasing memories
Barren trees, soon
Burst out in green
Foliage.

Waiting for blossoms
To follow and
Perform the rite of
Spring and time
As it runs down
The hill with the

Yellow carpet
No footsteps mar the
Velvet gold that trails
On and on and on
Harried birds flit
Among the branches

Dust balls swept
Out of corners
They rise and rest
And rise and move
Beyond the trees
Yellow wild flowers
Running down the hill
Chasing memories.

SO I SAY

We feel our way along, with
A little chaser of reason on
The side when it suits us.

An independent thinker
Becomes dependent as
A drinker
So I say.

We are carbon copies
Of our folks
Smudged by years of
Lies and jokes
So I say

Does it matter what
I'm saying
No one listens
Some are praying
So I say.

I've accomplished very little
All in all
Life is a riddle
So I say.

TIME

Time is closing in. Every now and then I panic. I won't have enough time. I won't have enough time. My panic is enclosed within my house. I have almost two years of the New Yorker in a magazine rack. I haven't opened a one and for some unknown reason, I have renewed my subscription for another year. I have other magazines waiting to be read or thrown away. A box in the garage is stuffed with more of them pulsating to be released.

But, the saddest, the tragedy that overwhelms me is all the books on all the shelves. Surrounded by so many words, so many pages I'll never read. They are an accumulation of years in bookstores finding treasures, carefully examining their contents before bringing them home to live with me.

I look around and in every room books are looking at me. I, guiltily, look away. I brought you home when . . . ten years ago or maybe longer. Some are relative new comers . . . a year or two and now they sit untouched, dusty and waiting. Will I perhaps read a few of them? I don't know. All the ones neglected sit like unwanted children. I can't play favorites.

My reading is limited to current books from the library. No loyalty is expected from these transient books. Local newspaper delivered every morning . . . scanned and then deposited in recycle bin.

It's the members of my family that cause me so much anguish. I care about all of you . . . classics, poetry, novels, and reference books. Everything I want to know or want to read resides with me.

I alone am responsible and so I will husband them untouched but well loved.

Where will they go when I am gone . . . a garage sale perhaps; strangers glancing at my lovingly collected books. I can't bear to think about it. Every imagined touch by a strange hand gives me a twinge and I shudder.

I am afraid to look closely at all my worldly goods; furniture, linens, rugs, lamps, televisions, C.D.'s, tapes, clothes, so many clothes and hundreds of small mementos of my life . . . a harem ring from Istanbul; a necklace from Athens; a silver bracelet from Mexico; beads from Venice; shells from Hawaii; a Gucci bag from Florence; Navajo ring from Arizona . . . so many, many.

Why now, do all the material things gain such great importance? The pleasure of obtaining and selecting is past. The knowledge of time running out propels me to look around and inventory my life.

INSIGNIFICANT OTHER

Today, I drove downtown. The traffic was heavy as usual and every other street was under construction i.e. new sewer pipes, replacing bad portions of the roadway, fixing potholes. By the time, I drove into the garage I was feeling tense. Maneuvering the car carefully past the obstacles and avoiding other cars in their mad rush to reach the intersection first, was unnerving.

I parked easily in the garage, took an elevator to the street and moved out onto the sidewalks of the city. I looked into the coffee houses and saw faces drinking coffee, faces staring out the windows. Men and women were walking hurriedly, passing each other as if each were invisible. All of a sudden, I felt totally invisible.

It was an eerie feeling and I felt I was walking among stranger but I felt the strangest of all. My whole life has been spent knowing there was someone who truly loved me.

As a child, my mother and father were always there for me. I was always sure that no matter what happened, they would be there. As I got older, my parents were still there but I had added others who were aware of my existence and cared.

Marriage solidified my being. I had a partner, a mate and even at the worst moments, there was someone who knew I was very much alive. I really did not think about my existence until I became a widow.

When I am alone now and especially among strangers, I have a feeling that I just arrived from another planet. Though everything looks familiar, I am the one out of place. The term "significant other" has been used over the last years to define relationships. I can only define myself as completely insignificant. This is not to be construed as self-pity; it just a fact of life that I will have to face.

The other in my life knew me when I was younger, could share years and hours of memories. The other knew my weakness and my strength. The other could laugh with me and hold my hand in sorrow. I have become so insignificant that I am at times inconsolable. Neither happiness nor sadness is real. I still feel the warmth of the sun, the chill of a cold wind. I still love the sound and smell of the rain. I still love the sunsets and the blue sky. I still love to hear the birds' sing and the sweet smell of flowers. Maybe I am still significant; I hope I am.

REVERIE

Fingers pressed against
My lips
Pensive thoughts, eyes
Closed, no peeking
Into my wayward
Mind.
Sighing deep, pleasured
By my breath as
It draws in memories
Sweetened by time.

Silence touches my
Brow, brushing tenderly
Through years, long
Gone.
Many, many years
Sweetened by time.

SILENCE

I have been surrounded by noiseless sounds most of my life. Growing up in a family of limited talk, my own voice was the loudest and often the only one. Intermittently, I became involved in the noisy world of people, music and always my own voice. I then moved into a marriage where most of my days and nights were silent. I read and read; occasional phone calls. No one really knew me, I knew myself less.

Ejected back into the world of a working girl, nine to five; the clicking, clacking of typewriters; evening spent in bars, restaurants, parties where silence had no part. Again, reemerged into a quiet life but an easy one with a partner that had a voice to match my own. We merged our sounds and silence stayed at bay. Phones rang seldom, parties were few, and events were shuttered behind closed doors. I thrived with a minimum of sunlight, sound and gentle words of rain.

Death cut my world in half, in pieces; hacked on a butcher's table of bits and scraps. I tried to reassemble something, anything to reassure me I was still here. I started to write and in the course of thoughts on paper, I became something; yet in the silence around me I was reduced to nothing.

I am back or really forth into my silent world. The phone rings seldom, a reprieve from my isolated cell to which I return reluctantly at conversations end. Again and again, I try to break out; am still defeated at day's end, darkening skies summon another long day.

THE DAY
MY HAIR TURNED ORANGE

Somewhere in my middle twenties, I began noticing gray hairs among my brown tresses. Eventually more and more gray appeared and I began going to a beauty parlor to restore my hair to its original color.

Years went by and I visited the beauty parlor more often trying to regain the color, which was fast disappearing. Time took its toll and after only one week between tints, a white stripe began appearing in the middle of my head. I began to feel I looked more and more like a skunk whose natural beauty is the stripe—but not on top of my scalp.

I took the skunk by the tail so to speak and decided it was time to either become a platinum blond or find out exactly what had transpired all these years. The objective was to first remove all color with a so-called color remover that was purchased at Walgreen's. The instructions seemed simple enough and the process began. With the help of my mate, solution was applied and the operation commenced. As the "miracle" color remover began its task, strange things began to happen. Step by step, we followed the instructions faithfully. After the last rinse and drying, "Lo and behold" I looked in the mirror and I had the brightest orange hair on this planet. I could now qualify for a job in the circus.

Was I condemned to this orange hair for the rest of my life? I was not prepared to give up easily. I returned to Walgreen's with a knit cap pulled tightly over my orange curls, some peeking out. I did not look around. I was determined to change my freakish persona. This time I purchased a tint labeled "Ash Blond." I really had no idea how ash blond and orange would blend but desperation is the mother of invention. Again instructions were followed; again the application of this new color, again the rinsing and again the drying. I was no longer eligible for clown school.

Actually, I wasn't a bad looking blond. All in all, I decided to let time and nature do the rest. My hair began to grow and grow and underneath the blond, I found I was platinum silver. All those years of tinting, all those years of being a brunette and now I found myself in the world of silver haired ladies. No more beauty parlors except for necessary cutting. Now and then someone will say "You have a young face with your silver hair." This age thing happens to all of us and I truly believe getting older isn't a big problem. Remembering the day my hair turned orange still fills me with the dread that I would be eternally doomed and end up somewhere with someone calling out "Bring on the clown."

ENOUGH IS ENOUGH

I never really dreamed of acquiring anything. It isn't that I didn't want things . . . . they just didn't have a name.

I collected Indian Head pennies when I was very young. I don't know why they seemed valuable to me at that time. There were many of them in existence. They were in the top drawer of the dresser and I would look at them now and again.

When we left Texas, my father stayed behind and sold the property and the furniture. My Indian Head pennies disappeared, obviously, along with the rest of the things. I know he either sold or gave away all of my books. I didn't have a lot but I always thought he did it on purpose. He didn't want to move but I did. My mother chose to come with me. My father followed a few months later.

Each time I moved, something was left behind. When I left home to get married I knew anything of value would still be in my parents house. Other times, I remember an electric broiler I was particularly fond of (even thought it did a lousy job of broiling.) I still miss it.

When I got married and was asked to register for silver, china and crystal, I refused. I wanted things I could use all the time and the thought of registering for gifts seemed rather pretentious. I think I've always been a snob or I should say a snob—in—reverse. I detested going to dinner parties, playing Mah-Jongg, joining women's clubs or the neighborhood coffee klatches.

I did want nice things in my house: nice furniture, the right colors for the rugs and drapes plus all matching linens, towels and kitchen appliances. Yet, if I were asked what I could live without if necessary, I would have said everything.

This must be my innate bohemian nature; never attaching too much importance to material things. However, here I am surrounded by elegant pieces of mahogany, rosewood furniture which I love, drawers filled with linens, shelves filled with books, kitchen filled with every electrical appliance made so why do I keep saying that it really isn't all that important.

I think perhaps "I protest too much." Since I have lost so many people dear to me over the years, I refuse to get attached to all the inanimate objects surrounding me. I find myself going into the store and buying another item to add to my collections of things. I remember my mother's words "It is important to keep wanting, it is in our nature and we know we are alive; never stop wanting something new, it rejuvenates you." That are words I live by or should I say, "I buy by."

HEAR, HEAR

"Did you hear the birds that just landed on the roof?" "What birds, nobody can hear birds on the roof." "Come out on the deck, maybe we can see them fly away."

We went out on the deck and within a few minutes, several birds flew off from what was obviously the roof. He said, "You must have extraordinary hearing."

I had never thought about my ability to hear more than I really wanted. Over the years, when traveling and staying in motels along the highway, I would spend the night listening to traffic. The sound of the stereo in the apartment directly under mine kept me up all night. There were many incidents of noise that I found unbearable. I thought it was a common complaint and never bothered to think about it much.

Of course, one of my first apartments in San Francisco really gave me trouble. I heard a grinding noise most nights and finally went upstairs and asked the people what in the world was going on. I got my answer. They were dental students and practiced drilling teeth at night. Needless, to say I moved.

We moved from our apartment because the people next door were fighting or partying and I couldn't take it anymore. We bought a house. Most houses in San Francisco are wall to wall; up close and personal. The first neighbors were gone most of the time but they moved. The new neighbors; well, that is another story . . . he snored, oh did he snore. We couldn't keep moving, so we hired a contractor. He removed a wall in our bedroom, installed heavy sheets of fiberglass between the studs on the wall, then two sound boards, then sheet rock covered in wallpaper. The snoring continued but at least it was muffled.

Travel has been a delight and a nightmare. You just never know how thick the walls are in a hotel. Some were better than others. Even on cruise ships, I didn't escape from the intrusion of noise. One cabin which I requested to be moved from because of the noise from the ship's engine, to be replaced by a cabin on the highest deck. Sounds good, hah, the shuffleboard was above my head and a few idiots liked playing at 2:00 AM in the morning.

I got a new TV a few years ago with stereo sound. The sound is so stereotypical, I called the Sony people to come and check. Maybe it needed an adjustment. They sent a man who said, "It sounds fine to me." "Oh, don't you think there's an unusual hollow sound." He said, "No, I don't think so, but I have very bad hearing."

I have tried to make my peace with all the extracurricular sounds I hear. Other people have told me "You must be wired different." I have tried to come to terms with my sensitive ears. However, I have found one place I simply refuse to enter . . . the movie theater. Apparently, most people are hard of hearing and this includes all ages. The sound track is so loud at the movies, I have put cotton balls in my ear, bits of Kleenex but now I just avoid going to movies. I can wait until they come out on video and adjust the sound for "my ears only." I love movies and in my life, I was an avid moviegoer.

I actually like sound, the sound of birds singing in the trees in my backyard, music played on my CD player, the wind blowing in big gusts and shaking my windows, loud thunder crashing against the sky and a heavy downpour on my roof.

Noise is my friend and my enemy. If it were true that I am wired differently, I would have wished they had put a bit more insulation. Could we please have a moment of silence? Thank you.

TRAVELS WITH MY MOTHER

Uncle Willie came by every Sunday in his big tan and brown
Nash. I would run madly out of the house and jump into the car.

"Uncle Willie, let me drive, please let me drive."

My first love was the car and the feel of the road as the wind
rushed past the windows. Not always, but often he would put me
in his lap, my hands on the steering wheel and off we drove
sometimes to Cameron Park and sometimes, way, way out to Lake
Waco.

I must have been at least four years old and was still sucking
my thumb. My mother had tried every method imaginable to
discourage my obsession so I would hide behind doors, guiltily
sucking my thumb.

One Sunday, Uncle Willie honked his horn and I ran out
quickly as usual. In my haste to get into the car, I slammed the car
door on my thumb. I spent a week or so looking longingly at my
swollen black and blue thumb. By the time it healed, I had
forgotten all about it.

I got sick, really sick when I was seven. I had spent the day at
Uncle Willie's and when I got home I had a very bad bellyache.

My parents gave me an enema but I got sicker and sicker. My
mother called Uncle Willie. He drove over and took us to Providence
Hospital. The doctor operated on me and my appendix burst right
there on the operating table. I was sick for a very long time. My
mother stayed with me in the hospital and slept in the big chair in
my room. When I got home, I had to learn to walk all over again.

When I was eleven, my mother took me to the doctor's office

downtown. This was the day he removed my tonsils. She had promised me a whole lot of ice cream when we came home. The doctor gave me ether and when I regained consciousness, we took the streetcar back to our house. I remember my throat was very sore and I was sick at my stomach. I couldn't even swallow the ice cream. As we came in the front door, there sitting on the table was a radio, our first radio. It was the most wonderful present I had ever received. So, who cared about ice cream? My days and the following years were filled with wonderful stories.

My mother and I traveled to San Francisco during the early years of WWII. The train was crowded and we could not even sit together. We sat at different places on the car and met for our meals. Our trip from Texas to California took three days two nights. My seatmate was a fellow Texan with a big guitar. He introduced himself "My name is Ernie Tubbs and I'm going out to Hollywood and become famous." He sang and played his guitar during the day. The whole car was delighted with his songs and time passed easily. The problem was the nights. As the sky darkened and the other passengers were adjusting their seats in a reclining position, I did the same. As I began to doze off, I felt a hand reach around my back and another hand on my leg. I quickly got up and went to the end of the car where my mother was already asleep.

"Mom, the fellow next to me is getting fresh, what can I do?"

"Don't worry." said my mother "We'll change seats at night. I don't think he'll get fresh with me."

And so it went, during the day I sat next to my Lothario and at night my mother became his nemesis. Later, I read about him. He had moved to Nashville and had become a big country and western star.

Years had past, I had moved to Texas, moved back to California and my father had died. My mother was still very viable but I was hesitant to take her touring with my husband and me. She was in her 80's but when we said we were taking a trip to Arizona, she had looked so crestfallen on being left out; we made additional travel arrangements so she could join us.

The first overnight at a motel, we went out for dinner and then to bed. It was our custom to take along instant coffee, some sweet rolls, oranges or other fruit and eat our breakfast in the room before starting a new day on the road. My mother came down to our room and saw our makeshift breakfast. Looking disdainfully at the buffet, she said haughtily "I don't eat like pigs." We said, "We always stop for a real breakfast later on." She sniffed and said nothing. I could not understand how my quiet, shy mother had become so arrogant. Obviously, to her travel meant luxury and we certainly weren't in her league.

At the lunch stop later, we entered a very ordinary coffee shop. She said, "I don't think there is anything I can eat here." My husband said, "You like fried chicken, order it." When the chicken came, she picked at it indifferently. He took a piece, tasted it and said, "This tastes good, eat it!" She looked up amazed but did proceed to eat and finish it.

When we arrived in Phoenix, the accommodations were fine. My mother now kept her negative remarks to herself, but we could hear her muttering to herself about the heat. We continued on to 'Tucson and moved into a cottage. The heat was unbearable and we realized this trip was a disaster. We hurriedly packed, drove to San Diego, saw the zoo and came home.

We were thinking of moving to Palm Springs. My husband had very bad arthritis and we thought perhaps living in a dry climate would alleviate his pain. We had been there for a few short visits and decided to rent a condominium for a month and really try it out. We wouldn't and couldn't leave my mother for such a long extended stay. She seemed enthusiastic about the trip. We took a leisurely drive and arrived in Palm Springs. The condominium was beautiful—three bedrooms, two baths, large living room and dining room; a wonderful kitchen—an atrium, a patio and back deck. The condominium was situated on a large golf course on the Palm Desert Country Club. Around the golf course tall palm trees, newly planted were swaying in the breeze.

We began house hunting and exploring all the surrounding

area. My mother decided she didn't want to leave the condominium; she said it was too hot outside and she preferred the air-conditioned interior. I told her about our plans and urged her to join me one night while I showed her some of the houses. Afterwards, just the two of us had dinner out. She was strangely quiet.

When we returned home, she went into her room. We heard her voice. My husband said, "Who is she talking to?" I went closer to her door and listened. She said, obviously talking to herself in a very stern voice "If those dam people think I'm going to move down here with all of those crooked trees, they are crazy."

I went back and told my husband of her anger. He said, "O.K. that's enough, we've been here two weeks and I want to enjoy the rest of the time. I'm taking her back to San Francisco tomorrow. I am making reservations on the Greyhound Bus. Go tell your mother, she is going home."

I went in and said "Mom, I know you don't like it here so you are going back to San Francisco tomorrow with Mel." She said, "Are you throwing me out?" I said, "No, but you don't want to live here, so we'll just spend the rest of the time by ourselves."

She seemed pleased and eagerly got on the bus next morning with my husband. He told me the bus ride was miserable for him. His back hurt most of the way. My mother however seemed to enjoy every moment. She sat by the window looking out like a child. Arriving in San Francisco, her first request was "Let's stop by the grocery store, I need to cook dinner." They stopped and he said he lugged bags of groceries to her house. She immediately began preparing a meal.

He returned to our house and flew back to Palm Springs the next day. He said, "Your mother must be made out of steel. I'm a wreck. I really need a vacation now.

Our last trip together, we were on separate planes. One plane was carrying my mother's coffin back to Texas to be placed beside my father and brother in the family plot. My husband and I were on the other plane preparing to join her at the cemetery for her last journey.

We arrived late Sunday evening; the funeral was scheduled the next day. The local newspaper called our room at the hotel asking me if I would like to place my mother's obituary in the Monday morning's paper. I agreed and gave them a brief outline as requested.

The next morning while having breakfast, I opened the paper and saw my mother's name in bold black letters. Reality took me completely off guard. As I sat there, my cup of coffee before me, the tears ran down my face as if my heart had sprung a leak.

I hastily went back to my room to prepare for the final trip. We drove out to the cemetery. I heard the Rabbi's words so eloquently spoken as if he had known her for many years. I saw the beautiful polished coffin with the large carved Star of David being lowered into the ground. I remembered my mother's words when we talked about death many years before. She had said, 'When I die, plant me in the ground. I want to be part of the earth and grow with the flowers and the grass." As the words were spoken over her grave, a gentle breeze caressed my face. I felt my mother's hand touch my hair, brush against my arms.

We stayed a few more days to pick out a stone. I visited the cemetery several times during those last days. Each time, the breeze followed me as I walked about. I didn't want to leave. This was our last trip together.

When we returned to San Francisco, a deep sadness enveloped me—not only because my mother had died but also now I no longer had her to share our memories, our travels and mostly the laughter.

A LITTLE MORE PRACTICE

My leg was aching. Actually, it was above my ankle on my right leg. It didn't seem to respond to the heating pad and a few of the odd and sundry pills I have in the house.

Finally, I made an appointment and went to see my internist. He gently prodded the sore area and said "Its tendonitis. All you need to do is keep taking the pills and place a cold pack on the area. It will clear up in a week or two." Weeks passed, no results—only more pain.

It was suggested that I go to a podiatrist. After all, their specialty is feet. I went. He said, "No big deal, we'll give you a shot in the sore area and some ultra sound and you will be good as new in no time". Also, I must mention, he made a couple of inserts for my shoes. A little extra padding when walking would alleviate the pressure on my leg. This treatment took the better part of two months. Two shots, several ultra sounds and four pads for my shoes. I thought I would wait a bit and see if positive results would ensue. No such luck.

In the meantime, I forgot to mention, my upper right thigh and right side of my buttocks were very sore. I was sure my car seat was putting pressure on this part of my body. I took the car to an upholsterer. He added more foam to the seat. For a few minutes, I thought it felt better but by the time I got home, I knew this was not going to work. I took the car back a few days later. Some of the foam was removed and sheepskin covers were installed. Again, I felt better for a few minutes—but again, I took the car back and had the sheepskin covers removed. They talked about making a pillow for the seat. I tried a few pieces of different size foam and nothing was going to make my body quit hurting.

It was time to go to an orthopedist. Made an appointment with a very busy doctor. He greeted me and looked at my file. He said "You had an MRI a few years ago and it looks like you have a bad disc in the thoracic area. You should go to a neurosurgeon. I don't work with discs." And so, he sent me to a neurosurgeon.

The nice young man greeted me with these words after hearing my complaint. "Well, it could be old age." Just the thing I had been waiting to hear." "However" he said after a cursory examination "You should have another MRI." I wasn't convinced I was moving in the right direction, but after all I'm not a doctor. I had the MRI. The next visit; he came in and began examining the pictures—there must be hundreds or so it seemed.

He said, "You don't need surgery." Did he really think that this is what I want? He continued, "I really don't know what is causing your pain, perhaps you should go to a neurologist.

I delayed making an appointment for a week or so. It seemed nothing was wrong with me, I just had a pain in my leg and it was hard to walk sometimes. I made the appointment.

I saw the neurologist. He did some kind of electrical test on my legs. Little pinpricks and a machine showing little symbols or something like that. When he finished, he said, "You have peripheral neuropathy. There is really not much I can do for you." I said, "What can I do about the pain?" He said, "Do you have any pain pills?" "Yes, but is that the answer?" He said, "The neuropathy is very mild and it is in both legs, so I am puzzled." He's puzzled, what about me. I made an appointment for two weeks in the distant future.

In the meantime, I needed to see my internist. He wasn't available but his nurse practitioner was on call. I didn't think I had a serious problem, so I went to see her. Outside of my original reason to visit her, I mentioned that a doctor told me I had peripheral neuropathy. She said, "The best thing for neuropathy is to take colloidal minerals. It contains trace minerals. You buy it over the counter at the health food store." At last, I had a solution. I went to the health food store, bought a bottle of colloidal minerals, which set me back over $20.00 and began taking them religiously. When the bottle was empty, my leg still hurt. So much for trace minerals.

Maybe, if I got a car with a bigger seat, the pain will go away. I drove out and sat in a Lexus. The seat looked good but my leg still hurt. I looked at a Mercedes; surely a luxury car would feel good. It was nice enough but the seat was still uncomfortable to my aching leg.

I drove over to the Toyota dealership and talked to the manager. I bought my car there and they have been very friendly. I would sit in a new Toyota. The manager said, "Sit where you like but your leg will still hurt." "Why, do you think there is no solution to my problem?" Well, he said, "You have sciatica." "I do, do you really think that is my problem. I've been to a lot of doctors." He said "Take it from me, you have sciatica. I have it now and then and the symptoms are the same."

After two weeks, I returned to the neurologist. I said "My leg still hurts." He said, "I don't think you have peripheral neuropathy, but I think you should have some physical therapy."

I went to the physical therapist. He talked about my ankle and I said "My thigh and the rest of my leg hurts." He said, "Did you tell your doctor that your whole leg hurts not just your ankle?" I said, "I talked about my car seat being uncomfortable, but I guess I didn't really stress all the places I have pain."

When I got home, everything that hurt before was magnified and hurt more. I called the neurologist and he told me to come in. This time I told him that I not only hurt around the ankle, I hurt along the thigh, I hurt in my right buttocks and I am miserable. He said, "I think you have sciatica."

At last a diagnosis. I should have gone and talked to the man at Toyota first. It would have saved me a lot of time.

Now, I went back to the physical therapist and was assured with an added exercise plan, I will feel a lot better. I still don't know the outcome but the better part of nine months has been spent going to doctors and taking tests. I haven't learned a lot except I wish these doctors were beyond the practicing stage. Or better yet, please don't practice on me.

MR. HAPPY, MR. HAPPY

Things happen, good things and bad things. One of the bad things, that isn't all that bad, is having sophisticated medical procedures.

I, for reasons only a doctor knows, was told to have an MRI. This process takes place in a long cylindrical tube. You are placed on a narrow bed or board and rolled into this strange device. The initials stand for Magnetic Resolution Imaging. How's that for a space age machine. I was asked if I was claustrophobic which I am not. I've been through this before and at that time I was asked if I wanted a blindfold. This time, I wasn't asked and I didn't request one. I thought, at least, I could look around and see where I am.

I was slud in (please don't tell me slud is not a word). I know this but I like to use wrong words to bolster my ever-fading courage and humor is my ally.

After I had been slud in—the games began. There is no pain, only the discomfort of lying still for thirty or forty minutes which for me is extremely difficult. The machine started. I heard a noise, or maybe it was just my imagination but I heard the words "MR. HAPPY, MR. HAPPY, MR. HAPPY". How nice, I would be hearing these pleasant words; but then it changed to "BLAH, BLAH, BLAH". O.K. That's not too bad either. Eventually, it became a quartet—"MR. HAPPY, MR. HAPPY, BLAH, BLAH, BLAH" accompanied by "BOOLAH, BOOLAH, KNOCK, KNOCK, KNOCK". My mind was singing along with the sounds. Perhaps, this was a tribal dance in Africa and the natives were singing "MR. HAPPY, MR. HAPPY, BLAH, BLAH, BLAH, BOOLAH, BOOLAH, KNOCK, KNOCK, KNOCK".

As I was slud out, back into the great outdoors—oh, did I mention this expensive piece of machinery was housed in a mobile van on the grounds of the hospital. I walked from the hospital in my hospital gown, down a path, up the stairs where I entered the ROOM. A very nice technician, who seemed a little bored by his job, which he monitors probably six or seven times a day. Then, back down the stairs still exquisitely clothed in a hospital gown to redress myself inside.

I had no idea what the results of this test would show but if one positive thing would come out of all this, I have a new song to sing when things become stressful "MR. HAPPY, MR. HAPPY, BLAH, BLAH, BLAH, BOOLAH, BOOLAH, KNOCK, KNOCK, KNOCK".

P.S. I went to see the great neurosurgeon today and got the results. He said, "I see nothing wrong on the pictures, perhaps you should see a neurologist". I asked, "Why does my foot hurt so much?" He said, "I don't know".

MR. HAPPY, MR. HAPPY, BLAH, BLAH, BLAH, BOOLAH, BOOLAH, KNOCK, KNOCK, KNOCK

AGAIN

The dying is starting
Again
I was only four or five
Swinging from shiny brass bar over
Empty grave
Six feet deep or was it more
I swing, playing
My mother grabbed me
Held my hand, no joyous ride
Across the emptiness
Someone died, funeral
I saw play in
Everything.

Then it happened again,
My brother barely fourteen
Frothing at the
Mouth as I looked
Across the hall into
The hospital room
He died, was he buried, was
I there, I don't know
A stone in the cemetery
Carries his name
"Beloved Son"
No longer play, no

Longer anything
My brother
Was he dead?
Yes, he was dead
I was alone, an orphaned sister

My dog, Boy, hit by a car
He died. My cats just disappeared
Years passed
My father made his final
Trip
I was there I sat nearby
Another black hole
Gathered around friends, his
Wife, his daughter
He disappeared
Like my cats.

My mom, my mother
Held on to life, and
Slipped away quietly
As she lived
So small, so fragile
Again, I feel the breeze
Blowing past me, my mother's
Breath, breathing
In the graveyard
My brother, my father, my
Mother
Together, they disappeared.

Time is closing in
A husband, don't go
I'll be alone
I am desolate with grief

Who is left to gather?
At my grave or visit once
I too will disappear
The dying is starting again
People I know are disappearing
I look out the window
My world is there
Will it disappear?

THE BIG ONE

"Come over here, hurry" I called out. The house was shaking violently. "It's an earthquake, come stand in the arch of the door" I said again. I felt frozen with fear. Would our house go toppling down the hill? Would all our big glass windows shatter or in a worse case scenario come tumbling through the room and cover us with shards of glass.

I looked over at my husband sitting in the living room, his attention focused on the television screen. "It's nothing, the game is starting." At that instance the power went off, the screen became a blank. He got up from the chair, looked around, and only then became aware of the rocking motion.

I stood in the hall, braced against the wall. The only warning that goes through my mind when an earthquake occurs are the words "Stand in the arch of a door. It's the safest place." Over the years, off and on during earthquakes, small and large, I immediately scurry to a doorway.

My husband was always very sanguine about earthquakes. He had told me about a big one in Los Angeles when he was a boy. He had been tossed on the floor from his bed. After dusting himself off, he returned to self same bed and back to sleep. Many the times, I would wake to hear the handles on my dresser clinking and clanking. Immediately, I would start to rise up out of bed and my husband's hand would stop me "Don't go into the hall, stay in bed. No big deal. Go back to sleep."

As he joined me in the hall, he said, "This is a big one." I looked over at my cabinets in the kitchen. The doors swung open; a few glasses fell to the floor. Thousands of houses being jostled about roared through the house like a herd of buffaloes stampeding across the plains. My husband's face-hardened and he called out in a stentorian voice "Stop it, I say stop it!". Immediately, the shaking subsided. I signed with relief. He said, "Damn, no power, no game tonight."

Why not eat all the ice-cream in the freezer for dinner. We sat and literally pigged out like a couple of kids. As night fell, I put several candles on the table and lit them. What seemed to be a romantic evening was only a temporary reprieve from the terror I had felt only a few hours before.

As the skies darkened, I looked out our windows. We live on a hill facing east and the red glow in the distance looked surreal. Could my beautiful San Francisco be going up in smoke? I sat up late into the night mesmerized by the crimson glow.

The next day, I looked around my house. Outside of a picture that had fallen over and a few broken glasses, everything seemed intact. I was listening to the radio and heard the news. The Bay Bridge had collapsed; eventually I learned that it was only a small section but tragedy had certainly been felt all over the Bay area.

There were suggestions of retrofitting your home. For instance, was your house bolted down? I walked down the stairs and looked into my sub-basement. Holding my flashlight carefully, I stepped inside and examined the base of my house. Sure enough, I found the bolts. I was becoming earthquake country savvy.

As I saw the television reports on the damaged and destroyed buildings throughout the city, I felt very lucky. Still I knew and still know I could be one of the unfortunate ones. I hope, oh how I hope, I'll never see or experience another big one.

SOMETIMES

Sometimes, I wish they wouldn't bother me. I sit down to read a book or watch television and they won't leave me alone. All those words scratching at the window of my mind. I close my eyes and try to pull the shade down. It does no good.

I can hear their relentless movements. I finally give up and let them in. They are so disorderly; all the nouns bunch together, the verbs are scattered about; adjectives and adverbs push each other from side to side and I want to scream out "Stop! If you want me to do something with all of you, give you a place in my stories, you must wait your turn".

Where do memories go? I have a large volume of stories about where I lived, how I lived, with whom I lived, whom I've met and what I did and didn't do. If memories could be incorporated into an art form, what a wonderful colorful tapestry it would be! Sometimes the word "memory" sounds trivial, its use so casually mouthed. When I start remembering, I am amazed at the experiences and the people involved in my life. They all have been incorporated into my life's resume.

THE YEAR I BECAME FERAL

All my life up to a year in the late '50's were spent in protective custody. My parents were lenient wardens but nonetheless there were rules to be followed, time limits were set. I merrily rolled along through my early years, pulling at my leash now and again. As my mother told me years later "You have to give your children a long rope" and she did.

I left my parents home to venture into marriage. This was not only acceptable behavior but also mandatory. My new jailer, and I use the term loosely, was benevolent. In fact, he was so removed from reality; the doors of my marriage were never locked or guarded. Actually, I tried to reverse the roles and attempted to hold the reins, hoping to guide us both in the same direction. I succeeded in part but eventually lost the battle. Reluctantly, I left and moved out on my own.

The terror, the sheer terror of being in charge of my own life; no one to turn to; it was now my responsibility to be what I was. Eventually, the fear began to lessen. I gave myself breathing room and looked around. What I saw was good. Freedom of a sort I had never known left me heady and confused. Slowly I began changing, becoming feral. I liked the feeling. I was daring to go where, when with whomever I pleased.

There were many new people moving through my life. Bea became my first new female friend. She tried to mother me and suggested clothing and accessories. I didn't need a mother but I needed a friend; then Louise moved in with me for a few days when her husband threw her out. I was part of a world in turmoil, but my hands were at the helm.

Art, the wannabe actor from New York, who begged me to marry him; Morris, the left wing lawyer, who suggested weekends in Acapulco; even my lawyer, Lou who thought I should have a bigger and better apartment (of course, at his expense). I settled down with one loyal friend, but my taste buds for freedom tired of the sameness. Two men who followed my car and got my telephone number from my license plate began calling me morning and night. I never went out with them or even saw them. They knew what I was wearing each day and who I was going out with. It was frightening, yet exhilarating. The feral creature I had become was leaving her scent.

Eventually, I moved away much further. I needed to broaden my horizons and explore my new world. And, that world was waiting for me. Jim in advertising, his friends in Sausalito living the rustic life surrounded by dogs, wooden benches for chairs and strange music from their stereo.

Dante, who spoke in tongues, actually spoke several languages; handsome, egotistical with very little to say unless it was about him.

There was the redheaded Italian travel agent who would take me around the world on a honeymoon. No, no honeymoon. I liked the world I had created.

Jack worked for a steamship company, very honorable intentions. Not bad for brief periods but much too methodical for my newfound independence.

Charlie, owner of an art gallery, lived on Nob Hill. No one said "No" to Charlie but I did. No saddle on my back. I was riding bareback and the wind felt good in my face.

Settled down for a while in North Beach. The fringe beatnik role I assumed seemed to fit nicely. Everybody was untamed and we reveled in our ability to thumb our nose at the rest of society. We all hurried out in the evening when the tour bus came up Grant Avenue, standing solemnly a row of black-garbed ravens of the night waving unsmiling at the tourists. The joy of non-conformity became joyless. The endless parties, the masquerading

as characters in some clever play, which would never be produced
left me feeling stultified. I needed fresh air and cut the cord, quickly
moving into new territory.

What happened to the feral me? I met the master magician
who put a spell on me and lured me into his life. I was never
bored, sometimes restless but mostly intrigued by his intellect
and temperament. I returned to my origins. My feral years were
over I look back in amazement and think, "Wasn't it a blast?"

THE MAN
WHO LOST HIS BALLS

Returning to San Francisco after having spent the previous ten years in Texas, I came home again. I volunteered at a community center and my social life shifted into first gear. One of my first dates seemed suave and worldly. He was a writer, or so he said, and was planning a trip to Africa. He wanted me to learn photography and accompany him in his research. Of course, he asked me to marry him. No gentleman would have acted otherwise. This all seemed a little far-fetched to me, but what the hell, I looked forward to a little excitement. He showed me snapshots of some very pretty women. He said he was subsidizing these aspiring actresses in Hollywood. I heard other tales of his philanthropy.

I must say my mother was impressed. I was staying with her until I had accumulated enough funds to be once again self-sufficient. On our first date, he presented her with a delicious chocolate cake from Blum's, the best deserts in the city. He took me to the best restaurants, literally the term "wined me and dined me" fit the bill.

One evening at the movies, I heard a clicking sound. It persisted. Finally, I asked, "Do you hear that noise?" "Oh", he said "I often carry two small steel balls with me. I find that rolling them in my hands give me greater concentration". I was immediately reminded of the movie "The Caine Mutiny". Humphrey Bogart played the role of Captain Queeg, a sociopath, who constantly carried two small metal balls in his hands, also rolling them for whatever reason maybe he need to concentrate too.

The movie ended and as we got up to leave, he exclaimed, "I dropped my balls! They must have rolled under the seat". Luckily, it was the last show. The theater lights were turned on and my escort frantically searched for his balls. The ushers were brought into the hunt. Up and down the aisles—up and down the rows of seats—no balls. The balls were lost. I was with a man completely devastated and I had to refrain from laughing. Maybe he wasn't "Captain Queeg" but I felt he had lost his marbles along with his balls.

Our last date, he told me he was flying his plane to Los Angeles. Not one to let an opportunity pass to find out the truth, I said, "I'll go with you". I had yet to see his plane. He said, "You have to work, don't you?" "No problem", I said, "I'll take off a few days". He said, "I'll call you".

I never heard from him again. Life is a lot like a casino—lots of games are offered for one's amusement. This time I really got the booby prize. I wonder if he replaced his missing balls.

STOP THE WORLD

Having spent many years in Houston and after a very civil divorce, I was leaving Texas. Looking back, I don't know how good or bad it was; I know there was some good and the bad was left behind. Time had placed me here and now I was going to be there, wherever there turned out to be. I only knew it was time to move on and as I looked out the window the landscape was flat and unsympathetic. Driving from one state to another, I had no plans and only tomorrow was my future. I had no tears, no regrets.

My newfound freedom left me heady, confused, excited but the best thing of all—here I was in San Francisco, a city that held the promise of a new life. When I arrived in San Francisco in the late '50's, I entered my new life. I got a job an ordinary job, in an ordinary office and spent time with a lot of ordinary people. Like my fellow workers, I ventured out on Fridays after work to participate in the bar scene. Up and down the streets of the financial district, bars were filled to overflowing with men and women consuming volumes of liquor and eating the tidbits put out on the bar. In the spring of 1957, Maiden Lane was my destination. The Iron Horse, a wonderful bar/restaurant dimly lit, seductively warm and everyone hoping to me "the one". A man with dark hair and shining brown eyes stepped out from the shadows and so it began, it began . . . . my sojourn into the world of North Beach and as a member of the Beat Generation. Len showed me San Francisco, the real San Francisco. At last I felt I had come home. I had a sense of belonging that I had never felt before anywhere or with anyone.

He moved into my life, like a gleaming black panther, sleek, mysterious with a hint of danger. His laughing eyes watched me in approval. His voice on the phone would start my heart pounding like a schoolgirl. Every day, he picked me up at work and drew me into his world, a world of art, beauty and adventure. He knew every curve in the city and drove to little known spots high on a hill where we drank ale, had our dinner out of a brown paper bag and watched magnificent sunsets. We parked on Powell Street and people watched, silently observing our fellow man. We spent hours in museums where he introduced me to his favorite artists as he talked of the light and shadows of the pictures. Evenings were spent at poetry readings, bookstores, and little Italian restaurants in North Beach where we talked and talked.

He took me to his apartment on Russian Hill. It was like entering a surreal world. The walls were black; the ceiling was painted black crisscrossed with white twine. Looking up gave me great pleasure and delight. I was in a giant spider web with no spider in sight. Thick white throw rugs were scattered about the black stained floor; two crimson couches against each wall and the sound of soft jazz coming from the speakers perched here and there about the room. There was certainly nothing ordinary about the room or the man. He was a cartoonist with an emerging greeting card line.

Everyday I entered the world of offices and machines but every night I returned to my spiritual home. North Beach beckoned and I answered its call. My jobs varied but not my nightlife. I entered his world and wallowed in it; submerged myself in it; I couldn't wait for the evenings.

We ate and drank our way up and down Grant Avenue. We spent evenings browsing at City Lights, a unique bookstore where you could walk down the stairs, sit among the books and read without interruption. We spent time in different homes with all sorts of people thinking up clever words for his greeting cards. Sitting on worn couches laughing and creating phrases; sometimes coming up with a great line. There were so many people, sensitive, intelligent and outrageous people.

Len opened a store on upper Grant Avenue, a store with no name. A manufacturer's rep became interested in Len's artwork and said why don't we use your cartoon characters on cups, ashtrays and other ceramics. Soon we had crates of small objects with the same character . . . . a funny blob of a man and underneath the words "Stop the World, I Want off". The front half of the store was stocked with tourist items but the back was an art gallery. Local artists displayed their paintings plus a few landscapes from France, which Len and his buddies stretched and framed. New art showing up continually. A small makeshift bar in the gallery was poorly stocked but always enough for hot toddies around midnight with a few friends.

Len decided to be innovative. He bought fiberboard and took it down into the basement. You had to descend carefully down a ladder into a dark, damp empty cavern where the toilet was located. He assembled several cans of paint, stood on a chair, calmly poured different colors on the boards with a twist of his wrist . . . . here and there . . . a large glob and a sprinkle. Eventually, the whole board was covered. He stepped down from the chair and waited for the paint to dry. With a small saw, he cut the board into small squares; rectangles and soon we were surrounded by dozens of abstract paintings. He printed my name carefully on each of them. He said he didn't want any of this stuff to come back and haunt him. He hung them in the gallery and they sold, literally like hot cakes. The going price for these masterpieces was anywhere from $25 to $50 depending on the size.

When business was slow and even sometimes when it wasn't, he would become bored and say, "Let's have a party". He closed the door, made a few phone calls. Within an hour, people began coming in . . . . men and women flooding the store. Everyone was welcome and soon the rooms were so crowded it was impossible to move. The men supplied the liquor; the music was loud and everybody was talking. I always sat on the counter up front and held court. After all I was with the King of North Beach. The policeman on the street would knock on the door and say, "Have a good time, just keep the noise down".

I would often wander down to the Black Cat, a rowdy, noisy bar with two of the local artists. It was really a place for serious drinking. Walt, a small man with a benign expression was a great artist but also a great drinker. He gave me one of his paintings. He said it was the face of God and I wasn't about to argue. Having no money for canvas, it looks like it was painted on heavy wrapping paper and maybe it was. Tom was very tall and very angry; even his blond unruly hair bristled. He always wore white overalls covered with paint. He worked part time in a silkscreen company but his love was beautiful abstract art in panels which when hung were a melody of colors. Both were always in need of money. Walt sold his paintings for food, drink or whatever his needs were at the moment, but he never signed his real name. Tom painted huge clown pictures, which he hated. They are still on the walls of a lot of restaurants throughout the city.

We would often stop at Leon's on Fillmore to buy barbeque ribs. Once he picked up some small sweet potato pies. I remember, I got mad at him in the car and threw a pie in his face . . . . he ducked and the pie flew out the window. We beatniks had no inhibitions; we acted out our hostility, our love, our ambitions (which were never taken very seriously). This was an era for action and reaction, all natural, fluid, ever changing.

Grant Avenue was alive especially in the evening when all of us felt a special bonhomie with each other. Ate most of our meals within the area; New Pisa was my favorite and enjoyed a meal for $1.25 . . . . soup, entrée and all the dago red you could drink. We might go down to the Matador on Broadway for drinks later or to Vesuvio's on Columbus Avenue to hear jazz and poetry readings. It was a favorite hangout for Jack Kerouac and other Beat poets. Drinking cappuccinos at Tosca's and listening to arias from operas playing on the jukebox; sometimes hearing customers sing along with the music. I discovered a wonderful drink at the Gold Spike, Amer/Picon with a brandy float. The Purple Onion, a nightclub with brick walls in the area once called The International Settlement, and the jazz clubs, so many, so mellow.

Once a week we would go to Blabbermouth Night at the Old Bagel Factory. Anyone could go up on the small balcony and perform . . . sing, story telling, poetry readings, maybe a chapter from their ongoing book. Whoever received the most applause at the end of the evening was rewarded with a bottle of champagne. The Greyhound Bus brought tours through North Beach, up Grant Avenue several times each evening. When we heard the bus, we all rushed outside to wave at the tourists. Most of us wore the accepted costume of the day—black sweaters and pants. There we were a group of grim faces waving solemnly at these unknowing people. We knew the secret of life. Sometimes we would drive out to Land's End and watch the sunset. Sundays was a brunch at the Buena Vista at the foot of Hyde Street; always a Ramos Fizz.

Reality began creeping into my life; I felt it was time to leave the party. Toward the end of 1959, we seemed to have become ordinary people and began having ordinary disagreements. We had talked of getting married in December. The magic was fading and I told him that the next time he saw me I would be married but not to him. I was angry, not really knowing why. He sent me cards and called but I was adamant; the exhilaration of the past years had become tiresome. I refused to talk to him on the phone. I was still mad.

Two weeks later I met another man at a dance and a week later I was married. I have called Len, my "springtime" but I left him and married a man "for all seasons". I will always love North Beach. Many years ago it gave me a new life, a sense of wonderment, which I had never known. *Don't stop the world yet; I'm not ready to get off.*

THREE GOOD SENSES

Glowering skies
Fog draped hills
Unruly clouds
Silently move
Stalking each other

Crashing against
Infinity.
Wide horizons
Expanding
Stretching, inhaling
Resting gracefully.

Drone of traffic
Ambulance weaving, twisting
Screeching, siren
At top of
Game

Halt, slamming doors
Voices, voices
Plaintive calls as
Disturbed sleep
Prays for quiet
Hush hush.

Poignant fragrance
Sweet rain puddle
Moist earth, mud
Pies never thrown

Bees sing, darting
Tasting pollen on
Painters' palette of
Early petals
Yawn and face
The sky
Dreaming of tomorrow

LITTLE BROWN MEN

WHOOSH! I heard the loud noise. I jumped up out of my chair and looked out the window. Down at the end of the street, I saw that a van had careened against the fire hydrant. The driver was struggling to escape from his watery grave. He backed the car and accelerated, his foot obviously jammed on the floor of the van. The car bounded hilariously about, in what I thought was a laughing manner, as if it was saying "Wow, this sure is fun!" Finally released, the dirty white van skidded across to the other corner.

Free at last, free at last. The doors of the car opened and out hurdled a group of little brown men. As I watched, they seemed confused moving about haphazardly. By this time, a group of neighbors had begun arriving to evaluate the damage. The fire hydrant was spewing water, yellow water, to a height of ten feet. It was a lovely amber fountain. I heard the fire engines in the distance and more people began to gather. I rarely see so many people in my neighborhood.

The men began dispersing, scattering and running away from the scene. Police cars began arriving and some of the people approached the cars, talking to the police, gesticulating wildly, pointing down the street. Several of the police cars took off in what I would describe "not hot" pursuit." If they were to catch up with the men who left on foot, it would be fairly easy to pursue them with their cars.

It did seem to take a fair amount of time for the firemen to control the gushing water. The gathering crowd seemed to leave reluctantly. The van sat sullenly alone on the opposite corner. I assumed a tow truck would arrive eventually and take it away.

And then, I thought about the men. Who were they? I think they must have been from Central America or Mexico. Obviously, they couldn't speak English and the driver fearful of his own skin, probably did not have a driver's license. The men were no doubt illegals and here they were stranded on a strange street with the sound of sirens approaching. Their only thought was to run, to escape.

How sad, how very sad I thought to be a stranger, in a strange country unable to communicate. The overwhelming need to work, to make some money, any money and the fear of being deported constantly hanging over your head. The men who cross borders and risk even death to come to this country; how heroic, how very brave and now they are scurrying away down streets like hunted animals. I don't know if they made good their escape, but I hope so.

BRIEF ENCOUNTERS

I saw a pencil box the last time I was in the PX at the Presidio. It didn't look at all like the ones I used to cherish in elementary school but the new-age colorful plastic container intrigued me. I couldn't resist and picked up one, turquoise and white.

I walked over to the register to check out and saw Ellen was on duty. She told me she's going crazy trying to find an apartment, working two jobs and visiting Pita on weekends. Pita is her cat that is temporarily residing with friends who live on Treasure Island. She says Pita is becoming cold and distant. After having a close relationship for twelve years, this is a blow to Ellen. I asked her once where she got the name Pita. She told me they were initials for "Pain in the Ass" and it looks like Pita is beginning to live up to her name.

Next encounter—Jay, visiting friends here from Virginia. He is involved in writing a book about the San Francisco Giants. He's not interested in talking to the players; he wants to hear comments from the fans, starting as far back as when the team came to San Francisco. He says he knows it's only a niche book but is traveling all over the country to find people who were or possibly still are fans of the team. He is a retired Army Air Force officer, a slim soft spoken man who looks like he should be doing research on some esoteric subject; the origin of the species or some abstract theory. He said he had spent the day in St. Helena and Napa. He gave me his card and web site: the words The Giants Journal under his name and the website included among other things . . . the words "members and giants". This man epitomizes "the love of the game".

Next encounter—Vinnie, Hawaiian, who sits at the desk at the entrance to the Presidio Commissary. We have exchanged greetings over the years. Her husband was badly mangled in an auto accident several years ago and seems to have recovered. She has long, long straight black hair, which she changes periodically, sometimes hanging like a window shade down her back, sometimes in thick braids; sometimes a mass of curls. No matter her hairstyle, she always wears a hat. She must own every color, every fabric (some straw, some velvet and on it goes). Around the brim of each hat there is always a circle of imitation flowers, or other decorations all-blending in with the color of the hat. She is the perfect greeter, colorful and solemn and nodding with pleasure as most of us tell her "I like your hat".

As we were talking another encounter approached us. This is Esther who is one of the managers. I know a little about Esther. For instance, she loves her dog, a Chihuahua and has a picture of him on her desk. She is buying a house, sorta buying a house. The owner has agreed to take the rent for the next five years, total it up as a down payment on the house. At that time, Esther will find a mortgage company somewhere. She has never had a credit card, never written a check, never ever made a purchase except with cash. Thus she has no credit rating making it impossible to qualify for a loan. At the end of five years, the owner will supply a report on her ability to pay and thus she should be qualified for an honest to goodness loan. She has an 18-year relationship with her boyfriend who is now in Ohio. His brother is going through a very unpleasant divorce and has periodically been suicidal. I think Esther is planning to visit her boyfriend in Ohio. She is taking her dog. She told me her house is filled with all the dolls from the Wizard of Oz. She knows them intimately and I think she fancies herself as "Glynda, the good witch". She says no matter where she goes; she is in Oz, which I can relate to. Many times I've said "I'm off the see the wizard" and my other favorite sentence is "I always follow the yellow brick road".

Back to Vinnie who looked at me intensely and said "Did you give Esther your phone number and do you have her number? Esther is one of the most giving people in the world and if you should need something or someone, she is always there to help. She has helped me many times". Esther gave me her phone number and took mine and said, "Yes, if you need something, call me."

Then all of a sudden, Vinnie looked at me and said, "What religion are you?" Esther answered "Helen's Jewish".

"Oh" Vinnie said, "You are one of the blessed, the Jews were blessed by God, truly blessed". I walked away feeling quite pleased about my blessing.

Four encounters in one hour; all with very kind and warm people. I'm off to see the wizard again.

OPEN FACE

The term "sandwich generation" is being bandied about again. Every few years, it appears on the news, on talk show and then all is quiet.

Once upon a time, people were not described as generations but my, how things have changed. We had grandparents, parents and children. Older people for the most part didn't live to be really old, which simplified things for the generation following. And, the generation after that moved out of the house got married and started a new generation.

Taking care of elderly parents or parent and children under the age of 18 qualified you to be a designated sandwich. I, myself, was an "open face" sandwich. No children were around to complete the sandwich . . . . only one parent, my mother. She, at first, silently moved into old age. Eventually, her inability to do the things she had always done became apparent.

First, I did most of her shopping. She would push her cart to the store several blocks away now and then. She wasn't one to give up easily. Her doctor visits, of course, were part of my duties. Manual labor too, which was minimal but time consuming . . . . knobs that she pulled off the TV, windows that wouldn't open or close, looking for missing items that were misplaced . . . . the list goes on.

On my return home after completing some of the above, the phone would start ringing. The requests were unlimited . . . . a spool of thread of a certain color . . . . a phone number she can't find . . . . and when was she going to see me again, it had been so long. She had completely forgotten I had just left her house.

My car went back and forth between our houses. At times I didn't remember in what direction I was driving. I used to say "the car knows the way, I'll just send it without me".

I didn't think she should live alone. She absolutely refused to move in with me. Looking back, I think she made the wisest choice. I checked out board and care facilities. I drove from one place to another, always taking her with me. She calmly walked through and shook her head "no". I agreed with her. I couldn't see her living in one room, joining several other boarders to eat meals together and go their separate ways. Each of them was living in their own world and no one was allowed to enter.

What was I going to do? What could I do? It was suggested that I enroll her in a complete geriatric evaluation. The day began at a local hospital.

First, a physical . . . . eyes, ears . . . . the whole body examination. She passed. Very good for her age.

The next step . . . . how does she manage her cooking. We entered a kitchen. "Please Mrs. G., would you mind making a cake for us? The mix is in the bowl, the cooking oil is in the cup, the egg and baking dish is on the counter".

My mother looked at the ingredients and said, "I never use a mix. I make cakes from scratch".

"Please Mrs. G. use the things we've placed on the counter".

"Mom" I said "Just make the cake, you don't have to eat it".

"Aright" she said and began to break the egg and pour the oil into the mix. She moved very smoothly through all her motions. She carefully poured the batter into the cake pan and walked over to the oven. She said, "This is an electric stove, I use gas. I don't know how to turn it on".

"Don't worry Mrs. G." The nurse said, "We'll do it".

My mother took the dishes to the sink and began to wash them.

"Don't bother with the dishes, we'll take care of them".

"I like to leave a clean kitchen but aright if you want to do them".

We were now led into a large room and sat at a long table. "Mrs. G. do you see the clock on the wall, what time is it?"

"I can see, it's two o'clock". She was right.

"Mrs. G., here is a sheet of paper and a pen. Would you draw us a picture?"

My mother said, "I'm no artist, I can't draw".

"Mom, please draw something; maybe just a funny little man". I was becoming more confused then my mother, who seemed to be taking everything in stride. "Aright, I'll try".

She began to draw. I watched as she drew a very well defined cartoon character . . . . a little man wearing a jacket with carefully drawn cuffs and buttons spaced perfectly down the front. I was amazed. My mother could draw.

The nurse looked down at the picture and said, "Very good Mrs. G. but you haven't finished the picture. Where are his legs?"

My mother looked up at her, a bemused expression on her face, and said, "Where is he going?"

A total silence fell over the room. How can you argue with simple logic?

On to the next room. A series of simple math questions. No problem for my mother. She could add, multiply, subtract in her head. I was always surprised by her ability with numbers and she hadn't changed.

One more question "Mrs. G. what is heavier, a pound of feathers or a pound of lead?"

I sat there thinking (a pound of feathers versus a pound of lead).

My mother replied almost instantly. "A pound is a pound".

As we left, I was told my mother was truly remarkable for her age; physically and mentally. She was ninety-one.

We returned to the car. As we drove away, I said, "Mom, you really put on a good show. You are one smart woman". She said, "What are you talking about?" I said, "All those tests you took".

"What test. I've been with you; we didn't go anywhere".

Oh my god, she had forgotten the whole day and I was back at square one . . . . a member of the open face sandwich generation with no clue at to what I was going to do next.

ASSISTED DYING

She was sitting in her chair, just sitting and then she slumped over. I moved over to her side and said, "Mom, mom, wake up." She didn't respond. So still, so very still. I said, "Call the doctor." My husband picked up the phone and dialed. I heard his voice coming from the kitchen. "Aright, I'll try but I don't think it will work. O.K. I'll call you back." He came into the room and said, "That nut, our doctor told me to slap her face, what an idiot." He gently touched my mother's face. "Wake up, you can't go to sleep yet." He looked over at me and said, "I'm calling the doctor back." Again his voice, "Send an ambulance, do you have the right address. Yes, that's correct." He said, "I talked to Anita, the nurse. She's got a lot more sense and is calling for an ambulance."

The sound of the ambulance in the distance gave me an emotional nudge. Would my mother ever wake up? Is she dying? I looked over at the small frail body, so peaceful in her chair. This quiet, gentle woman who gave me life and encouragement and laughter . . . . I needed her, oh, how I needed her. The ambulance pulled up in front, the doorbell rang. As the door opened, there stood a tall husky man and a small, chunky woman, carrying a stretcher. They put my mother on the stretcher and started down the steps. The woman couldn't go down the steps first, she was too short. When she took the stretcher at the other end; she was still too short. My mother's body was tipping up and down. My husband quickly moved and took over, carefully putting mom in the ambulance. Later, he would say, "I believe in equal opportunity, but for god's sake, that woman could have dropped the stretcher.

Your mother would have never gotten to the hospital. It would be straight to the morgue."

We sat waiting in the emergency room. It was late evening about 8:00 P.M. The nurse on duty came over to me and said, "I have to ask you this question, your mother is being attended to but we need to know if you want us to use heroics to revive her." I knew what she meant. "No, I don't want my mother to live the rest of her life connected to machines." The nurse said, "I'm glad you said that, I agree with you completely."

As we sat waiting, I began remembering the last few years. My mother's memory had deteriorated. When we left her home in the evening, my phone would be ringing as I entered my house. It was always my mother asking, "When are you coming to see me?" I would patiently say, "Mom, we saw you this evening, just a little while ago." She would say, "You did, and you're kidding me, aren't you." "No, mom, really we were just there, I'll talk to you tomorrow."

I had had surgery about six months before this episode. Even though I saw her and told her about myself, she had forgotten. My vocal chords had been traumatized. I had lost my voice though I could talk in a raspy fashion. I was told this often happens and I would regain my voice but the time frame was indefinite. She had been to my house many times, but as soon as she returned home her mind told her I was in danger. Who was the culprit? Who had hurt her daughter? She had appeared at our door with total strangers. My husband was the one who opened the door and was informed that my mother had told them he had cut my throat. Neighbors were told of this dastardly deed that had been perpetuated upon me. We had been called by the Public Health Department informing us that my mother was becoming a nuisance. We had to take steps. She was constantly going over to various houses in the neighborhood and asking to be taken to her daughter's home. She always told them that her daughter's life was in danger. We were advised to do something or else she would be put into a mental facility.

I tried to move her in with us for a few days. After only an hour or so, she asked to be taken home. When I tried to reason with her, she became adamant. "I want to go home, I'm not a prisoner." So, I took her home. I took her to several board and care homes, thinking possibly this could be a solution. She came with me willingly, but always refused to talk about it. I then took her for a geriatric evaluation with a group of experts; doctors, psychologists, social workers, etc. Not only did she pass all tests with flying colors, I perceived they thought I was the one who needed evaluation.

I was on the phone almost constantly with my mother. As soon as I hung up, she would call back and ask the same question "When am I going to see you?" I went to a support group for people with aging parents. It was a lot of talk, no action but I did learn one thing. Get an answering machine. I told my mother about the machine but this did not deter her continual calling. She left dramatic messages on my machine. The most prominent one was "You don't want to talk to me, o.k. The next time you see me I'll be dead!" That was guaranteed to make me call back. She always said "Don't be silly, I would never say anything like that." Months of trying to make sense of my mother's and my dilemma. Months of driving back and forth to her house. Months when I thought I was going mad. And, now my mother is lying in a hospital and I don't know whether she will live or die.

The day this happened, she had called me earlier and I had visited. I saw her sitting at the kitchen table and asked if she had eaten. "Sure", she said. I had looked in the refrigerator and it looked as if nothing had been touched. "Mom, let me make you a sandwich." "No, I've eaten. I'm not hungry." I stayed a while and left. I told my husband and after dinner, we drove over. She was still sitting at the table. He said "Let me help you into the living room and bring you something to drink." He took her arm and walked her slowly over to her chair. He went into the kitchen and returned with a glass of Dr. Pepper, her favorite. It seemed particularly frothy and she took the glass eagerly. After drinking several gulps, she set the glass down. Within minutes, she closed her eyes and fell into a deep sleep. There were the calls to the doctor and the subsequent arrival of the ambulance.

Now here I am sitting and waiting and wondering. I love my mother and yet, what am I going to do if she lives. The nurse at the desk suggested we go home; it was past midnight. We drove home and neither of us spoke.

The next morning, we returned to the hospital. We had called and were told my mother was fine. She was in her own room. We entered the hall where my mother's room was situated and saw her sitting in a wheelchair. I approached her. She looked up at me and said, "You know, those nurses aren't paying attention. I heard a woman calling them and they don't do anything." Lunch was served and we watched as she ate almost everything on the tray. They were going to do a few tests and then release her to a convalescent home for a month or so.

For the next three years, my life was an unending trip back and forth to the nursing home. After the first month, I took her for a ride and back to her home. As she walked in she said "Why are you taking me to this house?" "Mom, this is your home, you've lived here over forty years." She smiled up at me "You are wrong, I have never lived here. It's a very nice house, now take me back." I was soon to realize the convalescent home had become the only reality she could relate to . . . as far as she was concerned it was home.

I visited often, almost daily. If I stayed away for two or three days, I experienced pains in my chest. Pain that only left when I walked in and saw her sitting quietly. Her face would light up when she saw me coming down the hall. We talked of trivial things, but I would hold her hand remembering the mother who always told me "You can doing anything you want to do and do it well." My mother had been my best friend and confidant. I needed to be with her, she had always been there for me.

She fell at the end of the third year. Nothing was broken but she could no longer walk. She was confined to her bed. She had

ceased eating; over the years her food intake became smaller and
smaller. No amount of coaxing would help. She said "I'm not
hungry, don't worry about me." One day when I was visiting, she
was looking out the window and said, "She said . . . Old lady, it's
time to go." I asked her "Who is she, who said that?" She looked at
me in surprise "I must be crazy, am I crazy." "No, mom, you're not
crazy, it's just your imagination."

And, then the pain started. My mother was in pain. I called
the doctor and he prescribed a morphine injection. The last day,
my mother's last day, we both visited. I sat on one side and my
husband on the other. She turned to look at each of us, first to one
side and then the other. She said, "Can't you see, I'm smiling on
both sides of my face." Her face was beaming and my heart was
breaking. I rushed out of the room not wanting her to see me cry.

I failed her at the end. I couldn't go back that evening. My
husband did go. He asked the nurse if she had given my mother
the morphine injection. She said no, if she did my mother would
die. My husband told her the doctor had ordered it. He said my
mother had suffered enough and he stood over the nurse as she
administered the shot. He said my mother's last words as she
slipped into the final sleep were "Thank you, thank you."

He came home and told me what happened. He said, "I need
to tell you something." I was listening. "Do you remember when
your mother drank the Dr. Pepper and passed out"? "Yes, I
remember." He said. "I crushed a handful of Valium tablets and
put it in her drink. Do you remember how her glass was bubbling;
I didn't know what to do, she was driving you out of your mind.
You had been ill and I thought I was going to lose you. I took a big
risk, but I would do it again. It didn't kill her, for which I am
grateful. Do you forgive me"?

"Of course, I forgive you. It took a lot of courage."

How ironic that only six years later, my husband was taken to
the hospital and the dying began. Three weeks of dying, I never
believed he would die. I held his hand so warm and alive. This
couldn't be happening; I needed the courage to sign the papers

that took him off life support. It was so hard to let him go; and then he was given the same morphine injections as the pain became unbearable. My last words to him were "Thank you, thank you for being my husband". His last words to me were "Stay, please stay." And, I stayed.

THE SCENT OF LEATHER

I walked into the department store, past the men's shoes; the smell of the leather brought me up short. I inhaled deeply. I remembered my husband, dead now for almost seven years.

Long ago but not long enough for my heart not to break again, I fought back the tears. I always walk in this same entrance. Into the men's department, the scent of leather, men's robes, shirts, all men things. Things that no longer hang in my closets.

It took me a long time to give away his clothes. First, I gave away robes and pajamas to a convalescent home. Then slowly, a few shirts, then a few shoes and socks. I eventually hung the rest in garment bags in the garage. Maybe he will come back. I had a dream where he reprimanded me for giving away his clothes.

Finally, finally I gave away the garment bags. I still have some shoes, the Italian sweater I gave him on his birthday, many years ago. He did so love the sweater. I have his one and only hat in a hatbox on the shelf in my closet. A beautiful black felt hat he only wore a few times. He looked so handsome and elegant when he put it on. No one will wear the hat as long as I live, no one.

And now, the smell of leather conjures up images of him. I can feel his intense eyes looking at me. I wonder if he would approve how I've spent these last years without him. I have given myself permission to live but I use the term loosely. I get up each morning and go to bed each night. It's the in-between time the endless hours, the empty hours, I need to fill.

I looked down this evening at my cat, Finian, who is struggling with his aging body and I want to cry. I want to cry. My chest feels heavy with its burden of unshed tears. No, I don't want to immerse myself in self-pity. And, I say to myself, why not? You are this sad creature left to spend your remaining years alone. Yes, that is true but the optimum words are the "remaining years".

The smell of leather seems to awaken in me all the male garments and accessories, which have been part of my life. Now my life and closets are filled with women things and woman smells. No longer the masculine scents that made my life exciting, sensual and mysterious. I am truly living in a woman's house, a woman's world.

SLIPPERY SLOPE

My life now has become a slippery slope moving downhill like lava on a mountainside, its tentacles reaching out and destroying everything in its path. There is nothing potentially destructive about my downhill ride for anyone except myself. I find fewer and fewer people I can relate to or want to relate. Fewer and fewer things amuse me or entertain me. It is almost as if my life has become superfluous. I have lived long and well. The things I remember that are worth remembering give me great pleasure.

However, the pleasure is short lived because reality is all around me. I look in the mirror and see that I have become old. I cannot accept this mirror image; it is not the me I am. The me I am is faceless. I feel the wind; I taste the flavors of many foods; I hear the sounds some raucous, some melodic; I smell many scents pervading my space and the things I see, so many things part nature and part man. This is what I am or maybe what I have become. I have become a summation of all my senses and the body I inhabit is only a container, which has become weathered and yet still stands erect.

FINIAN'S WAKE

I think I loved Finian more than anything or anyone in my life. When I came home from wherever I was I would call out "Honey, I'm home". He would appear at the top of the stairs looking down at me. I would walk up the stairs and usually; he would follow me into the kitchen for a snack or accompany me as I took off my coat, put groceries away or just sit watching me from across the room. When he stretched out so gracefully in front of heater, I always found delight in his presence. Now he is gone and I mourn my loss. My husband is gone and other loved ones but Finian belonged only to me. No mother, no father, no siblings, and no friends to remember him.

Finian died December 31, 1999. Finian wrote the prologue to my book "Seduction of Silence". He was at my side through the long painful months after his master died. Now I am truly alone and the silence that surrounds me is unbearable. Maybe, I'll just write your biography, Finian. Your life was unique and as meaningful as anyone I've ever known. No one but myself can try to give you a place in history. I will try to recall the highlights

My husband fell in love with cats at a late stage of his life. I had several as a child and also as an adult. I had been catless for a very long time and now my mate was joining me in my secret desire. We finally went to the SPCA and began our search for that special someone. In the little cage, I saw him looking up at me with those beautiful eyes. I was in love. A small brown tabby kitten with a long plume of a tail, an insolent look in his eyes that said "Don't ever take me for granted". That was at the end of July 1981.

Little did I know then that he was to live with me for over eighteen years and share some of the most dramatic days in my life?

We adopted him and brought him home. I said "Now listen here kitty, I put your litter box in the downstairs bathroom, so don't go messing about upstairs". With that statement, I took the kitten into the bathroom, showed him the litter box and took him upstairs. A little later, our new "friend" scurried out of the room and I followed. He went to the top of the stairs, he couldn't quite reach the steps; he proceeded to slide down the carpeted stairs on his stomach and then jumped into the downstairs room and hurried to his box. I told my husband "We've adopted a genius, a real Einstein". And, Finian proved me right over and over again.

We couldn't decide what to name him. We placed him on the couch and started talking to him. He looked first at my husband and then at me. Whoever was speaking soft words of praise, he would move over to that side. Then, as he heard other words, he moved over to the other side. I said, "You know, he's a Finian". In the musical "Finian's Rainbow", there is a song that goes something like this "If I'm not with the one I love, I love the one I'm with". He is a Finian, lovable but fickle." We couldn't have picked a more suitable name. He was truly a son of the old sod, full of blarney and could charm the shirt off anybody, especially the two of us.

I said to my husband "You know in a few months, we will have to neuter him". "What did you say?" was his reply. "You are not taking away his manhood." I said "But, we want him indoors as much as possible and male cats spray, you wouldn't like the odor. Also I understand if and when he goes out, he won't get into any fights." Ha, the fights turned out to be one of the best things Finian got into. Actually, I think he welcomed them.

Finian was not a "house" cat. He would go downstairs look out the window at the outside world and howl. And howl and howl; especially if he happened to see another cat. He liked us well enough but (I hate to say this), he was racist. He liked us but we weren't cats. He preferred his own kind and though as he got older and stayed in more, the company of other cats was always his cup of tea. We had no argument with that, being the liberals we fancied ourselves to be. At times though, we did feel left out. People would say, "Finian thinks he's like you, a person". I always answered "No, he just thinks we're big cats".

Then came the big day. The day that Finian became a "man" or when I thought the time was right. He had been looking out the window downstairs again. This time, he wanted to go out and not to play. He had other things on his mind and so did I. My husband wasn't home and I did what a gal's gotta do. I took Finian to the veterinarian for a minor adjustment. He came through this surgery without a whimper.

Finian stayed out most of the day now and could be seen wandering down the hill. I used to say we have a green cat. He was very hard to spot with his camouflage coat among the bushes and weeds. I know he never met a cat he didn't want to fight and fight he did. Even the cats he seemed to like didn't seem to stop him from having a tussle with them from time to time. Our vet bills continued every few months or so. After all the other cats gave as good as they got. We soon began to call him a member of the Sinn Fein (the Irish terrorist group). Actually, I think secretly we took a bit of pride in his macho temperament. He walked about with such dignity, his beautiful full tail upright. He looked about with his large green luminous eyes carefully surveying his world.

Many evenings, he stayed out late. We had a cat door for him to come and go as he pleased. Of course, we never called him "Kitty, kitty, kitty". Never, not this cat. We started early on by singing "When Irish eyes are smiling" from the back door. If we sang loud enough and long enough, most times he would saunter up the back steps into the house.

I buried Finian on January 16, 2000. He didn't accompany me into the millennium. I requested that he be cremated and when I picked up the small box containing all that is left of my beloved, Finian, I began crying again. I knew where I would place him; I always knew where he belonged when he died. I went out to the national cemetery where my husband is buried and dug a nice deep hole in which to place the tiny coffin. In front of the stone marking my husband's grave is an unmarked grave containing a very special cat. I placed two American flags at the gravesite, attached to one flag is a small green battered toy mouse that Finian used to play with a long time ago. I have now lost the only living link to my late husband.

These last few years, there was a silent rapport we had with each other, just Finian and me. The book "Seduction of Silence" is now beautifully printed with an elegant cover of a cat and on the back is a picture of me holding my Finian. There are so many stories in the book about Finian, conversations with Finian and I wish I could hold him close to me again. If anyone tells me that by writing this I will have "closure", I will laugh. Not funny, never funny. When someone you love dies there is no closure. They stay with you forever and I wouldn't want it any other way.

BELOVED FINIAN
July 1, 1981—December 31, 1999

MURDER HE SAID

I had a very special cat, a cat that probably was a warrior, a matador or a gladiator in his other life. He never ran from a fight, in fact he had a propensity for battles. He would walk arrogantly across the yard, his tail upright, swishing from side to side, glancing in all directions. From the time this noble creature entered our home he demanded the limelight.

As a very tiny kitten, he immediately took center stage never to relinquish it during all the years we lived together. He was truly unique in his cat behavior. No one has ever heard of a cat bringing friends home for lunch, but he did. Once when coming home, I heard soft sounds coming from the kitchen. As I walked into the kitchen, there was Finian lying on the floor communicating with a big orange cat that was eating his food. I gathered Finian was being a gracious host but was urging his guest to finish so they could go out and play. This went on for a few months until his friend left town. After that, Finian became a loner. I think the many fights he engaged in were a display at the anger he felt at losing his best friend.

We took a trip now and then and were careful to secure a cat sitter to his liking. Bill, a retired Marine, was completely acceptable to Finian. He put out his food at the required time and always kept his distance unless Finian decided to acknowledge his presence, which was rare. Once when we returned from a trip, Finian rushed up the stairs and began bawling us out. He was so riled up, he continued until he literally lost his voice emitting croaking sounds that broke our hearts. We shortened our time away to appease his discontent.

I wasn't allowed to talk to other cats. Once he caught me on the lower deck in the act of talking to Fuzz, my neighbor's cat. He came up from the yard, enraged and chased Fuzz off the deck then returned to my side, looking up with an expression of displeasure. We bought a kitten into the house once, hopefully to give Finian a buddy. He took one look at his unwanted guest and chased him through the garage down the steps into the yard. Fortunately, the kitten escaped his wrath and was returned to a safe haven.

There were many other incidents but time moved on and New Year's Eve before the year 2000, my beloved Finian died. I had him cremated and saw that he was buried in a military cemetery with honors as one who served his country. In his case, an exception was made.

The other night I had a dream. I had a dream and there was Finian looking up at me. He now had a real voice and he said loudly "Why did you clone me?" "What" I said, "I would never think of cloning you." He said, "Look at this cat, take a look." Sure enough, there was a cat lying restlessly near Finian, a perfect duplicate. "Finian, I have no idea how that happened. I would never do that." He said, "What am I supposed to do with this clone, tell me?" The clone looked at me and said, "Did I do something wrong?" I felt pity for the frightened creature. "No" I said, "I don't know what happened." Finian spoke again "Well, there's only one thing for me to do, I am going to kill this damn clone." The clone pulled away and looked up puzzled. "Finian, just leave it alone." "No" he said "I'm going to kill this clone, nothing is ever going to replace me . . . I'm going to kill the clone." The clone looked up at him timidly and said, "I'm sorry, it's not my fault". Finian replied, "I don't care, I'm going to kill you" and off they ran, Finian in hot pursuit. I woke up and I am still wondering if he killed his clone.

I had been thinking, perhaps later in the year, I would adopt another cat. Since this dream, I wonder if this is an omen of disaster. I am not superstitious, yet until I find out what happened to the clone, I think I'll wait awhile. I was waiting for the dream to be continued . . . but not for long. I was asked to baby-sit a cat for a friend who was going on a Christmas/New Year's cruise. A cat looking very much like Finian, almost a clone was deposited at my house. Ten days with another cat was fine with me but I had a sneaking feeling that she would become a permanent part of my life. I was right. The previous owner urged me to take over the care of her cat citing that I had a larger home and a backyard. I have no idea what to call this cat . . . her previous owner called her Mary but there had been someone before that. I started calling her Merry Christmas since she was a gift of sorts. Even though she does look almost identical to Finian, he would never think of himself as a girl. Since the dream I haven't contacted Finian or is it the other way around but if he should return in the wee hours of the morning, I will not tell him about Merry Christmas. You can't be too careful dealing with the ghosts of New Year's past.

"Maggie" or "Merry Christmas" or "Mary"

SILENT VOICES

Lately I have been talking to dead people, my late husband to be precise. Nobody in the world knew me better than he did and every now and then, I think of something I want to ask or tell him.

Yesterday, I was trying desperately to remember a phrase he used. I was going to write e-mail to a friend and wanted to remember the words. I clenched my lips and thought. I sighed and mumbled to myself think, think. No luck. I went down the stairs and on the way up I said, quite loudly "What is that phrase?" Before I had even finished, the words appeared on an invisible blackboard before my eyes VIEW WITH ALARM. Yes, I said still speaking "Thanks, oh by the way how is Finian?" He was my companion for 18 years and eleven years old when his master died. "Oh" he said, "that little devil bit me." I said, "You know he doesn't like to be stroked unless he initiates it". The message came back loud and clear "I thought since he's dead, actually we're both dead, his manners would have improved." "No" I retorted "I think we just carry our good and bad habits with us." Then, I stopped; if anyone heard me they would think I'm crazy.

Just for the hell of it, I said again "Finian, behave yourself. You never knew how to appreciate a good thing." Finian's face flashed in front of me, no words, just his usual cool cat gaze. Oh well, I always had a soft spot for that dam cat.

I do believe this is going to be a good thing. I do have questions from time to time. No one knew the answers better than my mate. He always told me I was the intellectual. He admired by my eclectic taste in my reading material. I would always protest, "No, I'm smart enough but you're knowledgeable about so many things including philosophy, politics, history. You are not only perceptive but brilliant." "No" he said, "I read a lot of non-fiction; I've watched more political debates and shows. You have an innate sense of things that I miss completely." We came to a truce. We each thought each other was the smartest but this never engendered any long lasting argument.

Now he is gone and I come up against a blank wall with no answers more often than not. Not about little things; I am good with little things. I am used to living with a walking Encyclopedia Britannica, Webster's Unabridged Dictionary, Roget's Thesaurus plus the contents of most of the hundreds of books that surround me in my house. He has been dead over seven years and I think I can allow myself to start talking to him. I don't hear his beautiful baritone voice but a sense of him encompasses me; his penetrating dark eyes, chiseled nose and square jaw. I don't want to talk foolishness to him, only odds and end of information I need. He was never impatient yet I sense a need to make it brief and never overdo my welcome. He is living in a different world and time, which surely has a different dimension.

I clench my lips together again and say out loud "Finian, don't bite your master, do you hear me? He loves you." That little devil, how I wish he were lying in my lap. When I would carefully stroke him, I could feel his silent purr. He was much too private to purr out loud, but I can relate to that. I've always been a little embarrassed to show much affection, even to a loved one. I wonder if there is something wrong with me. No, not really. When it comes to emotions, I keep them close. Maybe I'm afraid of being hurt or maybe, I don't know . . .

"Hey, you guys, I love you, I really love you" I shout and I see my husband sly smile and the ends of my fingers tingle as I feel Finian's silent purr

LOVE AND WAR

I can't relive wars anymore, especially WWII. I was not a member of the Armed Forces and did not lose any close member of my family or friends. I started to watch a television program the other night called "Love and War" based upon a true story, so they said.

Over the last years since WWII, I have watched hundreds of movies, television programs and read many, many books all-relating to the war. This has now come to a screeching halt. When I started watching "Love and War" English soldiers were being dropped off a ship on the coast of Italy, plopped into the water and scurried to shore where the Germans were waiting. I turned it off! I became enraged, why am I immersing myself into a program. Do I get some kind of masochistic pleasure by having my senses abused?

I've been there, well not me, but Bob, my first husband. He was a member of the 36th Infantry Division. First he spent time in North Africa and then his golden opportunity to fight the enemy; taken by ship to the coast of Italy, Salerno to be specific, plopped in the water and scurried to shore where the Germans were waiting. He spent almost two years in a German prison of war camp; wounded in the leg he had tried to walk behind the truck taking his buddies into Germany, hoping to be recaptured by American troops. This didn't happen, but a lot of things did. When he was released at the end of the war and returned home, he talked very little about the war. In the ten years we were married, the stories unfolded like uncut pages in a book; there was an unheard tearing which at the time I was subliminally storing into my memory and psyche.

As I started watching the TV program "Love and War", I could feel the water surge around my legs and the fear that crept through every man become my fear. What am I afraid of; I wasn't there. Why now? Is it because we are again at war; a different war but still terrible things are happening.

My second husband, also a veteran of WWII was with an Ordinance division attached to the 92nd Airborne in northern Germany. He regaled me with stories about his buddies, in the states and overseas, some poignant, some humorous. He said he never fired his gun for which he was grateful and the closest he came to getting shot was by one of his own men on guard duty who failed to hear his command. Luckily, the soldier wasn't a good marksman. He along with fellow officers was headquartered in a large home in Ludwiglust, a small city in Germany. Ludwiglust was home to one of the lesser-known concentration camps. He gave me a bird's eye view of the horror contained behind the barbed wire fence. He told me of his trip by jeep to Paris for supplies. In the snow banks along the road, he told me of seeing so many dead soldiers lying in random positions; a frozen arm raised, a sprawled body whose face was covered in snow. On and on he drove literally through the white valley of death. He said that he forgot how to feel; he said if you allowed yourself to mourn for those frozen animal like carcasses, your brain would explode.

When he returned home to a military hospital, he told me life as he lived it prior to the war ceased to exist. He was filled with angry compassion most of his life. Now I am angry, very angry. How can I look at the screen and find "Love and War?" War, any war has reduced us to our most primitive emotions . . . . kill or be killed! Love and War do not belong in the same title or even the same sentence.

THE CROSS-EYED BEAR

I used to talk "lak" this a lot
Maybe 'cause Texas "shore" was hot.
I know it took a lot of years
To sound "right smart" so y'all could hear.

This "wo-man", she come up to me.
We talk "lil bit" about life and such
She say to me "Let's keep in touch,
Cause you don' know the cross-eyed-bear".
I looked at her, I saw a tear.

She walked away, I watched her go.
I feel so sad, but I "don'" know
"The cross-eyed bear" he "don' sound mean
Don' rightly know if, I have seen.

A cross-eyed bear must be a sight
If I did see, I'd sure take flight.
I told a friend about this bear
He started laughing "Never fear"

"You've been gone too long, you don't hear right"
"What you saying, I'm alright".
Oh yeah, "The cross-eyed bear, now listen here"
Say it slowly "The cross I bare".

Texas people talk real slow and slur their vowels
A "cross-eyed bear" would make them howl
Even if I still have my drawl, I love
That bear, cross-eyed and all.

NO, NO GET DOWN

Last year, shortly before Christmas to be exact, I was asked to baby-sit a cat. Her mistress was about to embark on a cruise. Shrugging my shoulders internally, I thought o.k. Why not? My own cat, Finian had died the previous New Year's Day, Jan 1, 2000. I had pledged not to get another cat or even entertain the thought until after the prerequisite year of mourning. Finian, my companion of eighteen years was irreplaceable. However, I did give him an elegant resting place. I went out to the National Cemetery where my husband is buried, dug a hole big enough to hold the small coffin. I placed a small American flag on my husband's stone plus an old battered toy mouse.

Back to the new cat. This one was a female and a Finian look like, which gave me some comfort. Outside of her external appearance, she had absolutely no resemblance in temperament, motivation or manners. I didn't know what to call her. Her mistress called her Mary but I thought that name was unsuitable for a cat. It wasn't long before I gave her a handle. She did not want to go in the large yard with trees and shrubs where Finian spent his days. Uh, uh! This was a house cat, a wily charming female that obviously thought I would be won over by her winning ways.

She would jump into my lap, purring and looking up at me adoringly; follow me from room to room talking in her small voice. Soon I found her climbing the walls, literally. My living room and hall are wallpapered. I began yelling, "No, no get down." She would jump to the floor and soon I found her at every elevation in the house; the shelves of my bookcase which reaches to the ceiling; the window ledges that are at least nine feet high. Glancing over, I would find her lying on the kitchen counter, dining table and just for kicks, she somehow jumped to the high shelves in the clothes closets or as a matter of face any closet where the doors were open. I find myself calling out daily, sometimes hourly "No, no get down."

It has been over a year since my replacement cat has lived with me. When her mistress returned from her trip, she convinced me that "Mary" would be happier in my house, a condition I accepted by that time "No, no" had endeared herself to me and at this very moment she has jumped into my lap, murmured a few cat words and is now lying in front of my space heater.

P.S. The wallpaper around the hallway has a new look, the grass cloth is shredded. She has tagged almost every piece of furniture in the house marking her territory. She has even managed to turn on the computer a few times. I have admitted defeat; symbolically waving the white flag of surrender. Before the day is over I will have shouted "No, no get down" and she will give me a puzzled look and I know she's thinking, "Why don't you give your voice a rest." She's right of course. Like most things we care about there's the old adage "take it or leave it." This leaves me with no alternative but to "take it."

PICTURES . . . .

Cover of the book
Author photo on back of book

1. The Arsonist
2. Gone with the Wind
3. Bride Wore Black
4. Somewhere
5. I'm a Caution
6. Babies on My Knees
7. Behind God's Back
8. Stand by Me
9. Lover's Leap
10. The Day Infamy Ended
11. Today, I Am
12. Where the Heart is
13. Oh Joy
14. Stalag IIB
15. East Meets West
16. Unshared Memories
17. Amazing Grace
18. Ships I Have Known and Loved
19. Terror in the Night
20. My Father
21. My Husband
22. The Year I Became Feral
23. Scent of Leather
24. Finian's Wake
25. Murder, He Said
26. No, No Get Down